THE TWILIGHT YEARS

THE TWILIGHT YEARS

Mohinder Singh

KALPAZ

The Twilight Years

ISBN: 978-81-7835-835-2

Published in 2010 in India by
Kalpaz Publications
C-30 Satyawati Nagar, Delhi-110052
E-mail: kalpaz@hotmail.com
Phone : 9212729499

Leser Type Setting by : Square Vision
Printed at : Chawla Offset Printers, Delhi

PART-I

A MISSED MARRIAGE ANNIVERSARY

PROLOGUE

Priti is dead.

What a tragic coincidence!

Priti, dying on the very day of her 50th marriage anniversary, the golden one. And Priti breathing her last a little before noon, the very time she was having her marriage *pheras* around the holy Granth Sahib, 50 years back.

Some coincidences are known in life. But this one may well rate as unique.

My dear wife's unexpected death broke my heart, shattered the very web of my life, and left me terribly lonely.

This coincidence later came up for discussion with my doctor-friend, Harbans Singh.

"Old people suffering heart attacks or strokes or dying on certain special occasions such as birthdays or marriage anniversaries, as if observing a pattern even in their death, is a phenomenon known to gerontology", says he. "Maybe, the excitement and activity generated by the occasion proves too much for some of them".

"Priti wasn't the one to suffer an attack of nerves".

"Can't say. Even after living together for 50 years, one may not fathom a person fully. The essence of your married partner may well escape you after living together for decades".

CHAPTER 1

The day Priti and I were married, the 25th of December, 1949, happened to be Christmas but that was simply a coincidence, nowhere intended or planned. "I didn't know on my marriage day it was Christmas", admits Priti.

Jogindar Singh (Jogi) our younger son, his wife Girija, and two teenage daughters, Mala and Lovely, are visiting a month in advance of the commemoration of that major event to work out the arrangements. They have driven down from Delhi in an official Ambassador. Jogi is combining the trip with inspecting a roadside Rural Development Block in Ambala district.

Early this year both got posted at Delhi, Jogi as Joint Secretary, Rural Development, and Girija as Joint Secretary, Shipping. They have moved into a CII first floor flat in Moti Bagh, a government officers' colony.

Jogi and Girija are of the same batch of the IAS (Indian Administrative Service), with her ranking ten notches above him. They fell in love while undergoing training at the Mussorie Administrative Academy, and married soon thereafter. Both got allotted to the state of Gujarat; Girija on the basis of merit, Jogi on grounds of marriage.

Jogi's first preference was Punjab but the two Punjab seats went to the persons scoring above him.

Girija, daughter of a Patel professor at the Ahmedabad Management Institute, is a gracious lady. A handsome figure with a wide face, milky-tea complexion, and 'good bones'. Breasts are on the heavy side. At 5 ft. 7 she's half an inch taller than her husband. Jogi evidently got my height, while Ravindar Singh (Ravi), our elder son at 5 ft. 11, has taken after his paternal grandpa, a towering six-footer.

Who knows? Jogi, with his enormous energy, may have been more relaxed, less combative, if he had been taller by a few inches. Jogi should rate himself lucky getting Girija, the way I deem myself blessed being married to Priti. Mala (17 plus) and Lovely (16) are charming. The younger one was such a lovely child she was named Lovely. And this has stuck on. Her pointed high breasts, set enticingly apart, are a sight under the thin cotton blouse, creased over by sitting five hours in the car. She has legs longer and sleeker than I remember; must have got them from her mother. Big brown eyes, cheeks sporting dimples as she smiles; it's the combination of a ramp model's body with a sharp mind. Whichever gods were present at Lovely's conception had been prodigal with their gifts. In her, nature is trying to come up with a winner. Will I see her develop into a mature beauty—a veritable eye-turner?

Both girls are at the Modern School, Vasant Vihar. They are known to be doing well in studies. Lovely is good in basketball, Mala excels with sitar.

"A trio of beauties", I exclaim, as the family alights from the white Ambassador on a cool, sunny noon.

"You're looking great", rejoins Girija, bending low in greeting. "The same merry man I met at my marriage".

The girls rush into me. Mala is an armful. Lovely's skin feels live and fruity when I stroke her bare forearm and pat her china-smooth cheek.

"Any boyfriends?" I ask in a jocular vein.

"Plenty", she said with an enticing swirl of her newly bobbed hair.

"Anyone special?"

"None. Am speaking for myself, not Mala".

"Shut up", shouts her elder sister. "And better keep your distance from boys. The lusty louts are too tricky".

"Mala is coming rather hard on boys. If I, for one, was 60 years younger, I'd love to be Lovely's boyfriend".

"I treat you as one even now", says Lovely, rubbing my neck. "And you haven't a rival to rout". Jogi steps in. As he makes a motion to touch my feet, I pull him up for a firm handshake. And then he hurries to hug his mother.

Later at lunch, Priti asks Girija, "How was the trip?"

"Mummy, rather tiring for me. Jogi takes over the comfortable seat by the driver as if it was the natural order of things. The girls insist on taking window seats, from where they carry on their wordy warfare, with me sandwiched in-between". "There was an Earl of Sandwich, a UK naval chief ...", I was remembering. "The earl was such an inveterate gambler, he would not break his play for meals but had asked his butler to bring two slices of bread with a piece of pork tucked in-between every two or three hours. The arrangement got named after him".

"A very well informed and read father-in-law", says Girija. "Reading is what he does the whole day", rejoins Priti.

"May be my mind is cluttered with all sorts of useless information".

"Papa, don't underrate yourself. It's never dull talking to you".

Girija wants to return conversation to the upcoming event: "Calls for a grand celebration. It has been such a perfect marriage", she says.

"Everybody tells us, it's a perfect marriage", I agree. "I suppose, Priti and I are happy to go along with the consensus".

Initially, Jogi had proposed celebrations at Delhi. We ruled it out. And in this we were supported by Ravi and his wife Nonita (Noni). Ravi and Noni, with their 5-year old son Viki, live in Cranford, New Jersey. He has a flourishing software business and she's high up at Merrill Lynch. "December 25 can get very cold in Chandigarh", says Jogi, brushing his jacket of the road dust. "It could rain, even produce a hailstorm". "I'm not in favour of a hotel. A dinner party at home will give the celebrations the right intimacy", says Priti. I nod in agreement.

And so at home it would be.

"A *shamiana* can be pitched on the front lawn; an enclosed tent that's warmed by a score of gas heaters", elaborates Jogi. "Elegant shamianas, fitted with chandeliers and all sorts of decorative frills, can be had these days. In an emergency like stormy weather or heavy downpour, there's sufficient space in the house to take in a hundred guests".

How many to invite, and whom to invite? Arguments are bandied back and forth. Jogi and I favour a smaller number, around 70; Girija and Priti want to go as high as 180—the more, the merrier, they say. Eventually it's agreed to invite 150—not counting children. As quite a few of my age group are in poor health, we'd be lucky to get a gathering around 130.

"Give priority to those who attended the marriage 50 years back", I say.

Yet the ones who survive and are in a position to attend are no more than a dozen. Pity, people haven't been living long enough or they're bedridden. That way, thanks are due to the Almighty for keeping the two of us in reasonable shape. Relatives have to be invited, though some are no longer on speaking terms with us. "We must rope in more of younger folks; sons and daughters of elderly friends", says Girija. "The evening party has to have some sparkle and zest, not a mere mass of old fogies nodding their heads". Prominent local officials known to me, Jogi and Girija, and that includes the Punjab Governor, are being added to impart prestige to the occasion. And Priti insists on getting in her teachers and their spouses. Her nursery school kids will be treated to an afternoon of toffees and toys.

Invitations are to go in the name of Ravi and Jogi, Noni and Girija, in the first week of December. The two sons insist they'll bear all the expenses; the invitations are from them. In what proportion they'll split I'm not privy to. Most likely, Ravi will pick up the entire tab.

Jogi has thrashed out details with his Director of Rural Development, Haryana, a person of influence and drive. This worthy would be entrusted with the actual arrangements. And he's expected to do his best. Jogi is sponsoring him for a study tour of Southeast Asian countries.

Invitations have gone out for the party. A dozen of the golden-coloured cards are with us to issue to anybody left out. The eye-catching card has been specially designed by an artist friend of Noni's in New York. Along with the cards, came a silvery Gucci purse—the size of a sandwich that can only hold her lipstick and cell phone—and matching shoes (Priti's shoe size obtained surreptitiously from an old pair).

The caterer and Jogi's Director of Rural Development have been around several times, sorting out where to pitch the shamiana, what will be the seating arrangements, asking our views about the dinner menu, and sundry matters.

"Why such an elaborate menu? I see some 25 dishes and 8 types of dessert, let alone a dozen pre-dinner snacks".

"Doesn't make much difference in price, sir", says the Rural Development Director. "The caterers know that a guest can only consume a certain quantity, no more. And, as per usual custom, it will be charged per plate".

"What about those who change to another plate mid-meal? In fact it is not the best of buffet manners to take a used plate for refill".

"Seasoned caterers have a way of determining fairly accurately the number of those eating. And they can also take into account where two or three guests eat from a common plate".

"And, sir, where should we set up the raised stage that has the high-backed throne-like chairs for the anniversary couple?"

"No, no. No raised stage, no special chairs. We'll sit along with others, at the most at a marked dining table. Mr. Ramdev, it's only a wedding anniversary, not a new marriage".

"As you wish, sir, I've also arranged for a couple of cops to regulate parking".

It promises to be a fabulous function.

The tiled part of the back courtyard is being set up for dancing. The wedding cake, we're told, has already been ordered; a rich torte cake, the shape of our home. Good. I opposed Noni's idea of fireworks. That would clearly be overdoing.

We have been lucky in our tenant, renting the whole of the first floor. Right since the house was built, we have had the same people.

Ramesh Chandra is chief engineer at a brewery ten miles out of town. His wife, a doctor, runs a private pathology lab in Sector 17. This has grown into a lucrative enterprise.

Aarti is big and busty, spectacled and dusky. Dresses in her skirt for work. Upturned nose, high cheek bones, and full lips indicate she must have been a fetching girl. Aarti greets us with smiles and is ever making friendly overtures. Often returning from work, she steps in to ask Priti about her health. And Aarti is solicitous in rendering medical assistance. She does not charge us for the medicines she gives or the tests she conducts at her lab.

"You're like my mother", she's apt to say.

To which Priti responds, "I take you as my daughter. I've no other. And, as they say, daughters are yours for life, sons only till they marry".

Talking of the coming anniversary, Aarti says, "Of your outstation guests, we can conveniently put up three couples".

"That would help. Waheguru has blessed me with a dutiful 'daughter'".

Priti deems it a distinct advantage having a doctor on the premises.

And coming events would prove how right she was.

CHAPTER 2

Four days before the planned event, the dawn sky was dazzling; bright, sunny, cloudless, the air invigoratingly fresh. Chandigarh winter under a warm sun is something to be savoured. You simply feel like lolling in chairs outside, more so in a quiet, bougainvillea-loaded walled compound like ours with greenery all around and winter flowers in full bloom—phlox, zinnias, hollyhocks, and dahlias as big as cauliflowers.

The day, however, hasn't been kind to Priti. She has nursed a low-intensity persistent headache right since morning. Two aspirins hardly afford any relief.

In the evening she consults Aarti. Yes, the BP is worryingly high, as high as 180/115. Priti is given a Lutensyl tablet, along with one more Natrilix; she already has taken one with breakfast, and is advised to eat light, preferably a bowl of soup and a glass of milk. Priti anyway takes a glass of hot milk as nightcap.

While she sips her cup of mushroom soup and swallows a bit of toasted bread, I, too, lose my appetite. Nibble at a piece of fried fish and a portion of mashed potatoes. I skip the custard, content myself with an orange.

Aarti comes down again. Gives Priti a Calmpose to calm down, induce sleep. And she plans to run a battery of tests on her the next day.

Priti is in no mood even to watch her favourite serial at 9. She just lies down, eyes closed, with a cloth band tied tightly to her forehead.

"Something seriously wrong with my head", she moans while preparing for the night. "Who knows my life may ebb out soon".

"This is talking nonsense".

"All right, I won't talk of it. But I can't help feeling that way".

"We'll see a specialist tomorrow. I'll ask my doctor-friend Harbans to fix an appointment in the PGI. In fact I can call him in just now".

"Don't bother Harbans at this late hour. By the way, when you get up at 5, wake me, too. I've a thousand things to attend to in the next 3 days".

And I commence pressing her legs lightly. She always liked me pressing her feet and legs. Tonight she waves me off; doesn't seem inclined for it.

I fall asleep. That's the gift of God. Whatever be the events of the day, sleep never forsakes me—an unfailing mistress, an undemanding consort. And I generally sleep the whole night through. It's still no midnight call for a pee, despite an enlarged prostate.

We have a Japanese Citizen clock given by Ravi that produces wake-up chimes, and its face can make out corresponding time anywhere in the world. I keep it close to my pillow on the bedside table so that the chimes don't disturb Priti.

As usual the alarm goes off at 5. Not feeling like getting up this morning, I press the buzzer down and doze off again.

Yet I nurse a vague impression of something amiss on the other side of the double bed. Leaning over I touch Priti. She doesn't react. It's past six. I give her a sharp nudge. There's no response.

Horror-struck I jump up. Grab her hand and grope for her pulse. Yes, the pulse is ticking, but she lies comatose. I pull down her cotton nightie over the exposed midriff and legs. And then rush up to call Aarti.

It takes five excruciatingly long minutes waking Aarti and getting her down in her housecoat.

She has one look at Priti. "It's a stroke. At what time it occurred, I can't say. She must be moved immediately to PGI".

Aarti rings for an ambulance and alerts the emergency room.

Priti hated hospitals.

"Let me die in my own bed, she used to tell me", I say.

"No question. Priti's in a coma. She must get the best medical attention, and that without delay".

Aarti goes to dress up.

I call Jogi. He and Girija would be here by lunchtime. They'd be informing Ravi. And I just have time to ring Harbans, get into my workday clothes, and pocket my purse when the ambulance arrives.

Two khaki-clad Sikh male nurses jump out. Led to the patient, they take Priti out on a collapsible canvas stretcher to the waiting van—a vehicle virtually bare of life-support equipment except an oxygen cylinder.

Aarti rides along and so do I—my first ride in an ambulance.

With the siren blaring and little traffic at that time, we are at the PGI Emergency door in minutes.

Harbans is reaching the hospital directly.

Within an hour in Emergency, Priti is moved all the way to the Intensive Care Unit in the Advanced Cardiac Centre. There isn't much paperwork; she's entitled to treatment in a government hospital, both as a former government servant and the wife of a retired IAS.

Harbans approaches me, after having had a discussion with the attending neurosurgeon, "Sorry, it's bad news. Doctors see scant chance of her coming out of the coma. They have put her on life-support systems: heart-lung machine, glucose drip, and catheter. And she has been given anti-blood-clotting injections. An MRI of her brain is being arranged. But essentially they're just watching developments for the next 2–3 days. Any surgical intervention is ruled out for the present".

Aarti, standing nearby, tugs at my shoulder, "Let's go home. There's nothing we can do here at this hour. You've to remain calm, composed. I give you a Valium. Eat something substantial at breakfast".

"I'll drop both of you", says Harbans, and hurriedly gets into his slate-coloured old Maruti 800.

As I get back, there's a call from Noni. They'd all be reaching Chandigarh by the 23rd, instead of the scheduled 24th. There's no way for them to come quicker.

"I faulted badly in not calling you in yesterday. You may have averted the nightly catastrophe. During daytime, I remained so engrossed in Updike's Rabbit at Rest, I didn't give the needed attention to her headache. And Priti won't let me summon you after dinner".

"Don't blame yourself. And my specialty, remember, is kids".

"You'd have done something effective. And, if she dies, I shall never forgive myself for this lapse".

A few droplets trickle down my cheeks.

Later, Aarti, going to work, forces me to gulp down a bowl of cornflakes and one boiled egg.

Numbed with the sudden tragedy and Valiums I stay slumped in the easy chair, till Jogi and Girija walk in. They are soon off to the hospital for a glimpse of Priti and a talk with her doctors.

On return they report no change in her condition.

Girija takes over the running of the household. She orders supplies in anticipation of guests and visitors. Jogi will stay the night at the hospital, sleeping on a bench outside the ICU.

I retire for rest in the afternoon. Jogi attends to phone calls. And he gets busy canceling the anniversary arrangements and conveying regrets to the invitees.

After a light dinner of rice and *dal*, Jogi has gone to the hospital. Girija, winding up the kitchen, appears at my bedroom door. I'm lying in bed.

"Girija, you had a long day. Take rest".

"Wish I could share your agony". She sits, drawing a chair close.

"To be frank, I don't see much hope of Priti making a comeback", I said, looking at the floor. "And in what shape would she be if she does survive!"

"While there's life, there's hope".

I don't respond.

"It's so unexpected, so tragic".

A sob escapes her.

"How life changes so suddenly!" I broke out. "You sleep secure at night. You wake up to find your life lying shattered. Last night I dreamt of dancing slow-waltz with Priti on the marriage evening. On rising, I find my cherished mate of 50 years half dead".

We stay silent a long time.

What's there to talk? In a way, the silence spoke volumes.

Girija gets up. Bends over me. Holds my head in her two hands and plants a soft wet kiss on the forehead.

And she's gone.

Wish I could bury my face in her ample bosom, cry my heart out.

I grew up in a Sikh home where you prayed in the form of *ardaas*, loudly invoking Waheguru to bring a beloved back to health, ask for His blessing in a new venture, or seek His protection against threats to life and property. By now I've lost faith in such a ritualistic prayer. And I've grown too rational to believe in magical cures; it's mostly medical science for me.

Yet that night I put forth a plaintive plea for Priti's recovery. It was more like pleading with the Guru as if I knew Him well. I argued that Priti's life was precious, and she hadn't done anything wrong to invite this catastrophe. I made out a reasoned case for her life to be spared, as if defending before a judge.

And then sleep must have come.

Getting up after breakfast next morning, "I want to see Priti".

Aarti sipping tea, "What's the point of your seeing her? She's in a coma. She can't recognize you, can't talk to you". Girija mumbles something in a similar vein.

I'm aware of their reasoning. They fear the old man is not up to it. He may suffer a shock, do injury to himself.

"No. I must see her. She's my lifelong companion, a vital part of me. Wish, I could stay all the time with her".

And so finally, there I stand, shoeless, in hospital-supplied canvas slippers and a green gown. See her with tubes in her nose, in her mouth, in her veins, and in all sorts of places, a dog-tag slapped to her wrist. It's such a mess for someone as fastidious as Priti about personal hygiene. She was presumably right in asking me off and on never to let her die in a hospital. I've been overruled—with the best of intentions.

Mercifully, she's oblivious to the humiliation being heaped on her. She's in a coma.

A patient nearby, a Sikh youth around 30, is dying, say the doctors. His liver and pancreas stand shattered with excessive drinking. And doctors can do precious little while his life peters out, the young wife sitting somewhat stoned by his side.

People outside have no idea how devastating a hospital scene can be.

You have to have one look at the dear ones' downcast faces, as they wait, interminably perched on plastic bolted-in-line chairs outside an ICU, to gain some sense of the same.

I touch Priti's cheek; a gesture I often made, more so on getting up after a good breakfast while she was still at it.

The touch elicits a frown from the portly nurse standing alongside. Your time is up, she says, and escorts me out.

Men are supposed to go first. I'd counted on that.

And I had assumed we'd always have time to talk things over before one of us conked off; to have a fair chance to work out an acceptance of the approaching end, let alone attending to practical arrangements.

This is so sudden, so unforeseen, so traumatic. No time for the surviving party to prepare for it. Not even the exchange of a few words at parting or a handclasp.

Aarti has another Valium for me when we reach home.

"Why don't you give me the bottle itself?"

"In the mental state you're in, I'd prefer to dole out a pill each time".

Ravi, Noni, and Viki arrive late in the evening. On the way they have picked up Mala and Lovely.

Ravi hugs me in a supportive embrace. Tears reflect the only light in his eyes, and so do they in mine.

Noni puts her arms around my neck. Yet she manages to keep a dry eye; she's tough, Manhattan-hardened.

Next morning they all go to see Priti, leaving Viki with me. I find it hard to explain to the five-year-old why he can't see his grandma, who, he well remembers, gifted him his yellow sit-in toy Porsche. And what exactly is Grandma doing in a hospital?

Coming back, they report that a night nurse did notice a slight movement in Priti. She was trying to move her right hand and babbling incoherently. But her condition, otherwise, remains unchanged, a cause of deep concern to attending doctors. "The doctors and nurses are solicitous in a way, I fear, that they reserve only for the attendants of the gravely sick", Ravi comments ruefully. Asked why they couldn't operate, remove the clot, Dr. Mann, the treating neurosurgeon, was frank: "Most of the damage is already done. We're mainly relying on injections, some innovative and very expensive ones. We'd watch for another 24 hours before considering surgery. I asked my noted colleague, Dr. Kataria, for a second opinion. He and his team hold the same view".

"Priti is health-conscious, diet-conscious, weight-conscious. She's a regular walker, walking briskly. No health problems barring an elevated BP that she also had under control with a daily Natrilix. No indication of any imminent bodily crisis", I tell Ravi. "Why's the stroke? And such a massive one at that".

"The same question we've been painstakingly posing to her doctors. All they say is that a blood clot in the brain can occur at any time, even without warning or symptoms. She must have suffered a major blockage of blood supply to the brain. And the brain has no capacity to keep a glucose reserve. It depends on constant, immediate supply brought to it by the coursing arterial blood. In minutes a brain starved of blood suffocates".

"Possibly something genetic", ventures Noni. "I understand Mummy's father died of a stroke at 50".

"I should have been alerted by her persistent headache that day. Why didn't I take her straight away for tests and treatment?"

"Don't blame yourself unjustly", rejoins Noni. "Nobody dashes to specialists over a low-intensity headache for a day".

'One day your life is orderly, running smooth. And then without warning the solid floor under your feet turns into a trap door, dropping you into a black hole. It's a sorry, sad world.'

Saturday, December 25.

The day dawned, the day of our golden marriage anniversary.

Ravi and Jogi rush to the hospital a little before lunch. They got a call from there. I am not told about it. Within minutes of their reaching her bedside, Priti is declared dead. She has been brain dead since morning, say the doctors. By now it's all over. The life-support machines, one the size of a mini fridge, could have possibly kept her alive for a few more days. But then what's the point of doing so to a brain-dead person?

Time of death as I saw later on the death certificate: 12.20 p.m.

What an utter irony of fate! We got married about the same hour. The marriage party had assembled at the *gurudwara* a little before noon. I didn't notice the exact time but it must have been around 12.20 that I and Priti were doing the four marriage pheras around the Holy Book.

Jogi gets busy sorting out the formalities for release of the body, settling dues, and bringing her home. At his level, he has decided against an autopsy or donating any body parts.

Ravi returns.

Watching his face, I know the worst.

"Is it all over?" I ask.

A slight nod.

And he breaks down.

Noni rushes to my side. She grasps my folded hands into hers. Simply sits, uttering not a word.

By this time the gathered women—her sister Uma, my widowed younger sister Pasho, other relatives, and a few neighbours—set up a wail. Mala and Lovely start crying. Even Viki joins in, unclear what's he crying for.

Noni steers me to the study. She shuts the door. Gets me a glass of water and another Valium.

I could only mumble, "What a quirk of fate! Dying on the very day of her golden wedding anniversary.

"Papa, that's life. You don't live it on your own terms".

"Even my wish to be by her bedside in her last moments has been denied".

"Take heart, she suffered no prolonged illness. We all want a sudden death but few are going to be provided with one. That way our end will be our ultimate bit of good luck or bad luck; the final addition to our piles of good and bad experiences".

Priti is dead.

Fairness, it seems, does not govern life and death.

The cremation is fixed for the next day at 11. And it will be firewood, not electric crematorium. Personally I'd have preferred a burial with its dignity and grace than the ordained extermination by fire. To have her grave sited in our backyard under the tall tamarind tree, with a marble plaque carrying Priti's name, and her favourite roses planted around it. Alas, it's not to be, the burning tradition overrides individual wishes.

The body, brought in by the evening, is kept in the spare room. On my expressing a wish to see her, I am persuaded to do so tomorrow morning when it's bathed and made ready for the funeral. A number of overnight guests are being accommodated with the tenant.

The irony of it!

Aarti had planned to put up guests coming for the anniversary celebrations. Now she has mourners in place of celebrants.

With the family sitting up after a scrappy meal of *roti* and *alu* curry, Jogi takes up the matter of *chautha*, the traditional fourth-day prayer meeting for the dead. He mentions that it's customary to decide the date, time, and venue at the earliest. Better if people attending the cremation are informed there and then.

"There'll be no chautha", I say.

"No chautha!" Voices are raised in disbelief, even alarm.

"Yes, there won't be any. Priti and I drew up a written agreement 2 years back that there would be no chautha for the two of us. It was initially my idea. She agreed to go along".

"But why?" asks Jogi.

"Death rituals may have no value to the dead", concedes my doctor-friend Harbans. "But they have value for the living. Our elaborate death rituals are meant to make the bereaved feel he or she is not alone".

"In recent years I happened to attend many a chautha. To me the ritual struck too cloying, too sentimental—well-nigh ludicrous. Same *bhajans* and *shabads* sung. Same facile sermons trotted on the transient nature of life on this earth. Same hope held of a great afterlife for the dead.

Frankly I've lost faith in death rituals. You die, and that's the end of it. All links snap, links of love, blood, friendship, and possessions. The whole point about being dead is that you are gone for good. What's this talk of meeting after death?"

"But there has to be an occasion for relatives and friends to pay their respects to the departed", shrieked my younger brother, beating his head with the flat of his hand. His insecurely-tied rust-red turban almost loosens with the blows.

And one could notice an unzipped fly, with the while underwear showing. No point drawing his attention to this lapse. It's no big deal; the bird inside the cage is surely dead.

He's a shriveled sickly man who had to undergo multiple bypass surgery. Apparently you feel older when you feel poorly.

"I always surmised I'd go before Priti. She said, she'd respect my wishes about the chautha. And then she sought the same for herself. I acquiesced. If anyone is interested, you can see the document itself, lying in the top right drawer of my writing desk. It also speaks of no obituary announcements, no photographs in papers".

And I see no point in telling the gathered ones that I and Priti had another compact; the survivor should get on with life, not grieve unduly long for the other.

Noni rising, "Papa, the wish expressed by you and mummy has to be honoured. There can be little argument over it".

"In that case, we could delay cremation to afternoon, giving more time to people to join in", argues Jogi.

"That's for you folks to decide. I have had my say".

I imagine inwardly there must be a sense of relief among my near ones. No lingering on for the chautha. No arrangements needed to make the function look impressive. No anxiety about poor attendance. Who is to be the principal speaker? Ravi would break down with emotion. Harbans may have to be called upon to speak.

Over a score of people are there at the simple vegetarian dinner. Mala, Lovely, and Viki are fed separately and closeted away.

When others have retired to their rooms or homes, Ravi, Jogi, Noni, and Girija sit by me in the study.

"Come on, Papa, have a brandy", says Noni. "A little bit of normalcy".

Ravi fetches a bottle of Cordon Bleu. Girija fishes out five goblets.

We sit, sipping in silence for some twenty minutes. Nobody feels like saying anything. And then they disperse, just saying goodnight.

Everyone is emotionally drained.

The ability to deal with loss is perhaps no less significant than the loss itself.

CHAPTER 3

Priti is no more.

Ravi and Jogi go next morning to pick up her bones. Another solemn group is busy doing the same on a nearby pit. No risk of a mix-up here; those collecting the remains know exactly where their near one's body turned to ash.

To Ravi it comes as a surprise that the bone collection, besides select pieces in the copper urn, fills a large Hessian sack. And he hadn't had a look at human ashes before.

All over the cremation grounds, you see slabs bearing names of the deceased. Ravi orders a marble one in Priti's name.

They drive to Kiratpur, an hour's picturesque drive. On the way Jogi stops the Esteem over a bridge, and empties the sack rather unceremoniously into the canal below.

"A lot of Punjab Sikhs are coming here now to immerse ashes", noted Jogi. "The gurudwara on this river, the Sutlej, is historic, and that longish trip to Haridwar is not necessary".

To immerse the urn ashes securely in the river, Jogi and Ravi go over the specially constructed footbridge. The urn is now upturned into the water below.

"There's something romantic in our custom of spreading ashes on sacred flowing waters", concedes Ravi.

Prayers and offerings are made at the inner sanctum of the gurudwara before they return.

In the following week the business of living gets on its way. So many things need looking into and sundry matters to decide. On Ravi's insistence some years back, both Priti and I had taken hefty life insurance policies. The money will come in handy.

Ravi, walking barefoot in the house (possibly looking for borrowed slippers), draws from my sister Pasho the remark, "Ambling barefoot. Hard to guess he's a big shot making millions".

It's not a bad idea to keep my mind focused on mundane matters while the brain adjusts to the enormity of the loss.

I sort out Priti's papers. Apparently she followed no system in keeping them. Obsolete receipts are tucked side by side with National Savings Certificates. Personal letters stay mixed with school records.

Pasho finds cupboards in the pantry and the kitchen choked with stuff; things that are in use or out of use. Priti, obviously, was hesitant to part with things, as if emptiness bothered her. Pasho is asked to perform some radical clearance.

It must be said that despite the clutter in cupboards and desk drawers, Priti ran an orderly house.

Noni and Girija sort out her personal belongings. They give away most of the clothes in charity to Priti's gurudwara in Sector 15, after our female cook, the cleaning maid, and driver's wife have had their pick. Priti, they discover, happened to have far more clothes than her daughters-in-law envisaged—a collection going back over 50 years, with scant propensity to discard.

"What about this heavily gold-embroidered saree?" Girija exclaims. "New, unworn, still in the original wrap. No matching blouse or petticoat".

Noni, handling it, "Amazing. Never seen one so ornate, gorgeous, and so thickly threaded with gold. It must be Papa's gift for the anniversary".

"You mean, a gift given before the event!"

"The slip shows it's from a shop in Amritsar. Date's not readable".

The two women bring the saree to me.

"No, I didn't give her this one. For the anniversary, I was keeping a solitaire mounted on a white-gold ring, I bought in New York at Tiffany's".

"Maybe it's a gift from her Amritsar sister when she visited her last", as Noni opens up the folded saree.

"No chance. Uma's a known miser".

"You mean Mummy bought it on her own?" asks Noni.

"No idea. She had money. She gifted me for the occasion an evening suit, the cloth and stitching charges coming to 15,000 rupees, plus an Italian shirt and tie. But then she'd have surely shown such a purchase as her own to me".

Noni admiring the saree: "Did she make a mention of it? Wives generally are wary of sharing with their hubbies full information about costly personal purchases".

"No, she didn't. Not even a hint of it. And why the hell would she buy such a gaudy one at her age?" I say, adjusting my glasses after rubbing them clean.

"Who knows, it may be an offering from a former lover? She's an Amritsar girl", I add after a pause. "Now I understand why she appeared so elated on her return from there".

Priti flagranting around! I could bet my soul against it. Even the thought of it is unworthy.

"Papa, you always took Mummy's fidelity for granted", quips Noni.

"Yes, you're right. I remain dead sure of it".

"What do we do with the mystery saree?" ask the two women at the same time.

"It goes to Girija. Noni rarely wears one".

Girija lovingly adjusting the folds, "I won't wear it, either. It goes to Mala on her marriage, a gift from her grandma".

Noni takes the brownish *shatoosh* shawl, knowing a law now forbids ownership and use in the country of wool from the rare Tibetan antelope. Girija keeps the other three *pashmina* shawls. The jewelry is divided between the two. Girija gets the lion's share; she has two girls to marry.

Noni is operating on the premise that the living should not be reminded too often and too much of the dead. Photographs and similar memorabilia are all right, but the rest of Priti's belongings better be out of her husband's sight.

Disposing of Priti's things, I speculate as to what she'd have done if I had died first. Giving away my clothes and shoes would have been easy. These are not too many, and are of average size for easy distribution. But what about all my books and clippings—writing men collect a lot of papers and reading material? Files of cuttings and notes she could destroy straightway or give to a *kabbadi*. But my book collection is so varied it can't even be given to one library; anyway, not to a school library, with all the pornographic and erotic content. She would have had a problem getting rid of them.

Johnny, the brown Labrador, lies listless in front of the kitchen door, with head in his paws—you've to step over him to enter the kitchen. Looks at his food and leaves it untouched. At one time he'd gobble his bowl of meat with gusto and let out a mighty belch. Now he growls at people coming near him; something he never did before.

Johnny was greatly attached to Priti.

How does the dog figure out his mistress is dead? Did he smell the corpse? Did he sneak into the room where her body was kept?

I ask my vet friend Sobti, "Can you take in Johnny for some time. I'll bring him back when the situation at home stabilizes". Sobti had given us Johnny as a pup.

"Sure, that's no problem".

Johnny is sent out, riding like a dignitary in the back seat of the Esteem.

CHAPTER 4

Girija and Jogi come into my bedroom after dinner. She sits on the bed near my feet and starts massaging them. I make a move to pull them back. In my family, nobody makes a physical show of affection. There's hardly any touching of body or feeiy gestures. I imagine, in Girija's parental family, and so also in Noni's, it must be different.

"You'd be haunted by her memories in this house. Better come along with us to Delhi. Wind up in Chandigarh. Stay with us permanently", says Jogi.

"I've to sort out many things here. I just can't leave for the present".

"OK, shift to our place after a month. I'll come to fetch you".

"Frankly, I'd prefer to live on my own here. I don't want to be a burden to others".

"We'd welcome having you. Presently you think you can look after yourself. But that may not be for long", chips in Girija, busily running her fingers through my toes.

I know that the invitation is more a formality than anything serious. Their government flat has only three bedrooms. And these are occupied by them and the two girls. Whenever a guest comes, Lovely has to be shifted to Mala's room, a situation unpalatable to both the girls.

Jogi and Girija are too busy in their jobs to attend to another live-in. And I am not unaware that living at the mercy of one's children is a sure way to hasten one's extinction.

"No, Girija, no. I'll live on my own. It would pose problems. I had become far too dependent on Priti, and so somewhat of a stranger to household matters. And I know it'd be terribly lonely. Nobody to unload my anxieties, nobody to talk to or squabble. But that's the life for me. I've to learn the art of living alone as widower, to live with discretion and dignity, to make each day as pleasant as possible".

"I respect your resolve. But do come and stay for a month or so after you've settled urgent matters here".

"We'll talk about it in March, April".

Jogi hasn't broached with me the subject of the house and my will. He had been pushing me and Priti to gift him the whole house, in any case the more attractive ground floor. Clearly he realizes this is not the right moment for it. But he did take it up with Ravi.

"Jogi wanted to discuss with me about your will and the house. I told him the time wasn't opportune for it", says Ravi the other night as he and Noni sat in my bedroom.

"That's between the two brothers. As far as I'm concerned you both would have equal share, with you getting the ground floor. You helped finance the house construction".

"Dad, can I make a suggestion?"

"Go ahead".

"Don't part with any property during your lifetime. The best beneficiaries are known to turn thankless, even hostile. I'd go as far as to say, one is rarely forgiven for being generous.

"If you've to make a will, keep it secret. And brook no discussion over it. An effective use of your property and other monetary resources is a must for your peace of mind. Nothing's more distressing in advanced age than dependence on others—and that includes the nearest and the dearest—for money or shelter. When dependent, others begin to club you as aged, even if you don't think of yourself that way. All in all, it's important to die with a healthy bank balance".

"And we're not asking you to live with us in Cranford", says Noni, sniffing her cognac. "We love you. We hold you in regard. And we can possibly provide all the needed physical facilities. But we know you won't be happy being totally dependent—unless, God forbid, you became disabled".

"Leave out such thoughts for the time being", interjects Ravi. "The ideal in old age is a full, enriched, and rewarding autonomy—an ideal few attain but very much worth striving for. We only expect dad to stay with us for a limited stretch every year. How about coming in June and celebrating your birthday with us? June weather is glorious in our parts".

"Let me see how it goes living on my own. A visit to Cranford could be discussed around May".

Noni, holding my hand, "Papa, keep up with your reading, and your writing. Reading offers us company, and writing gives purpose to reading. Writing, they say, is the best antidote to depression".

"Don't know I can accomplish anything worthwhile. A literary venture isn't a pleasurable sidelight. It's a hard slog, perhaps the hardest one. No fire left, while a writer has to burn a little within oneself. I even keep on forgetting names of people and places".

"Papa, everybody burns out; some do resignedly, others irritably". "Everybody forgets. And not everything is worth remembering.'

"Maybe, the only thing I may be good at is writing pornography. But writing porn at my age!"

"Write under an assumed name. Porn can be paying".

And then she clasps my shoulders and says, "You've published one novel and you're into writing another. Only ensure that the second novel breaks free of the first. I've faith in your ability and tenacity. The Adidas slogan for sportsmen, "Just do it", is equally valid for writers".

Yet, in my heart, I carry a keen awareness of my mediocrity.

Walking out, Ravi confides in Noni, "I had not felt so strong a love for Dad since I was a small boy".

My widowed sister, Pasho, younger by 2 years, lives in Amritsar. Her husband, Mangal Singh, was a powerfully built hotelier who did wrestling as a sport. He did push up and jousts at a nearby *akhara*, after he returned from his obligatory early morning trip to the market for buying meat and vegetables—a chore that brooked no delegation. Mangal was also an avid kite flier, who ran bets with other kite fliers as to who can bring another's kite down with their glass-smeared kite strings.

In later years he took to alcohol. It wasn't an everyday affair. But once a week or so, he'd spend a long drinking evening with a couple of buddies, returning home well-nigh plastered, to the mortification of his wife.

Mangal Singh died at fifty in a tragic train accident.

Pasho has agreed to stay on for a month. She can't be here longer; she has to look after two teenage girls whose parents, her son and daughter-in-law, are in UK on a year's training course. Both are college lecturers.

Pasho is a fat, cheerful dame, with a browning-apple complexion and double chin. She has a front tooth missing, and coarse gray hair sprouting on her chin. When young she was attractive, with full lips, a nice nose, and a buxom body.

Her total make-up now consists of talcum powder in generous measure after bathing—you see some sticking to her neck mixed with sweat—Ponds cold cream as a nightly treat for the face, and kohl for the eyes.

At Amritsar I mostly saw her squatting on a low *niwar pidhi*—sagged with her weight—in the central court that sported a frame of thick steel bars in the middle. This arrangement provided light and air to the floor below, as the house was bounded on three sides with other houses. She sat shelling expertly for herself the snacks called panaceas or *chilgozas*. She'd extract these out one by one from a side pocket, eat the nut, and deposit the shells in a *katori*. You could calculate the length of a particular sitting session from the contents of the katori.

At one time Pasho's diet consisted mainly of *kharoras* and ghee-smeared *rotis*, with a total absence of physical exercise. Of late she has largely given up on meat. It's only eggs.

"I had enough of meat in my life. Yet I can cook and serve. Even have no compunction to wring the neck of a chicken. Myself I don't fancy eating anything that walked or flew. A vegetarian diet may even pare down my fat".

Yet, for a body as heavy as hers, she can move with surprising nimbleness.

Pasho enjoys talking to people, and is fairly free with her smiles—the gap in the front teeth showing. At Amritsar her most socialization is with neighbouring women, not so much through visiting one another but from adjacent rooftops. During winter, women spend hours on their roofs, enjoying sunshine, doing things like knitting, and exchanging gossip. In summer, this has to be postponed to evenings when it's cool enough up there.

At Chandigarh she misses such neighbourly socialization, the next house being almost a hundred yards away. So she looks forward to women coming for condolence or otherwise.

Pasho is on the garrulous side, and possesses a high-pitched voice. I can't help overhearing snippets of conversation between her and the calling women.

"Priti died too early".

"She wasn't old".

"Wasn't young, either".

"Well, 67, they say".

"Was she 67?"

"That's not old. Not old for her family. Father-in-law lived beyond 90".

"The husband looks devastated".

"How will he get along without her?"

"They seemed so happy".

"An ideal couple, I'd say".

"Think, he'll remarry?"

"No, no, no. He's seventy-five".

"Doesn't look 75".

"Behaves as shy as someone seventeen".

"Men can always start again, can't they?"

"Seems to have a roving eye".

"Rubbish", says Pasho. "Don't say such things. My brother anyway is no pushover. No one can hustle him into marriage".

Pasho is strong and solid like an ox. It must be the good genetic material. But then my younger brother remains sickly, suffering bad lungs, bad heart, and bad liver. A waster, a failure in life, a loser—but aren't we all losers in the end? A widower at 50, he has been living with his son since then. Not an easy person to put up as a permanent houseguest, with his propensity to throw tantrums. He's ever harping on his illnesses. Yet his son, an engineer-turned-politician and rising in the Akali party hierarchy, has displayed remarkable patience and forbearance. Maybe politicians learn to put up with all sorts of people. Satwant Singh has even cajoled his busy teacher-wife to suffer the man. But in the process, my brother has earned his daughter-in-law's unremitting, subdued disdain.

Pasho may be short on expressions of sympathy. But she's the only one who may "stick around". She gets on with the day-to-day tasks of running my home while making very few demands. Her presence can be of inestimable value in warding off my sense of loneliness and helplessness.

She's willing to entertain my plea of living here longer, though her heart is not in it. She's essentially an Amritsar woman. To her Chandigarh with its spaces and greenery feels like a deserted place or a hill station. She has lived mostly in a place where the busy bazaar is at your doorstep and street noises come into your rooms. You have houses at handshaking distance, and a neighbourly chat whenever you are free for it. Straight from that bustling locality and the narrow winding lanes she's catapulted into open vistas and geometrical straight roads. She'd like to see more fellow beings than trees.

Even in my boyhood Pasho always stood by me, did a lot of odd jobs for me. Pity, she can't stay on till her son and daughter-in-law are back from UK by July.

Meantime her talk mostly veers around Priti. The two had

lived in the same house for over two decades.

"Amazing how calm and composed Priti could be", says Pasho. "No easy task with two active kids, her teaching job, and you absent. On top of that, our demanding father staring whole day, making comments, doling out advice. He could have helped us with the restaurant. But he could only teach, he said. And took merely those tuitions where students came to him; he was too old to go places, he said".

"Priti matured much earlier than many. Indeed, I'd say, she happened to display more natural intelligence than me".

"Only once I saw her lose her cool, the night Jogi went missing".

"Yes, Jogi gave her a terrible fright. Yet she counselled me to be patient with him".

"Priti was my choice for your marriage. And I had to push you into it. Thank me".

"I thank you Pasho from the bottom of my heart. I couldn't have married anyone better".

Loneliness is going to be my lot. I've so few male friends. In fact the only close one I have is the doctor-golfer Harbans.

How many male friends does a man need? Mine are mostly friendships of convenience. I have friends I joke with. A few others are there I play golf with or bridge or discuss books, and then there's the tenant couple.

Of late, Satwant, my politician nephew, is a frequent caller. We discuss politics. He's a jolly fellow, who enjoys narrating the peccadilloes of politicians, even making fun of himself.

I suppose men seldom make close friends after the age of fifty. Men are essentially failures at friendships. Maybe it's their drive to compete that puts others off. Anyway, I haven't made a new friend for some years.

Harbans, my one intimate friend, is younger by 6 years, and a widower, too. He renders me medical advice and assistance. He has time for me, as he does consultation work at his house-clinic only from 8 to 12.

The best about Harbans is his sense of humour, let alone bursts of laughter. And laughter is infectious. Hope he doesn't catch my depression, the same is also contagious.

"Harbans, you can't imagine how lonely I feel on some evenings, with Priti missing".

"Loneliness, I'd say, is a mental state. You take to Prozac or some similar pill for depression and your mood may lift. Or, it could change with the saying of prayers—the way it was with your father. Or companionship. You already seem cheered in my presence".

"But you'd be gone soon".

"Too much thinking gets a man down. Go more for activities, leave less time for brooding".

Ravi, Noni, Jogi, Girija, and the children all leave on 31st morning.

Noni is seen giving outrageously large tips to the servants. Rano the cook and Banta the driver get Rs 5,000 each. Gauri the cleaning maid and Bhura the mali, Rs 3,000 each.

"You could be spoiling them", I say.

"These are good people, Papa, and they'd work well for you".

"Knowing his weakness for alcohol, Banta's tip should better be handed over to his wife".

The two brothers sit in front, Jogi driving the rented Toyota Qualis. Their wives sit next behind while the children jostle in the rear.

"Mother's demise is clearly the most traumatic event in Dad's life. A horrendous blow. As bad as a disabling body blow", says Ravi.

"Well, all of us who are married know it's coming".

"But this was so sudden, so unexpected. He had no time to be mentally prepared for it. I don't know how he'll cope with the loss. He hasn't the solace of religion, something our grandpa had. It takes some time to comprehend a tragedy, like the death of a loved wife. You can't readily accept the reality.

Presently he's numb. Doesn't cry. Soon it will turn to pining, followed by spells of depression. It's only six days as a widower and he already looks like one. His hair is messy and clothes unkempt—someone who used to pride himself on his tidy get-up. "

Jogi, levelling up after overtaking a truck, said "I assume papa's mentally tough to tide over it".

"Hope so. Old men are known to die within a year or two of the demise of their long-term spouse. Not so much from a broken heart—you wouldn't find grief on a death certificate—but from sheer loneliness".

"Papa has got his writing and his golf. He may play more bridge. Stay more with you and me".

Ravi adjusted himself comfortably in his seat with the same lazy movement he might use to scratch a not-very-pressing itch, "You know it was Mummy who ran the whole show: house, kitchen, garden, servants, purchases, family budget, social obligations. She took care of umpteen details, right up to sorting out dad's clothes.

Wish Pasho Auntie could stay on, perform mundane tasks, and give him company. Dad could be quite helpless in day-to-day routine".

"Who knows, he may fall in love again. Acquire a mate. Give himself a second chance to find the love he lost; a frantic attempt to bring love into his life. He's young at heart and fond of female company. Has money and property".

"Most unlikely, though I won't rule it out altogether", says Ravi, suppressing a smile. "To be frank, I'd welcome such a development; someone to give him company, someone to look after him; some familiar female face—not Rano's—he can see last thing at night and the first thing in the morning.

That would also relieve us partly. We, I'm afraid, are too preoccupied to take responsibility of an ageing parent. Pity that marriage or live-in among the elderly continues to be frowned upon in India".

"At his age and with his independent spirit, Papa isn't unduly concerned about what others think".

The brothers stay silent for a few minutes. Jogi is concentrating on negotiating a road patch under repair. Ravi is lost admiring the vast spread of yellow mustard fields.

“Sometimes I think we’d all be a lot happier to underplay sex in our lives. It just does not last long enough to support all the expectations we place on it”.

“You’ve a point”, concedes Ravi. “Sex can cause disorder. At Dad’s age, for one, compatibility on shared pleasure in food, or of TV programmes, or books, or gardening may be more rewarding than merely fooling around”.

The two ladies in the back share their own concern about the widowed man.

“As far as I can make out he’ll be simply miserable without female companionship”, says Girija.

“Pasho may well stay on”.

“No, I mean intimate female companionship”.

“You assume him to be sexually active?”

”One can only surmise”.

“You may be right. But how does he secure the needed female companionship?”

“No idea”.

“We can get him into a high-class old-persons’ home in the U.S. They pick up companions there”.

“That won’t work. He’ll only be comfortable with his home, his books, his golf course”.

“Girija, you mean second marriage?”

“Something of that sort. Hope he hits on someone really suitable. A wrong choice can spell misery. Of course, Jogi will fume at the prospect of another claimant to the old man’s property. But then it’s Dad’s life that matters at this juncture, and he hasn’t much left”.

For me, this New Year’s Eve was the first without celebrations and expectations.

Pasho and I eat an everyday meal, me having one more whisky than usual. Pity Pasho doesn't drink. Her husband's bouts of drinking developed in her an abhorrence of alcohol. The only concession she makes tonight is to have a late cup of tea. Pours two heaped spoons of sugar, stirs the same relentlessly.

We watch some celebrations on TV. In a corner Pasho struggles to wriggle out of her bra and panties under her nightie. As I remember, for years she slept in the same *salwar / kameez* she had during the day. Only recently she seem to have taken to the nightie—a loose, shapeless garment gaining fast popularity these days. She's still wearing her heavy gold chain, with a gold toothpick hanging to it. Though I often notice she uses more of her tongue tip than the gold toothpick to ease out food particles from her teeth. She tells me, she never takes her chain off, not sleeping, not bathing.

We exchange memories of our childhood only. Pasho and I grew up together in the same household but our recollections don't come out identical. Memory, anyway, retains no more than an infinitesimal bit of the lived life. And it is mysterious how one little incident is retained and not some others.

"You were the first fully nude female I chanced to see when I came upon you getting into your school uniform".

"I've absolutely no recollection of you barging in while changing".

"Do you remember blaming me for spilling ink on your desk and Mother shouting at me?" says Pasho.

"I do recollect the incident of spilled ink but I don't think I specifically blamed it on you".

And so this goes on.

"Never did anything special on New Year's Eve", she says. "They (she always spoke of her dead husband as 'they') deemed it all a thing for white people". Pasho has the habit of quoting her husband for corroboration of her views.

In a way her husband was right. It's the Christian Gregorian calendar that forms the basis of such celebrations.

And then we sleep without waiting for the midnight hour, sleep through to the dawn of the new millennium which, one discovers, turns out no different from the preceding dawns. Except in one major way: Priti wasn't there.

The obligatory New Year merrymaking, I have always felt, is a bit fake and phoney; the fun somewhat forced. Maybe the festivity is mostly dancing, and I'm no good at it.

Last year we were at the golf club. I did join Priti for the hectic dance at the stroke of 12, embraced her, and kissed her. But then another acquaintance of ours, a tall sprightly Sikh pushing eighty, managed three dances with her. And he danced damn well. I felt a pang of jealousy, seeing him hold Priti close by her waist, and Priti apparently enjoying it. It made me down more whisky.

Mind, this gentleman had once confided in me that he had forsaken sex, marital or otherwise, for over a decade; he couldn't get it up. And yet I didn't fancy his dancing arm in arm with Priti.

Eventually, I pressured her to leave for home within an hour of the midnight shouting and bursting of balloons.

Once I was a true Resolutionary. I used to greet the first January morn with a full set of resolutions; often the same ones year after year—a sorry indicator of those remaining unrealized.

No resolutions this year. I'm too grief-struck to think coherently.

Priti is dead.

And, unlike joy, grief is the hardest emotion to convey because so much of it is numbness.

The last year was simply tragic. Life, it seems, plays all sorts of jokes on you. Let's see what it has in store for me during the coming year.

CHAPTER 5

Only six months back, Priti and I celebrated my 75th birthday in style at Ravi's place in the US

"Dad, you'd be 75 tomorrow, a major milestone in a man's life. Calls for special observance", says Ravi, dispensing drinks at the cozy, well-stocked bar, adjacent to their large living room. Their bulldog Othello is snoring loudly, spread on the carpet.

With everyone noticing the heavy snores, Ravi mentions, "Bulldogs have a problem with breathing. It stems from the peculiar shape of their nose".

Noni and I are perched on back-supporting bar stools that swivel. Priti, who disdains alcohol, lounges on a leather settee, with a glass of fresh cranberry juice. Back home you don't get cranberries.

We're at drinks before dinner.

"Poet Auden says seventy is a good age to die; he died at 66. Here I've reached 75, surviving illnesses and injuries, accidents and riots, lightning and earthquakes, let alone plain wearing out", as I take a gulp of Glenlivet.

"And all that red meat and those sugary snacks", rejoins Priti. "Tons of fat must have passed through his system".

Noni, sipping her lime-spiked Absolut vodka, pipes in, "Papa, with your genes, coupled with a trouble-free heart, liver, and lungs, I give you another 10 years, if not 15. Your dad died at 93".

"Mother packed off at 45, less than half her husband's age.

"That was from tuberculosis, not old age", corrects Priti, now engaged in nail filing.

Ravi, combing his curly short hair with fingers of the left hand, "Dad, you got grandpa's longevity genes. I should get yours, if there's anything in the doctrine of hereditary longevity. Anyway, the average lifetime stands extended to 80. Better plan that in mind. Old people are now a sort of protected species, courtesy medical science".

"So long as his dad is living, Ravi's freed from fear of his own mortality", quips Noni, biting into an olive.

"Dad, take my suggestion for whatever is worth; a glass of red wine daily with dinner. It helps the heart. I understand, India's into making drinkable red wine".

"I am taking a measure of Scotch, mostly Famous Grouse, before dinner for some years. I have been getting used to the colonial poison. At your place this time I got a taste of great single malts, brands like the 24-year-old Highland Park and the 16-year-old Lagavulin. Never knew of such fantastic stuff.

"Red wine should be good for your mother's heart, if you can persuade her. She has high BP.

"At one time I was taken in by single malts", says Ravi, with a clink of ice cubes in his Chivas. "You'd find some excellent ones in the cellar below; bottles of 25-year-old Macallan, said to be the finest of the 100-odd malts. Take away a couple. Soda or ice mars the flavour. Single malts are better drunk neat or one part water to two parts whisky".

"Why are you munching away so many cashew nuts when a nice dinner is waiting?" Priti calls out. She has finished the nails of her left hand to her satisfaction.

"He must show restraint in eating. You see him polishing off a bowl of cashews at a sitting. Such fatty stuff. Thinks dietary laws don't apply to him".

Dropping a big salted cashew back into the bowl, "Yes I must reform. No surprise, I've aged faster than I meant to. My doctor-friend, duly goaded by Priti, cautions me to go easy on snacks between meals".

Noni, doing bottoms-up on her vodka-lime, "Don't change too much. You're doing OK. Only a bit of bulge at the tummy. Treat it as a reserve to tide over an illness". Actually, every single person I've known who's switched to healthy living died rather early. Live as if you're going to live forever".

"What about his teeth?" Priti intervenes. "By now six front ones stand capped. And every time he goes to the dentist, they discover new cavities or a missing inlay. The dentist gobbles a good part of your papa's pension".

I have come to dread the dentist's bill, not his drill. In fact, it's such a comfortable chair, I wish I had one at home.

"I've started the practice of rinsing soon after I eat anything sugary. But eat I must, more so when at writing. Writing drains energy. A chunk of chocolate helps: a stimulant, a comforter. Something to soothe the nerves when a piece of writing isn't going well".

"You'll find a goodly selection of bittersweet, black chocs in the fridge. I prefer Toblers, the triangular ones filled with honey and crushed almonds" says Noni.

"Dinnertime, folks".

We are here on a month's trip, our third to Ravi in the US

The visits don't exceed a month. With the sort of lifestyle Ravi and Noni keep, we may well overstay our welcome beyond such a stretch. And back home Priti has her nursery school to attend to.

Twice we travelled economy on our own. Our Lufthansa flights happened to be choking full, with little leg room and tortuous waits at toilets.

At the Frankfurt transfer hub, said to be one of the busiest in the world, we were hard put to find a place to sit. People lay sprawled in every nook and corner, as if the airport designers wanted to create the architectural version of coach class.

Being airborne engenders a high for me. Indeed, few seconds in life are more releasing than when a plane ascends the sky.

Accompanied by the controlled rage of its engines, it roars into the atmosphere.

An immense horizon opens up. From the new vantage point the whole landscape looks more serene, more orderly: roads curving to avoid hills, rivers tracing paths to lakes, streets that from ground looked like they were laid out without much thought emerge as well-planned grids. Within minutes you have snow-like clouds floating underneath serenely.

A thin metal wall and cheerful-looking plastic separating some 300 people from minus 60 degrees and rarefied air at 35,000 ft.; people having the same angle of recline, the same TV.

Food that, if sampled in a home would appear unappetizing, acquires a new taste and interest, as if one was on a picnic. With the in-flight plastic tray, I make myself at home in this unhomely place. Lucky, this time we get cloth napkins and china.

Journeys are said to be the midwives of thought. Few places are more conducive to internal conversations than a moving plane or train. Introspective reflections, which are liable to be stalled when one is stationary, are helped along by the flow of the landscape. A sort of dreaminess comes over me, fostered by the motion noise; a dreaminess bringing on thoughts and memories that may not arise in more settled situations.

A month earlier Noni had phoned, "Papa, have the two of you ever been to Paris?

"Afraid not".

"All couples should go to Paris, the world's lover capital. The city exudes special love chemistry".

And she rang back after a week. "Your tickets will now include a flight from Copenhagen to Paris and back. A room at the George V, a top traditional hotel, has been booked for 3 nights".

The Paris stay turns out a wondrous experience. One can't envisage a city centre better planned and more meticulously preserved.

The hotel itself is beautifully built from days when space wasn't an overriding consideration. The entrance lobby's so high you squint looking at the ceiling. And what elegant furniture, as we wend our way through to the lifts.

Our room, a suite, shows up a radiant river as the porter draws the thick drapes. The heavy door closes with a solid bank-vault click.

The moment the uniformed bell-boy with his 5-euro tip steps out, Priti catches me by the waist and drags me to the king-size bed with its high headrest and long milky-white puffed pillows. Nether garments come off and we have the most satisfying sex—the best for months. Across the enormous bed is a gilded mirror that takes in the entire bed. No point in letting it go to waste.

I feel young, and Priti acts young, all because of being catapulted into a grand room of a grand hotel in a grand city—courtesy Ravi and Noni. How important an environment can be!

A new place has this effect on Priti. It excites her sexually.

I do caution her: "Don't touch the minibar. The prices amount to daylight robbery. A tiny bag of cashews can set you back by as much as Rs 400".

"Do they keep a count of all those little things?"

"Most of these minibars are now laser-set. Any item removed for more than twenty seconds automatically gets registered in your room account".

We go up the Eiffel Tower, take a cruise under Seine bridges, and visit Versailles. Priti finds museums tiring, if not boring. At the Louvre, she's only interested in seeing the Mona Lisa. Spends more time in the museum shop buying prints than viewing originals in the galleries.

On Noni's insistence, we have an evening at Folies Bergère, with its compulsory complement of a champagne bottle. Priti won't touch it. I get tipsy drinking the bulk of it—you can't waste costly champagne.

What a splendid sight! Topless dancers, equally tall, equally slim, are sporting identical breasts with their pink nipples; gorgeous, round, full, seemingly firm.

I always imagined breasts varied a lot but in the champagne-filled haze all those on the stage look exactly alike. The show selectors must be doing a smart job.

Being walkers, we walk a lot. Luckily, we have glorious sunshine during the whole of our stay. Paris shimmered under a shimmering sky, a charming place, awash with sunlight.

We enjoy walking to the Tuileries Gardens, to Concorde, and to the Champs Elysees right up to the Arc de Triumphe. Passing Les Invalides Priti remarks, "What a lot of gold is up there! Reminds me of the Golden Temple".

"The French Republic nearly went broke paying for all that gold, they say".

We sit at open-air cafes and bistros, savouring typical French cuisine.

Only one meal misfires. On the recommendations of a chatty, friendly waiter, Priti orders an exotic fish delicacy, going by the name *petite friture trouvillaise*, costing 200 francs. She's fond of fish; deems fish better for her high BP than red meat.

When the dish arrives, she's shocked. Within a deep plate lie ranged two dozen tiny fish—whole, complete with mouth, eyes, ears, and tail, heads facing one way, tails another. These look more like uncooked worms that have been stunned senseless.

Forthwith she takes over my pork chops and passes on the fish to me. I peer around to see how others are tackling it. No one's eating this strange stuff.

There's no point using knife and fork. I simply pick each little fish by the neck with the thumb and forefinger, dip it in sauce (an excellent white sauce) and chew it whole. And find these tastier as I get along.

When we relate Priti's mishap to Noni, she almost chides her mother-in-law, "Mummy, you missed a known delicacy of Normandy cuisine".

"Let's have a pavement café breakfast", I suggest one morning.

"But our hotel breakfast is paid for".

"Treat it as an adventure".

"Back home you're averse to experimentation in food. Outside, you become bold".

In a narrow street behind the hotel, we're assaulted all of a sudden by the fragrant, mouth-watering smell of fresh coffee.

"*Café au lait, s'il vous plait*", I tell the lady proprietor of a small café, exhausting nearly all my French.

She puts up a pot of coffee and a jug of steaming frothy milk. The first sip was simply delicious.

The good lady places before us a basket of different breads, small slabs of creamy butter, and a dash of dark, raspberry jam. "I've just brought them fresh from the corner bakery", she says in broken English.

I take a croissant. Find it warm, flaky and golden on the outside, soft tender layers within. Break off a piece, add a bit of butter, and a touch of jam. It melts in the mouth. Never tasted bread like that. And then we munch a cinnamon roll.

"Only when you come out of India, you know what good bread is", I tell Priti.

She looks as if she doesn't agree; she's always backing her country, a pronounced Indophile.

CHAPTER 6

Ravi, Noni, and Viki are at Newark airport when we land on a sunny Sunday afternoon. As I come out of Customs pulling a trolley (no pushing ones here because they are deemed unfriendly to others walking around), Ravi touches my feet, the traditional greeting reserved for respected elders. Noni gives a hearty hug. In return I peck her inviting cheek.

I suppose one nurses a soft corner for one's young daughter-in-law.

The hour or two of heightened conviviality upon fresh arrival is heartwarming.

It's a cool, cloudless day, the air unbelievably fresh and clean. On the 20-minute drive, miles and miles of forest flank both sides of the 12-lane expressway. New Jersey calls itself 'the Garden State'.

I wanted to hold Viki in my lap in front. But he sits back belted in his special chair, noisily running his toy Ferrari over the left armrest. "Children below 7 aren't allowed in front as a safety measure", tells Ravi. "And they've to be strapped to a seat, not sat up in a lap".

"You've taken to short hair", says Noni. "Is it some new trend back home or just your way to show less of gray?"

"Thrift, simply thrift. My barber charges Rs 100, here it would be $20".

Cranford is a pretty small town. It boasts of a public library, a 24-hour supermarket, a cinema complex, plus the usual complement of stores, schools, restaurants, and parks. You can make to Manhattan by train or bus or car in less than 45 minutes.

Ravi and Noni leave for work by seven in the morning, he for his software company near Newark, and Noni to her finance job with Merrill Lynch in Manhattan. Both have breakfast at office of coffee and bagels.

Ravi is casually dressed, often sporting no tie—he wants me to take away some of his neckties, but then I rarely wear one now. He's the boss and has nobody to impress. For important meetings or visitors, he keeps a couple of suits in office.

Noni always goes turned out immaculately.

"Years of work in Manhattan's money street have taught me that a working woman has to look great", she says. "People notice you. Look sloppy and they notice the sloppy part, mismatched clothes, even chipped nail polish".

Noni drives her BMW XS 4.4 to the local rail station—in existence since 1865— takes a train, and a short taxi ride at the other end. She isn't back before seven. Ravi drives to work in his light-blue Mercedes. He's usually home by six.

In the care of his nanny, Viki is off to the kindergarten between 8 and 11.

Priti and I have most of the weekdays to ourselves. She is either enjoying Viki's company or frequenting stores. On some days she busies herself preparing lamb, pork, or chicken curry; she isn't averse to eating beef but dislikes handling it raw.

She buys the cuts herself from the butcher, not the plastic-packed stuff from a supermarket. The stocky middle-aged butcher and his youngish wife wear white coats like doctors, and run a spotlessly clean place.

Her dishes evoke high appreciation all round at the dinner table. She happens to be a first-rate cook. And that's when it isn't her kitchen. She has to ferret out various ingredients and condiments.

Ravi and Noni attach much importance to dinner, the only meal, and hot meal at that, the family eats together. No disturbance is brooked. Mobiles are shut off, phones put on answering mode. "Telemarketers, knowing that people are home for dinner, often call at this time", says he.

And there's always a quality wine to go with the meal.

Our breakfast, taken late, is an elaborate meal of Sunkist orange juice, Kellogg honey cereal, boiled eggs, bacon, sausage, fruit, and espresso coffee. With the anticipated cold lunch of a sandwich, emphasis has shifted to cooked breakfast. The hearty meal makes you feel all is well with the world.

I while away a good part of the day at the public library, only a 10-minute walk away on Walnut Street, next to our Chestnut Street.

"Why don't you spend more time with Viki", Priti is apt to remark, seeing me readying for a walk to the library as we finish our breakfast. "At Chandigarh you talked so much of playing with Viki".

"I'd play games with him when he grows bigger".

"You said the same when Ravi and Jogi were small".

"But I was mostly away on jobs during their boyhood".

Frankly, I find it hard to amuse a kid of five for long. Maybe, I lack the needed communication skills, let alone being badly out of fathering practice.

My only contribution to Viki's growth: one day I took off the stabilizers from his bike, put him on the saddle, and ran and ran holding the bike till he could ride on his own. The venture left me panting breathless.

"Papa, don't overreach yourself", warns Noni.

But Viki is vastly impressed with my feat.

He, however, doesn't display the patience to learn and play marbles, my favourite boyhood pastime. He enjoys handling the multi-coloured glass globes I bought for him, treating them more as a collection than playthings.

Viki's a friendly, lovable kid. He's always kissing people, embracing people. Praises everything given to him in superlative terms. "That's the best car I had", he tells his grandma over the gift of a toy Rolls of Chinese make. "The best nuts I ate", he tells me when I gave him a fistful of cashews.

What usually annoys his parents about Viki is his picky eating, going for a few limited things: fries, bread, sausages, nuts, ice cream. They want him to eat beans and salads, pulses and meat curry to introduce him to all sorts of foods.

This often spells trouble at the dining table. At times it culminates in Viki being hauled off to his room, or left to sit alone at the table till he eats his slices of bacon or snippets of okra. Often his offence of picky eating gets compounded as Viki begins playing with his knife and fork or fidgeting in his elevated chair.

I commonly come out in Viki's defence. "Picky eating is an evolutionary survival strategy. By the age of four kids are old enough to find food on their own, but not old enough to judge what's safe to eat and what's not. An ingrained fear of new foods protects a child from poisoning".

Noni, near exasperation: "Come on, Papa, nobody is poisoning him".

"His picky eating should be taken more as a temporary inconvenience than a serious long-term problem. By the way, forcing a kid to gulp down a vegetable it doesn't like, before being allowed to eat the pudding, could simply make him hate that vegetable more as well as love the pudding more. Humans are hardwired to prefer sweets and avoid bitter. Bitterness is a sign of toxicity. No wonder the human tongue comes equipped with an elaborate bitter-alarm system".

"He's pleading his own case for sugary stuff", Priti smirks.

"In due time, Viki should be eating everything, at least all what his peers eat at school lunch",

And I can't resist commenting. "Lucky, he hasn't to finish his food, the way we had to do ours in childhood. We were made to eat everything heaped in our *thali;* wasting food was deemed a sin. It's altogether different in plentiful America".

Viki came after 14 years of marriage, his mother notching 40, father 43.

Initially it was a conscious parental decision—despite persistent prodding from parents on both sides—to delay a birth till Noni built her career. Thereafter, it took Noni an anxious year or two to get pregnant; the couple quite keen but the kid didn't know about it.

I do have a strong suspicion Viki is the product of an embryo first formed in a Petri-dish and then implanted in the uterus. In all probability, the semen and the egg belong to his natural parents, who keep cagey about the mechanics of his conception.

I wished Noni had given birth to twins, something not uncommon in IVF. That would have completed the family.

We were there at the great event, Viki's caesarian birth.

Pity, by the time the lad—a sweet kid, mostly smiling, rarely crying—is fifteen, I'll be eighty-five, if living. I won't see him mature into manhood.

Priti's latest plea of giving Viki a sibling is simply laughed off.

"An only child, with no brothers or sisters to share things, can grow selfish, self-centred", she argues.

"Mummy, that's old hat. Recent researches indicate that the onlies are no different from other children in social mixing, let alone being better achievers. Bringing up Viki takes a toll on all our attention and time. We've got what's called a full plate. We have absolutely no inclination to add to it".

"The subject, I suppose, hardly merits a discussion", shrugs Ravi as he gets up for a stroll in the backyard.

Viki has a room to himself, with an adjoining bath and a closet for clothes. It's a specially painted, decorated room that's already crammed with toys. And now houses a computer with sound track and kiddy software.

Since birth, he sleeps alone at night, with a monitor by the bedside that alerts his parents as well as the nanny. His room is now being fixed with a closed-circuit TV with extensions in various parts of the house.

Viki has graduated out of Huggies. He had started showing discomfort with diapers. A boy could have more reason for unease than a girl.

They have a professional, full-time, live-in nanny. Myra, an American of Polish descent, had joined soon after Viki was born. Short and busty, the upper lip hairy but curved prettily, deep-set green eyes, Myra is a smartly turned-out figure of thirty-five—marital status indeterminate. She has done a two-year nanny's course and put in another ten as nanny. Speaks correct English.

Everyday she fills a page or two of a book-size notebook in her neat, upright hand: what Viki ate during the day, how much he slept, details of his bowel motion, a resume of his other activities, and his general behaviour. This is gone through minutely by his mother on return from work.

Viki has a busy schedule, busier than mine, it seems: meals, bath, school, visiting the library or baby-power classes, reading, swimming, watching his favourite Nickelodeon on TV, sitting at his computer, the regulation outdoor walk for air, and so on.

Myra is paid $3,000 a month. She has a suite to herself and sole use of a new Astra. She is allowed to buy all the food she wants with a store credit card. In the process she also buys groceries for the house from the same supermarket, Noni leaving a list on some mornings.

Myra eats separately, with a kitchenette to herself. Indeed, the food demarcation is so marked, Priti's suggestion of passing her India-brought mango pickle was vetoed.

"Suppose she develops stomach trouble. It will be blamed on the pickle", says Noni.

Myra, hired through an agency, has a contract running into three full pages. Besides pay and perks that include health insurance, it lists holidays, hours of work, overtime rates, travel terms if asked to accompany the kid on tours, and so on.

And the crucial part: what she'll do and what she won't. For example, she'll only iron kid's clothes but along with his clothes she will load the family wash into the washing machine/drier and later take these out. The same applies to Viki's used utensils and cutlery for the dishwasher. She is to feed the family dog if the masters are delayed at work but has nothing to do with the dog's grooming or taking out for a walk. It's another matter, as a goodwill gesture—generated by the gift of two Bangalore silk scarves—she occasionally irons a blouse of Priti's.

Rules regarding nanny work are rigid. And there's some rationale behind this highly "unionized" approach. In middle-class American homes all other staff has evaporated except cleaning women coming for a couple of hours once or twice a week. The nanny, the only full-time employee at home, is left vulnerable to do extra work as she constitutes the sole pair of hired hands. There is almost an irresistible temptation to load her with household chores: turning down beds, emptying trash bags, watering indoor plants, shopping.

What's a nanny doing while her ward sleeps, runs a popular line of employer thinking. To the expensively trained nanny, the usual tasks of a maid are beyond her brief.

Priti can't help voicing the view, "Anybody can do a nanny's job. It calls for the least technological skills. You just need commonsense and patience".

Noni has her own version. "On weekends when Myra is off, the house is a shambles of clothes, toys, napkins, with us usually on edge by the evening. But when I return home weary on weekdays, I can see exactly what I'm bankrupting myself for; Viki bathed, powdered, neatly clad, ensconced comfortably in Myra's care, cooing contentedly".

In fact, Myra is deemed so good, Noni apprehends she may get headhunted.

A professional nanny, trained in child hygiene, health, and psychology, is someone confident, purposeful, with a businesslike efficiency. She's taught to take particular care of her ward's safety when driving about. Mothers feel much better having their babies in such care than of the inexpensive raw girls, commonly illegal immigrants.

Once I ran foul of Myra. She had given Viki a 3-minute 'time out' for spilling his Sultana Bran cereal on to the kitchen floor, to the delight of Othello, the family bulldog.

As she was making him sit in a chair facing a corner, Viki set up a piercing howl. Hearing the shriek in the next room I hurried to the scene—I thought he had hurt himself. I picked up a tearful Viki in my arms.

Myra wasn't amused. She noted the incident in her diary; how Grandpa had interfered in disciplining her ward, the kid—a canny manipulator.

Taking advantage of our presence, Ravi and Noni pull off a 4-day dream holiday to Bermuda, an island about which Mark Twain, a frequent visitor, had remarked, "Folks on their way to heaven stop off in Bermuda and think they have arrived".

They leave Viki in our care—no small responsibility to take charge of an only child.

What particularly fascinates Priti in her shopping forays is the operative "Rule of Returns". You can return anything you bought within a month and get something in its place. No questions whatever are asked on returning a purchase. Only for a cash refund, do stores require the purchase receipt, and Priti doesn't discard receipts. Big stores often operate a separate desk meant only for return.

Once or twice a week, Myra drives us out to the nearest suburban shopping mall. She picks us back after 3–4 hours. We love to spend half a day at the mall.

"If you had to pick one thing that would typify civilization in the US in the twentieth century, a front-running candidate would be the suburban shopping mall", says one writer on the American scene.

Malls are coming up in our country, too. But these are more city malls, and the shops inside are often owned. In the American malls, all space is only hired by the developers, with strict control over display of goods. Our malls have yet to reach the standards of upkeep and facilities of a typical American suburban mall.

The latter are entirely designed for people coming in cars. And are so located as to be well served by a network of roads. The mall we visit is a typical one; a fully enclosed area at two levels, no windows on the outside, department stores at the three ends, the fourth a food court.

Many seem to spend hours in the comfort and safety of malls. Older people can sit in peace amidst the overall bustle. Quite a few elderly go there on doctor's orders.

The sheltered, comfortable, and consistent mall premises are ideal for walking. This shopping mall has even instituted a walkers' club for senior citizens. Older people, heart patients seeking a safe place to exercise, arrive before the shops open to walk a measured route around the corridors.

I love the town library. It's a capacious, centrally air-conditioned complex that includes clean restrooms, drinking-water fountains, and dozens of computer workstations. Books ranged in bright new covers gleam in plastic library coats, catching light from overhead.

The liveliest part is the children's section, with its extensive assortment of illustrated books, educational toys, and other recreational-cum-instructional material, all amidst a colourful setting. This is clearly the most patronized section, the hub of the library. Children as young as two-year-old are brought in for "cuddle-up" story-time. Singing sessions are held for pre-school kids, often helped by their mothers or nannies. The local public library functions as an important educational-cum-cultural tool through which American children from a tender age are socialized to the world of books and computers.

Once, libraries loomed as forbidding places. But here is something of a club atmosphere. At the circulation desk, mothers bringing in children often chat with the staff and gossip. And nobody really minds a kid running about, or a toddler screaming. The idea is to create a hospitable place for kids, at the same time making them aware of the imperatives of library discipline.

I find the library staff most friendly and helpful to me. Maybe they can spot a serious reader.

Wish I had access to something similar in Chandigarh.

Near the library is a Ben & Jerry's ice cream outlet, known for its extra-creamy products. It's fun to take a break from reading and refresh myself with a scoop of rum & raisons, my recent happy discovery.

Located in an exclusive town quarter along the perennial riverlet Ramway, my son and his wife have an elegant two-storey five-bedroom house, with a guest wing. It's a 50-year-old house that has undergone extensive renovation. Rooms have parquet flooring. And the modern kitchen is as large as the living room, with a breakfast table in the middle, and a TV set. The house sports several interesting paintings, including an original sketch by Picasso.

A vast lawn on front goes up to the road. A bigger backyard lawn slopes down to the river.

Plucked to peer at, a single plant of grass isn't any arresting vision. But banded with five others in each square inch of lawn—making a turf of over 850 plants per square foot, or about 8.5 million in each 10,000-sq-ft lawn—it's an impressive sight.

What really sets apart a typical American suburb from that elsewhere is the distinctive character of its front lawns. In most other countries and places, and that includes Chandigarh, the upper middle-class house garden is a private place hidden behind a wall or dense hedge, such walls and hedges progressively getting higher. Americans hold the pastoral faith that nature was a kind of garden, which meant that hedges or walls were inappropriate to a suburban community, even deemed unneighbourly.

Cranford authorities, I'm told, forbid high hedges or walls. Peer pressure is brought to bear on those who do not keep their front lawns up to the standard of the area. And neighbours often pitch in with equipment or labour when someone is incapacitated. If all else fails, the local authorities take the responsibility of mowing the lawn and bill the owner. This is justified on the ground that long grass can harbour snakes and vermin.

Today suburbanite Americans live in the middle of lawns that by urban standards elsewhere are enormous. The borderless expanse of green in front of houses, broken only by a chain link, a bush, or tree, creates the sense of a park. Front lawns are thoroughly integrated into the whole landscape.

The American front lawn is a holy place, constantly worshipped but never used. Family members rarely venture on to the front lawn except to maintain it.

Of course, the front yard is still purely private property. No one else can use it or walk on it. Though often seemingly unmarked, its territorial sanctity is unquestioned. Even house dogs coming out to pee seem to be aware of their master's territory.

A very pleasing sight in the backyard is the mid-sized swimming pool, filtered, heated. Mostly we sit around the greenish water. Spend hours in the pool on weekends. Viki now swims beautifully.

They also have a deck on the river edge where one can try one's hand at fishing. I tried a few times but didn't display the patience to wait for a catch.

Let's barbecue today, Ravi is apt to remark on an evening promising fair weather. And such a proposal meets ready response from Noni. To her, it signals a release from cooking dinner.

Barbecue is an occasion when Ravi dons an apron and sets about enjoying the process of cooking—the ability to barbecue is the accepted image of an American male. It is evidently a hangover from human hunting days when men cooked parts of the killed animal, such as liver, kidneys on the spot, while bringing the rest home.

One beauty of the Cranford June evenings; daylight lingers on till 9 PM. It's the generosity of the late sun that seems to pause before setting as if wanting to give more company. And then there's the longish twilight.

One thing in Cranford never fails to please me. As I walk the well-kept pavements of this tidy town, passing women—mostly in shorts—almost invariably reward with a smile when I smile at them. Most smiles that way are started by another smile. Maybe it's because I'm a smallish, gray-haired chap in mid-seventies, with an unthreatening demeanour. Passing men muttering 'Good Day' are welcome but the really satisfying part comes when women, young and old, some pushing prams, others carrying groceries—complete strangers—smile back at me in greeting.

"I can well visualize your satisfaction at smiles from pretty women", says Noni with her mischievous grin.

"People smile more here because they have no bad teeth to hide", puts in Priti, busy clearing a clutter of Viki's toys.

Ravi, helping Priti in toy clearance, "Not that people don't smile in India or elsewhere. But Americans smiling so often and so easily may have something to do with their history and tradition. That country has no rigid class structure, no caste barriers. The American smile is a democratic version of a courtesy or doffed hat. Every stranger is deemed a potential equal.

The typical American smile is simply a parting of the lips and stretching the corners of the mouth—a bit muted compared to the British smile of lips curling upwards".

What strikes me most here is the utmost feel of safety and security.

The laundry driver on his bi-weekly rounds picks up clothes kept for washing in the front verandah and hangs the laundered ones instead. UPS, DHL and other transport agencies leave all sorts of packages—some quite expensive, such as a dinner set—at the doorstep without asking for a receipt. Indeed, no one is normally home during the day to take delivery or give receipt.

Mind, the house has no boundary wall or gate or even a hedge. It's simply a stretch of lawn reaching up to the road.

Cars—they have three—often stay outside unlocked for

the night. And it is not unusual for items to be left in: jackets, running shoes, toys.

When we wanted to have a key for the front door, we were told we could always enter the house from the kitchen dust-bin door that stayed unlocked.

In the open backyard itself, you come across an expensive lawn mower, a fancy barbecue grill, or $300 bicycles left there for days. The only feared raiders are raccoons rooting for kitchen garbage.

No one locks anything. In the town itself, people leave their cars unlocked, even windows rolled down. I was told that the employees of the local cinema come out if it starts to rain and roll up all the windows of cars parked along the front street on the assumption that most of them belong to cinema customers who don't know it was raining.

The fact is, there is just no theft. None. It sometimes seems so unreal, but there it is. Banks have glass doors and free access; they look no different from other offices or shops.

You might reasonably wonder why, then, this is not a thief's paradise. One reason, I suppose, is that there is no market for stolen goods. If you sidled up to somebody and said, "Would you buy a car stereo?" the person may turn back and retort, "No, I already have one". And then he would report you to the police.

The police in these small towns are special. All of them are appointed by the elected town council and can be summarily dismissed by it. The police are mostly local boys and girls who grew up there, studied there, and know everyone in the town. They'd take no time to spot a suspicious character from outside as they patrol intensively in their cars. And they know full well that any spurt in crime or a lapse in security could mean a loss of their jobs.

You can't visualize a more alert and sensitive police than what these suburban towns manage to have.

One morning when Priti is preparing breakfast, a slice of bread gets stuck in the toaster and begins emitting smoke. Engaged on telephone, it takes her some time to pull out the smouldering piece. By then the fire-sensor system in the kitchen has sounded an alarm.

Within four-five minutes a cruising police car drives in. We explain the mishap.

But lo, in another five minutes a huge white fire engine shows up. Viki, when back from school, expresses his deep disappointment at not being present when the fire engine arrived.

It's an astounding scenario. You feel fully safe and secure, both in person and property.

"Care for some gambling and fun?" asks Noni the next morning. "We can take you to Atlantic City on Sunday".

"That would be a welcome outing", I say.

It's a two-hour drive from Cranford. Starting early, we plan to return the same day. Viki is left with Nanny.

Atlantic City lures over 50 million visitors annually into its oasis of luxury, and showers them with gifts.

Some say its main industry is fleecing visitors who drop something like $15 million a day in its casinos.

Ravi and Noni have no weakness for casino games. But they aren't averse to an occasional round of blackjack on moderate stakes. "Of all casino games, blackjack possibly offers the best odds to a good player", says Ravi.

Both of us have been given $300 each to play. And a book on blackjack is there in the BMW to read on the way.

Grasping the basic features of the 21-game, I have every intention of trying my hand at it, preferably on the same table with Ravi and Noni

"I won't participate in gambling", Priti persists. "It's against my principles. Here's your money back".

"Mummy, keep it for the time being. Maybe you can buy us food if we lose all of ours", kids Noni.

"Mummy, gambling is a human condition. We all gamble, not necessarily at casino tables. Life itself is a gamble; you play, you win, you lose".

Atlantic City presents a fascinating sight, a sight almost unrivalled for a city. There's the mile-long Boardwalk, with eye-catching hotel-casinos on one side and the Atlantic on the other. A weekend crowd is enjoying the wide wooden Boardwalk, with its benches, restrooms and shaded pavilions.

"Atlantic City's Boardwalk was the country's first elevated walkway", tells Ravi. "The idea was born when the owner of a beach hotel became annoyed with sand on hotel carpets from the feet of beach strollers (the vacuum cleaner hadn't been invented). One Alexander Boardman came up with the solution: an elevated wooden walkway from the ocean to the hotel, with cracks between boards to allow the sand to fall through". Seems the walkway, named after him, was built in 1870. By 1890, a permanent steel-girded, 24-ft-wide Boardwalk, towering 10 feet above the ground, made Atlantic City even more famous. Over the years the boardwalk has been strengthened, widened, and extended.

The city has a gargantuan Convention Centre, midway on the Boardwalk. Miss America Beauty Contest, the first contest of its type in the world, dubbed the Mother of Beauty Contests, is held here on the second Saturday of every September. Winners, one from each state, compete. The festivities include a Boardwalk parade of contesting beauties, even former winners. The organizers claim, the contest is not only of body and looks but of brains and accomplishments as well.

Priti is persuaded to try a rolling chair. She and Noni ride a cushioned wicker chair on wheels, pushed by a burly bloke.

Shops on the Boardwalk are small and sell cheap stuff, some offering every item in the shop for one dollar. Indians and Pakistanis own quite a few of these. Priti picks up several trinkets as gifts back home.

We make for the Taj hotel-casino complex. In garishness and flamboyance, nothing beats Trump's Taj Mahal—in sharp contrast to the aesthetic elegance of the original Taj

Mahal. The 42-storey glass structure, said to be one of the costliest buildings in the world, sports a spectacular facade of incongruous multicoloured domes and turrets. The wall-to-wall carpets are a swirling dazzle of colour. As a concession to the name Taj Mahal, the complex carries many Indian motifs, even restaurants named Delhi and Bombay.

"Let's begin with their buffet lunch", suggests Noni. "You always get a good deal in casino meals. The food is subsidized, one of their measures to attract and retain prospective gamblers".

The extensive buffet tables stand laden with all sorts of foods. Only one tended to overeat with such a staggering variety on offer. You feel a little bad leaving out an inviting item, more so when you see some others, who have paid the same entrance charge, merrily tucking into heaped plates.

We take our seats at a minimum $5-bet blackjack table; one that will convert to $10 by the evening. A middle-aged Chinese couple is already at the seven-seat crescent green table. They seem well conversant with the game. The young woman dealer, a pretty Mexican, gives me basic tips when I confess to being a beginner.

"You're there to help me play particular hands", I tell Ravi.

"Yes, I would. And a general suggestion; make no show of emotion winning or losing".

By the end of a 2-hour session—plied with free drinks—Noni loses some $250. Ravi wins 90. I, with the beginner's luck, rake in $310. I must have been dealt blackjack a dozen times—an exciting turn at the table.

Looking for Priti amidst all those rows and rows of slot machines, we find her perched uneasily before one that demanded a minimum of a one-dollar token for each pull of the lever. Around her you see mostly older people playing at the machines. Evidently the older crowd has the time and money for it; retired with their homes paid-for and few other financial liabilities.

Priti appears distraught. The one-arm bandit has gobbled 30 one-dollar tokens without yielding anything in return; a highly constipated machine.

Noni persuades her to try one more hand at another machine. And lo, it begins to rain tokens; in all 60. Gleefully, Priti scoops them into her money bowl to be exchanged for cash.

"Now you'll get hooked to slot machines", says Noni.

Priti shakes her head—but not as determinedly as before.

"Mummy, it's a lucky day for you. Just play one hand at roulette".

"No, I won't. You can play on my behalf".

"What's your fancied number?"

"34, the number of our Chandigarh house".

"I prefer cards to dice. But a bit of roulette is all right", says Ravi.

Noni puts a 10-dollar token at 34.

Slowing down, the wheel makes the white ball bounce and bounce till it clatters to a stop. Comes to rest on 34. That's a clear gain of $350. Priti is ecstatic. She's persuaded to give a $10 tip to the courtly croupier.

Emerging out into sunlight and fresh air, Ravi remarks, "We have had fun at the casino, and it didn't cost us a dime. We actually pinched a few hundred bucks off the owner Donald Trump. In all probability we would have lost these and more if we had persisted in playing. One can well understand why casino managements have no love for bettors who play a bit, win, and walk away. Casinos ply you with free drinks to make you play longer. They even pump oxygen into gambling halls to keep the players awake far into the night".

It's another hour of boardwalking and ocean viewing. And then the long drive home. We are back by dinnertime.

"You have done the usual Manhattan sights on your previous visits: the Statue of Liberty, Central Park, top of the World Trade Center towers, the U.N. building, even a walk through Chinatown. This time you see the musical *Miss Saigon*", says

Noni. "I'll get matinee tickets for you. After the show, you take a taxi to the Port Authority. I'll join you there at six for a bus ride back".

"What about our buying cheaper theatre tickets at Times Square? At half the price, they say".

"Firstly, it's a little more than half. And the ticket queues are dauntingly long".

And she adds, "By the way take good care of your purse. New York isn't Cranford".

"We won't carry much cash".

"Things sold in Manhattan shops carry a city purchase tax. It's cheaper buying in the suburbs".

Myra drops us at the bus stand after breakfast. We deem the train trip, with a change in the middle, too complicated. Being largely empty at that hour, we get the front seats with the best view.

Getting on the New Jersey Turnpike is always exhilarating; 12 lanes of traffic moving smoothly. You get a magnificent view of the New York skyline prior to the dramatic ride through the Lincoln Tunnel. The driver tells us, "This tunnel business is so expensive, there isn't money to build another, despite mounting pressure on the Lincoln".

Getting down at Port Authority—an imposing steel structure with buses operating four-storeys high—we walk on the 42nd up to the acclaimed New York Public Library.

To the world at large, 42nd is known as the premier porn street. Nowhere else was such a concentration of peep shows, nude shows, and stores selling pornographic material and all imaginable sex aids. You see video stores as large as hotel lobbies and as well lit as libraries. And you often find a Gujarati owner at the cash counter, with a black muscleman at the entrance. Customers breeze out business-like with book-like tapes in paper bags.

We step in from a world of din and clamour into the calm and quiet of a marble palace. Climb to the Main Reading Room.

What a room! Possibly the greatest reading room in the world. It's an enormous circular hall with painted ceiling, miles of bookshelves, and scores of readers bent at their separate lighted desks. The first sight of the room makes one go weak at the knees.

Anyone can come into the library any time. At a counter in the centre you give a chit of the books you want to read. Within minutes they are delivered at your numbered desk, having been sent up from underground stacks—six storeys of them, extending under Bryant Park itself—through moving ramps.

We sit for another half-hour on the library steps, watching traffic and people go by on the fabled Fifth. All sorts of people are hurrying past: white and yellow, brown and black, tall and short, fat and thin, handsome and not so handsome, people seemingly from all over the globe. Even pigeons on the pavement strut fast.

And then we stroll up the Fifth to the Rockefeller Plaza. What a street! Possibly the most glamorous anywhere. Even on a weekday Fifth Avenue is thronged with people. With the sun coming strong, we take to walking in the shade of tall buildings. Priti is an avid user of a sun umbrella back home.

On the way we pass the diamond district. Nearly every store is displaying fabulous jewellery. Orthodox Jews in black frock coats and tall hats, with flowing beards and rimless glasses, can be seen making deals in doorways.

"They say, deals worth millions of dollars in diamonds are made over a handshake", I tell Priti. "They carry samples in their pockets".

"I'm not interested in all this. Better buy me a diamond, an imperishable piece of the earth".

"You'll have to wait till I write a bestseller".

Her reaction is a hollow laugh.

Thereafter, we proceed on to our Broadway theatre.

The musical is fantastic. Let alone the lively music, the story itself is moving.

But it's no go getting a taxi at that hour. You see those huge yellow cabs cruising past without stopping. Even a Sikh driver I hail vigorously motions, he isn't available.

Perforce we wend our way on foot through crowds to the Port Authority, crossing busy streets well buttressed by throngs of pedestrians. Noni is already there with the bus tickets. Covertly I buy a copy of *Hustler* at the adjoining Patel-run newsstand when Priti and Noni wait in the bus queue. It should afford some heady moments of private viewing.

All in all, an enjoyable day though it left us a bit fagged out. Amazing how our gutsy 5-ft 3-inch daughter-in-law has withstood daily commuting for 15 years? And how she operates in this unique, yet challenging city?

Noni must be damn tough, mentally and physically.

CHAPTER 7

June 20, 1999. I am 75.

How has life gone so far with me? Beginnings, ends, and mid-points of decades now have become even more significant as times to sum-up, in case time runs out soon.

What have been the good things, and what the bad? That's all one's life amounts to, the aggregate of the good luck and the bad luck. To tote it up; to look at the respective piles. Of course, there's really nothing one can do about it.

The good:

Satisfactory 35 years of government service. Rapid promotions. No setbacks. Well-off. Comfortable living quarters in pleasing surroundings. An enviable garden. Good health for someone 75. Sound sleep. Bowels never failing. A stable marriage—something that every couple has to save for, anticipating their old age. Both the sons successfully launched into the world. Understanding daughters-in-law. Likeable grandchildren.

Spared of a life-threatening illness, financial disaster, or other major calamities.

What I want to save most at this stage of life is the wife; the one who stood by me for 50 years through thick and no little thin.

The bad:

The feeling of a failed life. Seventy-five-year-old and not accomplished one single act of consequence. Once I had entertained hopes of some signal achievement.

Staying unhappy, unless reading something interesting, playing golf, drinking, or engaged in sex.

Not to mention the trouble with floaters in the eyes, troublesome teeth, impaired hearing, and periodic bouts of acidity.

I keep on fearing the worst; I'm essentially a pessimist. What saves the situation is a bit of inherent buoyancy that does not let a phase of despondency last too long.

Busy years in service had kept unhappiness at bay. With every upward step in service, came a rise in power and perks; power to order people around, to be waited upon, to be listened to. Your phone calls were returned promptly, your orders carried out. Priti tells me that those days I would be the life of a party, coming out with one witty remark after the other.

"Now you slink in a corner", she pouts, "and are wanting to go home early".

On retirement, I got reduced overnight to nobody. No one to sort out day-to-day hassles with lower bureaucracy, no one to run errands. Even the renewal of passport or the rectification of a bloated electricity bill could be a protracted tiresome undertaking.

The scenario feels all the more stark when you're retired from a high official position.

My 60s were plagued by mental anguish from jealousy. With news of any former colleague doing better, a part of me died. The revenue consultancy work did bring some money but it was no fun 'sirring' people whom you once lorded over.

Things improved during my 70s. I got better adjusted to old age. The pressure of ambition relented. Ageing, that way, is not all losses. In certain respects I am happier, more at peace with myself, than I was in my sixties.

Totalling up, the good clearly outweigh the bad. But then life is not a business account where losses can be written off against the gains.

And heaven knows what the future holds in store for me.

By this stage of life I'm supposed to have accumulated possessions, responsibilities, achievements, experience and wisdom. Some possessions are there and some experience, but no achievements to talk about—unless you count a hole-in-one in golf—and hardly any wisdom.

People tell me I laugh a lot, must be happy. Actually I remain dissatisfied with my life much of the time, my chief occupation being, "If only … ." It's a saga of regrets over past mistakes and missed opportunities, whether in service career or child rearing. And all that is happening when I know full well the past can't be redeemed, it's another country.

And now I'm not doing well in my latest venture—that's fiction writing. Doubt whether I have the stamina and the essential optimism that would make the effort of such writing possible. But then reading and writing are my only means against despair. Reading can be both a blessing and a curse. You learn writing techniques, but you also get more aware of your failings.

Of one thing I'm getting increasingly certain. If ever I accomplish anything, it will be as a result of being alone, i.e., creative writing.

And what if I fail to gain recognition as a writer? Fail to get my books in shops? Well, I should accept it as nothing more than loss of time.

Priti keeps telling me, "Live contented and happy. Your state of mind depends not as much on externals as on your attitude to externals. Just let go, relax. Take to yoga; it would calm your mind, let alone improve your health. Anyway, accept whatever comes your way. And you haven't been dealt an awful deal".

"Contentment is tantamount to death. No, that's not my way to live. That way you die, even when you're alive".

"But don't sacrifice your peace of mind for the sake of some will-o-wisp achievement. Maybe, it's fashionable for writers to be unhappy. But please don't dramatize your miseries".

Today, as usual, I get up at five. Being troubled since retirement by vivid, nasty dreams in the early hours, I've taken to rising with the birds.

"Why do birds rise so early?" I once asked my vet friend.

"Like our babies, their chicks start crying for food".

Priti sleeps late, gets up late.

Apparently it does no harm to a marriage where the sleeping and rising hours of the partners don't sychronise.

I slink noiselessly out of the bedroom as is my wont, so as not to wake her up. And then I stand naked before a full-length mirror in the dressing room. This shows some slackness at the neck. Skin's drooping near the ends of the mouth. Furrows on forehead. Upper arms no longer round. Losing hair though not yet balding. Eyebrows nearly grey. Legs gone almost hairless.

Looking down, the bulge nearly obstructs a view of the genitals. In the mirror, nothing seems wrong with the sexual equipment, hanging rather low. It has given good service for all these years, and could well be coaxed to go on a little longer.

Once, the mid-section body throw-outs—urine, semen, stools—tended to burst forth. Now each of these has to be coaxed out. Excretions of the head—sputum, tears, nasal deposits, earwax, however, are more copious, often come out quicker.

All in all, the 75-year-old body doesn't figure too badly in the mirror. There's the sharp nose and broad forehead, fair complexion and hairy chest. Pity, not enough chin.

"I could grow a beard to hide my small chin", I have been telling Priti.

"Forget it", she pooh-poohs the idea.

"A smartly-trimmed white beard would also make me look a real writer".

"Beards don't make writers".

And there the matter stands. I haven't given up the idea for good.

Wonder, what will happen if all the mirrors in the world vanished! You'll have to ask others how you're looking, and that would be mostly clothed, not nude.

For an hour I watch TV, the size of a small cinema screen, and leaf through the latest issue of *The New Yorker* lying around. What I like most about the acclaimed magazine are the cartoons; imaginative, funny.

At six, I make tea, using Assam Pekoe. Tea bags are unacceptable at this hour. Indeed, they are a vile invention; yield no taste, no fragrance, only colour, simply a ploy by tea companies to pack off their dust teas. Dunking a tea bag into a cup of hot water has taken away the whole ritual and romance of tea making.

I enter the bedroom in an exaggerated swagger, not unlike a senior butler, holding the tea tray with a plate of crunchy wine biscuits. Priti, up by now, gives me a long, loving birthday hug in her cotton nightgown. She scorns provocative intimate apparel, such as a flimsy silk nightie. Unnecessary, she'd say, if the systems were in good order, and only confusing if they weren't. Mercifully she hasn't taken to pajamas at night. I find these off-putting.

I lay my hands upon the back of her head, and we have a long, long kiss lasting nearly a minute—a real birthday or anniversary kiss—till we break off out of breath. I grope her buttocks. A breast slips out of a fold of her nightgown, like a puppy's head. She is as attractive as a sixty-seven-year-old could be. Often it needs some persuasion to make the trade and other service-givers believe she's entitled to the concessions of a senior citizen.

Priti retains a compact, tight butt and remarkably slender legs—must be from a lot of walking. And the breasts, right size, round, a handful, hardly sag.

Women, I suppose, age from top down. I can discern a little looseness in the neck.

I'm old, too. Yet, I tend to look on other old men as old—without clubbing myself as one. In my imagination I'm often someone 45—a younger man, screaming to be let out. Maybe, the true, essential self is ageless.

And a sexual spark still strikes between the two of us. We have our share of lovemaking. She's game for recreational sex. And Priti isn't one of those horrid wives who'd only permit in the missionary position. However, when I initiate anything different, she's apt to ask, "Where did you get this?"

"From a magazine or book", is my standard response.

Here's someone with beauty and brains, balance and backbone, someone ageing prettily, gracefully. She retains the same lively laugh at 67, she had at 17. A woman's charm, they say, is for life. But then you must pay attention to it.

What better bargain can I have in marriage?

Priti hands me a mammoth birthday card, akin to a good-sized wall calendar—didn't know they made cards as large as that. And she gives me a silver Mont Blanc set of a pen and ballpoint. These would have to be kept in my study. The star brand is too expensive to be carried around, especially in libraries where you're often asked to lend your pen 'for a minute.'

Of late she has been giving me gifts related to writing. Last year she bought a leather straight-back work chair to replace the old cane one.

Ravi and Noni look in before going to work. Noni plants a peck on my cheek and hands over a carton that reveals a compact Italian coffee percolator, complete with bean grinder. The percolator can make four cups at a time. Ravi's gift is a Cannon photocopier (110 volt with an adopter), and a length of beige-brown Harris tweed.

"As American ready-made clothes don't fit Papa, we've bought a jacket-length for your Indian tailor to stitch", says Noni.

"The robustness of tweed is proverbial", explains Ravi. "'Heart of oak, soul of tweed.' It's one of the world's best-known woolen textiles for durability, warmth, and rough use".

"Tweed is trendy again, the softer, lighter version. You see it being touted in fashion magazines", adds Noni.

"Dad anyway is sold on things British. And Harris tweed is the most British as clothes go".

Later on waking, Viki is walked in by his nanny, lugging a biggish white box of chocolates, the famous French Richart chocolates, being made by the Richart family since 1925. Viki sits in my lap displaying a bewitching smile. Hugs me tight.

And he helps me open the box. Viki likes opening presents, even those not meant for him.

The white cardboard box holds six trays, each tray containing several varieties, in the shape of small cubes or thin strips. And every strip bears the percentage of cocoa used in it and its country of origin; no cocoa percentage less than 70 percent.

Forthwith both of us eat 3–4 strips each. What a treat! Such wonderful taste and feel as these melt in your mouth.

In these chocolates, it's the high percentage of cocoa butter—the fat squeezed out of cocoa beans and then added to impart chocolate its unique qualities—that mostly makes for the quality of a chocolate. Cocoa butter is said to be non-fattening; the only butter of this kind on earth, because of its property of being poorly absorbed in the body. Another endearing property of cocoa butter; it remains solid at room temperature but melts in the mouth. And in this process of melting in the mouth, heat is absorbed from the lining of the mouth, giving the eater a pleasing sensation.

The birthday gifts are thoughtful.

Myra gives me *Lord Jim*, a novel by the Polish writer Conrad. I receive the book with all possible indulgence and evident pleasure, though I already own a copy of it. One important principle of gift-taking, I presume, is to receive with grace, whatsoever the gift may be, the way a prima dancer receives flowers at the end of a performance.

CHAPTER 8

No library; Priti lays down the law for the day.

We walk to the local Japanese restaurant for lunch. Eat portions of succulent beef and lamb cooked right in front of us, the middle of the table figuring as a sizzling-hot steel plate. I chase the meal with sake, the Japanese rice wine served warm in tiny porcelain cups. Priti drinks Perrier. Slices of sweet orange are offered in lieu of dessert.

Later in the noon, we have slow, satisfying sex, both coming in unison; the slowness itself lending more meaning to it. It's not a performance to be sneezed at on one's 75th birthday with a spouse of 67, the two mated for nearly half a century.

At 75, a man's body is like an old car with over 1,00,000 miles on it—and with no reverse gear. You've things like starting trouble, exhaust problems, misfiring, and loss of power.

You have to go slow but you often get there.

A luxurious tub-bath is taken late afternoon. At Chandigarh we don't have tubs; it's all shower. I immerse myself in warm water, mixed with scented bath salts. The limbs feel light, borne in water.

I emerge vastly refreshed.

"We should install a proper porcelain tub at Chandigarh".

"Where's the water for it? You're getting spoiled", says Priti.

"We can use garden water, run the tube-well".

"There are several tubs here, even a Jacuzzi. Yet Ravi and Noni content themselves with shower on most days. Noni tells me, a good shower is not only faster, it's more hygienic. Lots of Americans have been shifting away from tub to shower".

We are going out in the evening. I have been asked to don an evening suit, my best suit and the only one I've brought. Details of the entertainment are being kept under wrap. I suppose, if they are giving me a surprise birthday party, they wouldn't advertise its details.

An elongated white Lincoln limousine, incredibly long, pulls up in front by six.

Ravi, adjusting his digital Nikon, asks the liveried driver to take a group photograph of the four of us all dressed up and standing by the side of the stretched car.

"Papa, you look great", Noni enthuses. "The gray hair really suits you".

"He isn't getting older, he's getting better", pipes in Priti.

"That's a good joke. Getting better at what?" I ask.

More photographs are taken with me holding Viki in my arms. Viki likes being photographed. He puts forth a special pout for it.

And Viki makes no fuss at being left behind with his nanny. He's now trained to it.

The alert chauffeur gets us all in. And then moves swiftly around the rear of the behemoth and down to his door—possibly scooting some 30 feet.

We are driven to Manhattan.

What a car! I've seen these giants from outside but never ridden one. A virtual sitting-room on wheels, enclosed within heavily tinted glasses. Deep leather seats along the sides, long enough for a tall man to lie down. A floor carpet your feet sink in. A TV set, 4-speaker hi-fi music system, a fridge, a cocktail bar, and cup holders for every seat. The whole area is separated from the driver with a glass partition that slides with the press of a button.

By the time I get over my initial amazement, Ravi has fixed a martini each from the contents of the cooler.

We reach the Rockefeller building on the Fifth. And travel up to the top floor, the Rainbow Room. A table is there for us by the glass wall, with a flower bouquet in the middle.

What a breathtaking view of the city and the harbour from the 65th floor!

A bottle of Veuve Cliquot, its neck wrapped in a dazzlingly white napkin, is brought in a bucket of ice. Ravi opens it, putting the wrapper in his pocket. He removes the wire net, holds the bottle at an angle, and eases the cork by rotating the bottle, not the cork, thus releasing it without the usual plop.

"No cork popping? I've once seen a champagne cork hit the ceiling", I say.

"Nowadays it's deemed better to muffle the pop, especially with strangers around".

He pours the celebratory drink gently into the champagne glasses, the long stemmed narrow flutes, spotlessly clean.

"I'm pouring a little in the first instance. A regular refill will follow."

The bubbles are a delight to watch; smaller bubbles in the middle, bigger bubbles on sides.

"Best of luck, Dad" he says as everyone lifts their glass. Priti has been coaxed to taste the stuff. It's her hubby's 75th birthday, no ordinary day. We clink glasses, sip.

Caviar is offered on tiny toast, and so a bowl of hazelnuts.

Noni gets up to take a few snaps of us around the table. She's keen to take a snap of Priti drinking.

"Mummy, sip a bit more before it becomes tepid", says Noni.

"I've taken champagne for the first time. Doesn't feel tasty".

"Taste-wise, champagne isn't great", concedes Ravi. "A top sparkling white wine like Chardonnay would do better. But champagne gives a heady feel within minutes, a special kick".

We are at the Rainbow Room for 45 minutes. And then are driven to Café Paris, a famous French restaurant on 62nd East. Noni frequents it with her business clients.

"You can't get a table in this place below a month's notice. The management knows me".

We are invitingly received at the classy restaurant and seated at a window table. Ravi orders a 1993 Rhenish red wine.

I go for Russian salad, smoked salmon, and short rib.

After ice cream, it's a shot of espresso and a glass of vintage port.

"This Port Fonesca", Ravi remarks, "is a 1982 vintage, bottled in 1985. The longer the port remains in the bottle, the more it improves in elegance, unlike whisky that only improves in the cask. Port is probably the finest of all fortified wines, fortified with Portuguese grape brandy to bring it up to 20% alcohol".

"I read somewhere that the best patrons of port are English dons".

"That's correct. But now port is proving popular in the US as a prime after-dinner drink, more so with a blazing log fire in winter. There's only one problem with this great gift of Portugal: you drink three-four glasses at a sitting, you're likely to have a headache next morning".

And he winds up sipping Priti's untouched glass.

"As a matter of curiosity, what would be the price of this bottle of port", I ask, seeing Ravi pay for the meal with his Visa Platinum Card.

"$173".

And I'm a bit shocked to find him adding a tip of $100 to the dinner bill.

"Isn't the tip excessive?"

"Well, 15% is customary in such restaurants. Mine's 20%. But that's on food alone. For wine, you tip the sommelier, the wine steward, separately". And adds, "Dad, take a tip from me. Always tip generously. It pays in the long run".

As I assume the meal is coming to a close, two waiters dressed in black suits like casino croupiers, wheel in a high circular trolley bearing a birthday cake; that's with the compliments of the management. It's a solid nut-studded chocolate cake with 75 boldly etched on in hardened sugar. "Happy Birthday" is sung in a low tone, so as not to distract other diners. Priti offers me a largish slice, rather pushes it into my mouth. In the process the tip of my nose catches a bit of the white frosting to the merriment of everybody.

By this time it has been a martini in the car, two glasses of champagne at the Rainbow Room, red wine at dinner, and a glass of port. I'm nearly tipsy. Ravi and Noni who must have taken double of my intake are as comfortable and controlled as peas in a pod, only a little more loquacious. Who says, women can't stand alcohol? Everyone is in an expansive, reminiscent mood.

By the time the meal finishes, I'm full of food and alcohol.

Noni had plans of going to the Temple Bar, a posh place in Greenwich Village, for drinks and dancing. Priti, backed by me, wants to call it a day. It's already past midnight, the time when the elderly find it hard to hold back sleep.

We head home on the long drive. Stretch ourselves on the leather couches. No one feels like talking.

By the time we are half way, I start experiencing an embarrassing complication, an urgent pressure to pee. I had urinated in the restaurant at the start of the meal, but overlooked bladder emptying at finishing time.

"Why can't they fit a tiny toilet in such a car, this house on wheels?" I muse.

I nudge Ravi; the distress of a man with an enlarged prostate finding urine coming with a near non-negotiable urgency. I moan, stamp quick steps on the floorboard.

"It's only 20 minutes to the house", says he.

"I'm afraid I can't hold beyond five".

The driver is told on the intercom to pull into a service station. And if that's far off, to stop at kerbside. The driver keeps an impassive face, yet I sense a flicker of smile.

The long limousine veers to an abrupt halt. I get down at an unearthly hour in windy conditions to do my business behind a chest-high bush on a major motorway—an act that could attract a penalty in law.

It took an age to get started, and an eternity to wind up. In the anxiety to hurry with others waiting, I zip up, after a vigorous "shake of the tree". To my consternation a warm stream trickles down my left leg. Hope, nobody notices the spreading wet patch.

Reentering the car I don't notice anyone sniggering or laughing, despite the comic connotations of the situation. Maybe, they are too sleepy or just too nice to the "birthday boy".

"It's the best birthday I ever had. Must have cost you a packet. Many, many thanks for it", I tell Noni and Ravi. "I'll cherish the day as long as I live".

"Come on, papa. Cut it out", says Noni. "We wish you a long happy life. And you deserve it. You aren't a bad bloke".

"Thanks for the compliment".

"And one who has been made better over the years by his good wife", Ravi jokes.

We'll be leaving for India in a week, two days after celebrating Viki's birthday.

This promises to be a grand affair. A firm has been hired to pitch tents in the backyard, do decorations, and provide food for some 20 couples and their children. A magician, a youngish lady, is there to amuse the kids. And they have a tented net to jump on. A table is heaped with presents to be given away. Hundreds of inflated balloons are strung all over.

Various drinks are there, including a huge silver salver of vodka-sherry-orange punch. A suckling pig is stuck on roast grill. Delicacies are in plenty. And, of course, the traditional birthday cake. The brown cake is in the shape of a convertible Rolls, in tune with Viki's inordinate fascination for luxury cars.

The party goes on from noon into late evening. Men, women keep coming at their convenience, and in casual clothes, mostly shorts. The whole atmosphere is astonishingly informal. Some even bring their swimwear. We feel rather over-dressed, I wearing a full-sleeve freshly-laundered shirt, matching trousers, and black shoes. Priti moves in a fancy silk sari. Ravi is in jeans and Noni in shorts.

At the end of it, there's a heap of presents. Viki, though fagged out with the excitement of the day, insists on opening all those packages. I render assistance, and enjoy doing so. Only I'm enjoined by Noni to draw up a list of every present, with the name of the gift-giver marked boldly against it.

Finally, Viki is allowed to take one gift—a *Star Wars* Lego box—to his room, the rest stored for future use. "Too many gifts received at one time lose their novelty", cautions Noni.

Our gift this year is a ride-in battery-powered car, a bright yellow Porsche, with lights, horn, seat belt, even a radio. We had bought a red Mercedes one day before but found to our dismay it was too small for Viki's legs. After obtaining his brave consent for a replacement (in turn, invoking the rule of return), Priti and I take him along to a top toy store.

The kid's mind is clear. He ignores all other items, makes straight for the battery-car section. And forthwith he climbs into a Porsche, the most expensive of the lot, costing $650. He just couldn't be fobbed off with anything inferior.

And it's a sight, seeing him motoring gleefully on the circular tar road in the house compound, blowing the horn, waving at us, and slowing down at corners.

Viki going round gaily in the play Porsche brought me memories of my 13th birthday. Father had gifted me a brand new Raleigh bike, because I had stood first in my class. What exciting hours I spent cycling up and down the town's steep roads, overtaking tongas, dodging carts. Few things match the thrill of cycling downhill at free speed.

Nothing makes a boy smarter than being grandson, they say.

Grandparents are mostly liked for the gifts they give, and the way they indulge their grandchildren—"people who come to your house, spoil the children, and then go home". To an extent we must be getting viewed in the same light.

Our relationship with Viki, I believe, is possibly passing through its most benign phase. By the time he's ten, he may become distant, move away from his doting grandparents to his parents and peers.

Anyway, we are immensely happy with our current role—all fun for us, all responsibility on his parents.

And as Ogden Nash says: "The entrance requirements for grandpahood are comparatively mild. You only have to live until your child has a child".

Viki's parental gift this year is a DVD fitted into the ceiling of the BMW. While being driven, he can see cartoons and other kiddy films.

"Noni, it isn't exactly a gift to Viki", I say. "You've bought peace for yourself from the backseat. On longish trips no more demands from him for Coke or stops for toilet".

"There's something in what you say".

"I'm afraid I don't fancy this transformation from a chatty, question-firing Viki to the one who sits quietly, watches a cartoon movie, smiles at times, or bursts into a guffaw. I prefer the former Viki, with his ceaseless chatter and candid comments, such as calling someone driving dangerously 'Bad driver!"

Our stay is coming to a close and so also the end of my pipedream—till the next visit—of winning the New Jersey Lotto.

While in the US, I play this lottery. I wager weekly two entries of a dollar each. I play on fixed six numbers that revolve around birthdays of Viki, Ravi, Noni, Priti, Jogi, and me. The first prize is often in the range of $10 million, even a bumper one of $20 million. And despite drawing a dismaying blank till now, I do entertain hopes of winning a first prize when I'm here.

And this hope of a great win engenders endless fantasies. I day dream of getting the 6 numbers right, visiting the lottery office with Ravi, Noni, and a lawyer to redeem the winning ticket, and receive all the win in lump-sum instead of the usual 10 yearly installments—the state disburses at the winner's bidding.

Banks and businesses would be vying to give me their platinum credit cards. I'd be gifting an Aston Martin to Ravi—to him, nothing rivals an Aston Martin, a diamond set to Noni. A hundred thousand dollars deposited in Viki's account, to be given to him at the age of 21, along with accrued interest. Jogi is gifted a Honda Civic; Girija, a diamond bracelet, not to mention money for the marriage of the girls. And Priti can have whatever she fancies.

The Chandigarh house would be transformed into a luxury home. No tenant to share the place, despite our liking the present one. Both I and Priti would equip ourselves with entirely new wardrobes. And in the garage would nestle a new Mercedes 300 and a Toyota Camry.

Enough money will be left to set up a charitable hospital, preferably an ENT hospital specializing in hearing problems.

Don't know whether I'd keep up with my writing; the rush of money may prove too distracting.

I lose hours lying in the backyard hammock at the river's edge—oblivious to the appealing surroundings—dreaming of untold riches, working out various schemes of enjoying this windfall of wealth, all the time a book lying upturned on my tummy.

Isn't fantasizing one of the most harmless ways of enriching one's life?

"You're wasting good money on lottery tickets", Priti keeps telling. "Nothing will ever come out of it".

"The numbers lottery is mainly played by the poor and lower middle classes. The smart, upper ones know that the odds for a win are too high to merit investing money or attention on it", Ravi had once remarked.

Yet I persevere. A major lottery win is one hope that has me buoyed over the week—till the dismal results are out.

It's the day to depart. Ravi and Noni are seeing us off at the airport.

"I wanted to discuss this matter of your sending money. Somehow, we didn't get a chance for it", I tell Ravi and Noni.

Priti and Noni talk for hours. They talk in the kitchen after dinner when Ravi goes down to the basement for his software business work and I turn to TV.

Once or twice Ravi and I did go out for a short walk but Viki taken along monopolized attention. His pet activity is swinging by the arms between the two of us while chatting non-stop.

"We don't need the money you keep on remitting", I say. "In fact, the money you send is mostly accumulating".

For the last 8 years, since Priti retired as headmistress of a government high school, $1,000 gets transferred every month into our joint bank account.

"You need some cushion for an emergency, more so a health emergency", says Ravi.

"Government is expected to render us free medical aid. And we've a sizeable bank balance. The way we live, we do comfortably from rent of the first floor, and our two pensions. Pensions and rents have been going up over the years. On top, Priti has her nursery school. And this is now proving a steady money earner".

Noni butts in. "You could live better, eat better, dress better. Take more holiday trips. Acquire stylish furniture and fittings. Have more of kitchen gadgets. A microwave is a real convenience, and so also a washing machine. Install more air conditioners. Keep a decent car, not that tin can of a Maruti 800. That car is a killer if involved in an accident. Better engage a full-time driver.

"We have more furniture than we need, more pieces than we can have dusted. You installed an air conditioner in our bedroom during your last visit. It's doing well. You had put in another one in his study. And our door-size water cooler does alright for the rest of the house. What else do we need?" says Priti. "We don't use the car except for his going for golf three days a week. I walk to the market, walk to my school, walk to the gurudwara on Sundays. The Rose Garden is just across. With Chandigarh's sector-wise planning, most places we go to are within 10-minutes walking distance, and perfectly safe for pedestrians. Walking anyway is supposed to be good for the old bones".

"Up to you", as Ravi rubs his eyes with the palms of his hands after taking off the glasses. "$1,000 will keep on coming. Give some in charity, if you've no other use for it. In fact, the amount will be stepped up in the new millennium".

"You're spoiling us".

"What's better: ageing spoiled or ageing deprived?" retorts Ravi.

We part at the security entrance. Noni gives me a hug, her hair tickling my face and the Givenchy perfume in my nostrils. Ravi, taller to me by nearly five inches, bends to touch my feet. Actually touches them instead of the customary pointing of hands towards the feet. Rather embarrassed, I pull him up for an emotion-laden embrace.

He seems more substantial than what I had assumed. Ravi is thickening in the middle, though it doesn't show with his height. Says he doesn't find time for regular workouts at the gym, what to say of tennis. He may be sparing in eating but he does drink—the empty calories.

He has started graying gracefully at the temples. Keeps short hair and is not fastidious about what he wears. The most noticeable feature of the face is his genial smile.

Jogi, by contrast, is a jogger, a health freak. He has a flat stomach, narrow hips, and powerful calf muscles. Dresses in natty clothes. Favours long sideburns. And there's the masterful nose and a cleft chin.

CHAPTER 9

We have a comfortable, uneventful journey back. I exhort Priti to take a little walk periodically, a safety precaution against developing blood clot in legs on long flights.

Our Customs posed no problem, though I always miss a heartbeat pushing a trolley through the Green Channel. And this particular trolley kept veering sideways as if inviting inspection. The Cannon copier and the coffee percolator, tucked amidst clothes in the biggest suitcase, went undetected. Other things—chocolates, two single-malt whisky bottles, golf accessories—fell well within permissible limits.

At one time we brought bottles of sauces, bundles of Camay soap, cans of shaving foam, and a host of other everyday items. On our first visit, I clearly recollect, it led to acute embarrassment when at the check-in counter, one big bag was found overweight. Asked to pay extra or reduce the weight, I opened the bag with Ravi and Noni watching. And to everybody's mortification, I had to offload four one-litre cans of Bertolli olive oil, three bottles of HP sauce, two of Lea & Perrins, and several packets of Iranian pistachio and California almonds. Don't know whether Ravi and Noni took those items home or left them at the airport itself in sheer disgust. Since then we take care to travel light on return.

Most of what we need is now available in the country. Yet three items I don't forget to bring: two dozen Pilot ballpoint pens, curved toothpicks, and two 200-tablets bottles of Tums. I haven't found an Indian ballpoint that can match the Japanese Pilot in writing fluency, and I write a lot. Our toothpicks tend to break in gums. Tums, the anti-acid pills are simply unavailable and no local substitute matches Tums in flavour. Indeed, I always carry one or two Tums with me whenever I go out for golf or any extended outing.

Ravi had spoken to Jogi about our arrival at Delhi airport. Jogi wanted us to break journey for a few days before proceeding to Chandigarh. We are keen to go straightway, already feeling homesick.

Jogi's PA is at the airport when we land at ten in the morning. His boss, he tells, had to go urgently to Mumbai. An Ambassador car is there to take us to Chandigarh.

Priti gets busy opening up the locked place, having it cleaned, stocking food, and sorting out the mess of clothes. And she's getting into gear the various household services, let alone sorting out matters pertaining to her nursery school.

Returning from abroad, a sort of emptiness, grips me, especially after an enjoyable stint; I feel like going back. It takes a few days of activity to shake off the queasy feeling.

We take two papers in the interest of marital harmony—what if both of us happened to read at the same time. As it is, I'm done with papers before breakfast, even on Sundays. She has no time to look at them before lunch.

I always start with *The Tribune*, the paper I had read from boyhood. Father, when he lived with us, went a step further. He read no other paper except *The Tribune*; he said he had been reading it since some 70 years, and that was the only newspaper for him. As to magazines, it the *Illustrated Weekly* of India. Pity, it has gone off publication.

Rano, the cook, is allowed to sell the old papers as *raddi* and pocket the proceeds. She takes damn good care in collecting and storing these. But she's often outwitted by the "buyers on bicycles". As she haggles for a better raddi rate, the wily kabbadi more than makes up through weighing less with his doctored scales.

I'm at what I call my "catching up on the country" phase. That means reading through the accumulated copies of *The Tribune* and the *Indian Express*, arranged date-wise. I like to read in the same order the papers arrived.

The whole exercise takes three solid days of reading. But when over, there is hardly any development to take note of, except the obituaries of a few known persons.

The first thing I look in an obituary is the age of the deceased. And, curiously, uncharitably, I sense a sort of satisfaction if he or she died younger than me, as if I'm fortunate to be alive when younger ones are kicking the bucket.

An intriguing feature of these obituaries; almost every notice proclaims that the deceased has left for his "heavenly abode".

A permanent stay in Paradise or what's conceived as a heavenly abode, with its classy accommodation, sumptuous on-time meals, perfect health of the residents, ideal weather, crystal clear streams, pure air, and pleasing scenery could well tend to be boring after some time.

Visualize a scenario where no one ages, no one falls sick, no one suffers an accident, no one dies, no one is in a hurry, no one is angry or crying. No work, no challenges, no successes, no failures, no hopes, no fears, no enemies. And how dull it would be with the total absence of money; getting it, spending it, running short of it.

That way, the good old planet earth, though not designed for paradisiacal existence, may be a more interesting place to live, if one has the cozy cushion of wealth and health.

Most of the current issues and controversies, I find, are practically at the same stage at which we had left them a month back; the same accounts of power failures, the same stories of water shortages, the same saga of unborn girls being done away with (courtesy of sex-determination tests). Women are still waiting for their Representation Bill to be passed.

"Nothing much changed in our absence", I tell Priti, at the end of the marathon paper-reading sessions.

"We should have discontinued the papers, saved money".

On the long homeward flight I had resisted all those tempting offers of alcohol and meat. Only did justice to breakfast—an excellent breakfast of Danish breads, ham, Lupark butter, pastries, thick coffee—served an hour before landing. This was in line with my friend, Harban's suggestion that one should eat light on long air journeys but fill up a little before landing.

Johnny is back, licking us and rubbing himself against our legs. He seems to have gone fatter since being left with our friend Ram Sobti, the retired vet.

Sobti had given us the brown Labrador pup 3 years back. Johnny's grown into a hulking creature that consumes half a kilo of buffalo meat. Once, Priti was critical of the added expense. Now she's grown fond of Johnny. He's a well-behaved dog who doesn't upturn garbage cans or defecate on walking pavements. Mostly he sits or lies outside the kitchen door when Priti or Rano are working within. He rarely ventures into my study; maybe, he has an aversion to books.

In that way, dogs and cats are the only pets that are allowed freedom of our homes. Unlike all other animals, these two can be trained to urinate and defecate outside.

With the large lawn in which Johnny can romp about, it isn't compelling to take him out for a walk. In fact he never strays off the property and has a keen sense of where he belongs. There're no sex complications, either. Our friend Sobti got Johnny neutered.

On the fourth day of our return, a Sunday, gathering clouds make the day dark by breakfast. A few swollen drops hit the ground. Soon rain is falling hard, heavy, bouncing off the tarmac with such force that at ground level it is hard to tell if the rain is coming up or down. You could see drops land, and go straight up; an amazing sight.

Rain is hammering at windows, water gushing down rooftops into gutters. You see children dancing excited on the road, shrieking at each other. And then they disappear on seeing a car sloshing through the surface water like a snow plow.

The rain suddenly doubles, a blanket of water falling right across the city. It changes the colour and texture of streets, polishing every surface to a shine, drowning all other sounds, till it falters, slows down, falls gently, then fades. Indeed, raining alone doesn't seem to do justice to the umpteen different ways in which water had descended from the skies over the last few hours.

Daylight returns. People are out again, avoiding puddles, saving themselves from splashes of cars.

Harbans phones, "Our golf is off for the day. The course lies flooded. Haven't seen such downpour for years. Heavens opening up".

Priti is out to assess the damage to new flower beds, walking barefoot, with salwar rolled up to her knees. She is seen handling the damaged flowers with exceptional delicacy and care; she should be handling human beings likewise. She's already unhappy with mali Bhura over the upkeep of some potted plants during our absence abroad.

Rano is asked to make *pooras* for evening tea, a celebratory fare for the rain god. Ramesh and Aarti, the overhead tenants, are invited to join in. They report no leakage in any rooms. Sound construction, comments Ramesh.

Priti's architect cousin who built the house used to say, "It's the *mistris* who matter, not so much the architect. Good mistri, good construction; bad mistri, bad construction".

With the four-pound packet of Columbian roasted beans brought from Cranford, I set up the Italian coffee percolator and grinder on a sideboard in the dining room. What an enveloping fragrance as the beans are ground! And we always have thick freshly-brewed coffee, with a dash of cream, not milk.

I break off around 11.30 for coffee.

I'm required to see what the cook and the cleaning woman are up to. And to talk to Bhura, the Bihari mali. He's dwarfishly short, no more than five feet one and coal-black, his heels scissored like ravines. But he seems sturdy and wiry, more so with his shirt off. Over 30, he looks like 20. His wife and children live somewhere in Darbhanga, northern Bihar.

Previously Bhura came for two hours on alternate days. On our return from the US, we have hired him full time. Noni is keen, we keep a grand garden.

It's all between Priti and Bhura. I know precious little about plants and flowers. My total contribution is restricted to plucking off ripened yellow petals from money-plants and other creepers—leaves that would be dropping down on their own. Indeed, I've become so obsessive about it I pick out yellowing leaves on the verandas of other people while waiting for them to welcome us inside.

Bhura, by now, is fully in the know of my abysmal ignorance in gardening matters. He treats my suggestions with amused tolerance. If I tell him something, like pruning an overgrown bougainvillea or lopping an overhanging branch, he doesn't proceed without first clearing it with Priti. Once, on my asking, he had trimmed one bougainvillea creeper. Priti made her annoyance clear: How can you trim a creeper in its flowering stage?!

Yet whatever be my ignorance in horticultural matters, I derive much pleasure from the garden, its various varieties of plants, properly "grouped", not "plopped", and set on walkways of red stone. Even obliquely boast of it to others.

After four weeks of sleeping in separate beds at Cranford, we are back to our double bed.

When the double bed was acquired a decade back, the use of a common coverlet posed no little problem. In summer I felt hotter than she, and in winter colder; our temperature responses obviously different. In winter, I take on an extra blanket on my side, in summer I sleep nude and stick out my feet.

Handling a common coverlet, I wake up in the middle of the night to discover that there's nothing to handle. She's taken the bulk of what's at least half mine.

I tug at it gingerly. She stirs, and seemingly unaware, tightens her grasp and rolls further away, taking another foot and a half of it. I'm left in the cold or exposed to a blast from the air conditioner, my side nearer to the machine. So I pull up the pathetically small segment of the coverlet left available and scoot up next to her. She should be warmer than me.

And in the beginning, it was a challenge to find room for four arms and four legs; arms and legs that didn't bother you all the day.

Yet we have come to appreciate the virtue of the double bed, more so as a breach healer. Minor infractions give rise to marital tiffs or sulks; my favourite dish ruined by sharp chillies or the pencil missing near the phone, her finding my urine drops on the toilet seat or curry spots on the tablecloth. It's not the gravity of the original lapse but the consequent behaviour of the guilty party in not owning the lapse or not showing due remorse that aggravates the tiff.

I go in for silent sulks that may well last 24 hours or more. She, with her household obligations and possessing a more amiable disposition, is apt to breach her punitive sulk. That's the trouble with sulk; once you unsulk, you can't resulk.

In beds separated by night tables, it means crossing that horrid chasm of some three feet.

Why not end up the silly quarrel? Why not snuggle in besides the partner; no doubt erring but still loved? But who's to make the first move "to eat crow"?

In a double bed things work out easier. A tentative toe meets a leg. There's no obligation to withdraw the toe. So it stays. Maybe, in time it is rewarded by return pressure. The underlying yearning for amity begins to flow. Arms reach out, heads may draw near. The physical contact has broken the ice, even if no formal reconciliation results before falling asleep.

Of course, occasionally we run into marital tiffs that even a double bed can't assuage. We lie back to back, as if signaling that the other party doesn't exist.

When sleep comes, it commonly sees me resting on my left side with the right arm flung over her and a leg over her legs. Her warm breath fanning my face can be a disturbing factor. To spare her similar discomfort, I often pull myself up on the pillows. The latter in my case are double pillows. Sleeping mostly on the side I look for a higher headrest. She prefers a thin pillow as she sleeps more on her back. And justifies the same, saying doctors advise sleeping on the back vis-à-vis the side.

The double bed, the quintessential mark of marriage, doesn't necessarily pressurize you to make any given night magical. The good thing about marriage; you know you can have another shot tomorrow. And the next. And the next. That's the beauty of Some Other Day.

We share a bed. But our bedside tables remain entirely personal, private, unshared spaces.

Anyone tinkering with the arrangement of things on my bedside table upsets me, even changing the angle at which I keep the bed clock. The cleaning maid has instructions to leave the table alone.

Books, aspirin, Tums, German cuticle scissors, and a US-made nail clipper find a place there. Other items include the TV remote (unless commandeered by Priti), a flashlight, and a hand towel, let alone Anglepoise lamp.

Hers is clearly more cluttered. Bottles and tubes of all shapes, colours and sizes are there. A thick volume of the *Bhagwad Gita*, her *gutka* of *Sukhmani*, along with a pair of reading glasses, enjoy pride of the place. You see bills, letters, odd bits of paper, cuttings from magazines. And in the midst of it all, an uncovered glass full of water for the night.

A bedside table, it seems, isn't just a convenient surface to hold inanimate objects. It's a significant player in the drama of one's daily living. A bedside table offers an inkling of a person's lifestyle, preoccupations or worries, all the more significant if the person happens to spend chunks of waking time in bed.

Since we moved into the present house 15 years back, a major source of marital friction has been neutralized.

Earlier, sharing a bathroom was proving endlessly contentious. It gave rise to the perennial question, "Who left it messier?" I genuinely believed my use was tidier, as my ablutions were seemingly simpler. Of course, with glasses off, I may be missing wet spots or any other lapse.

Her usual complaint: "You left water spread outside the washbasin, even water on the floor".

I've shifted my washroom activity to the bathroom adjoining the spare bedroom. And have moved my clothes to a wardrobe there.

That leaves Priti with an almost autonomous zone for bathing, dressing, and various other intimate matters women are supposed to attend to. Such personal space is all the more welcome to her as she is seeing too much of me otherwise; I don't go out for work.

A well-appointed bathroom all to herself is a luxury. She doesn't have to "adjust" to anyone else's convenience. She can use it undisturbed, unhurried. Can spread out her stuff, and there's none to pry into or tinker with it. Whether she cleans the place immediately after use or leaves it in a mess is entirely her business. What a change from Amritsar where she lived for over 20 years; a shared bathroom with nothing but a leaky 4-ft.-high tap.

Now I only use her bathroom for a nightly "emergency".

In the US, I spent little time with Viki. But back in Chandigarh, I feel nostalgic about him. I yearn to write to him, though aware, he can't read it well—anyway, can't appreciate the sentiments expressed. Still, I write. Maybe, the letter is partly addressed to his parents.

Dearest Viki,

It was great being with you this time. Indeed, as you grow up, it's more and more fun to be with you.

We got the latest batch of your photographs. You look like a princeling in that Udaipuri pugree and the embroidered black sherwani, your grandma brought for you. You've the uncanny knack of posing for pictures.

Whereas I was slightly irritated with the juttis being too loose for you and the pajamas too long, you bore these imperfections with an aplomb that would be the envy of adults. And you had the patience to keep on the toughened red turban for hours while we, the elders, hastened to relieve ourselves of our pink pugrees at the earliest opportunity in that marriage function.

The batch of photographs contains quite a few with you and me in the shallow part of the pool. To me these are treasured snaps, the two of us topless and cheery, splashing water playfully on each other. My protruding belly is a shame, you seem to say, pointing your hand at it.

Grandma and I are happy you're enjoying the yellow Porsche. The red Mercedes we bought earlier proved too small for your legs. And I was gratified to find that you, notwithstanding your intense fascination for ride-in cars, displayed a remarkably rational approach in agreeing to its return, before acquiring another one.

The Porsche was entirely your choice out of all those cars in the store. And I concede you showed an unerring instinct to go for the best.

I am aware a kid can learn a language with the greatest of ease—a month in India would get you going in Hindi. Yet I found an astonishing sophistication in your use of the English language. I heard you using expressions like, "I want it, too".

And your telling me, "I need some help" when you were trying to climb into the BMW through the back hatch opened by me at your behest. Now you didn't want me to haul you up. In fact you resisted when I tried. Evidently accepting total help in this manner went against your self-image; you just wanted a little heave up to supplement your efforts. And for that purpose, the expression "some help" was the most appropriate.

How exactly children learn to speak still remains a mystery. As I see you, children may well be coining a few expressions on their own, without having heard these from anybody.

Viki, you remain as playful as ever: smiling, laughing, brimming with fun and activity. Indeed you have developed into an adorable kid. Playfulness, I believe, is a learning process—a combination of imagination, creativity, and curiosity that nourishes the brain. We are a playful species.

Yet your playfulness (on occasions, bordering on hyperactivity) can land you in trouble.

I clearly remember the evening when you were exiled to the kitchen with face to the wall for fishing an ice cube from my drink—rather blameworthy on my part to encourage you to it. Both of us happen to be fond of chewing ice cubes.

And when I rescued you from the kitchen, you appeared too tardy in cleaning up the clutter of your toys. Peremptorily, you were removed from the scene, much against your wishes.

As you were being chastised, I saw for the first time in your eyes a peculiar expression; an expression of sorrow, mixed with what looked like anger. I couldn't sleep well that night, that expression of yours kept haunting me.

It's all right for grandparents to be indulgent. They come and go. But the parents bear a far heavier responsibility. For them it is of utmost importance how their child develops. It often makes them wonder whether they may be making any mistakes; mistakes made with the best of intentions?

When one ponders on the enormous importance of childhood—they say, you learn as much in the first 7 yeas as in the rest seventy—about how much is at stake in the fundamental act of raising a human child from helpless infancy to successful adulthood, one begins to realize what an awesome challenge it is. No surprise that parental anxiety and guilt are so widespread these days. Perhaps conscientious parents have it too hard on themselves when their youngsters "go astray".

I am not a child expert. And my own record as a parent is patchy.

You're lucky. You've parents who are mature, well-informed, and in a position to give you an excellent start in life. And I have high hopes you'd develop into a person of exceptional ability and goodwill.

Sometimes I feel, it wouldn't be a bad idea if you could round up your school education with a year of studies in India. This should give you a more rounded personality and a better exposure to your cultural roots. There are good schools here and the atmosphere quite congenial to serious studies.

The only hitch, as far as I am concerned: I'll be 87, if living, when you're 17.

Looking forward to seeing you during the forthcoming winter. You'll be here on our golden wedding anniversary.

Your grandpa,

Swarup

CHAPTER 10

We are now into our customary routine.

I get up at five, aided by an alarm clock.

I like the morning darkness and its silences. Look to an hour or so of solitude. No phone rings. And I don't turn on my computer; prefer to read a book or notes.

Reading continues till Rano brings in tea and morning papers around 6.30.

I'm always waiting anxiously for the papers. By 70, many people cease to care about news. But my interest in the world around has stayed undiminished.

I'm through three cups of weak tea, a banana, and the two papers in another hour.

Rano is supposed to have her morning tea, too. But only recently it came to light that she was taking away to her room over the garage a large brass pan brimful of highly-sugared milky tea laced with cardamom and garlic. One morning, carrying the open vessel in both hands, Rano stumbled on the stairs of her room that had become slippery from a downpour. The contents of the pan spilled over her body covered only by a nightie. The burning-hot tea badly scalded her left breast, parts of her abdomen, and her left thigh.

Rano ran back, shrieking in agony. And she simply lifted her nightie to her neck to show us the extensive burns. It was a sight, the full frontal nudity of that massive frame. Now one saw that she had two separate, rather asymmetrical breasts, not some sort of an undifferentiated mass at the chest.

I took her to Harbans who got her admitted into a hospital. Rano returned after three days.

The matter of taking tea for her no-good son was never discussed. But the exposure, let alone the physical suffering, has made her discontinue the practice. Priti, however, is certain Rano continues to steal tea leaves, sugar, ghee, garlic, and other costly ingredients.

"Why not give meals to the no-good son, too?" I once suggested. "That would eliminate food pilferage".

"Feeding another wide mouth! Not a bright idea", she shot back. "It's enough that I let Rano take away many a leftover dish. She must be sharing it with her son".

Priti stirs by seven. She sips tea sitting in the open back verandah, barring the very cold months; the tea kept warm in a thermos flask. Johnny is there, having got his biscuit and made his obligatory trip to the hedge.

"They call it bed tea but I like to sit out for it", says she. "Nothing's more soothing than seeing the sun rise. Birds chirping merrily. All around green and peaceful".

Yes, it's delightful out there, the city at its best. Yet, notwithstanding her prodding, I don't stir out of my study. I prefer controlled temperature, controlled light.

After ablutions, Priti gathers some flowers, preferably jasmine, to proffer at the Guru Granth Sahib, positioned in a small room, which we call our gurudwara. Then she reads parts of *Sukhmani*, the first 5 *ashtpadis*, in 15–20 minutes. By now she can almost recite them by heart. Priti hails from a Hindu family but has taken to Sikh scriptures and gurudwaras. She finds *Sukhmani* eminently intelligible and comforting.

The breakfast remains unvaried, unchanged throughout the year, with no concession to seasons. It's mostly fruit, a boiled egg, toast, and a cup of milk.

Priti has been suffering from hypertension since the age of 50, her BP in the region of 145/95 if left untreated. She has a home monitor. Checks her blood pressure every Sunday morning. Records it in a notebook.

Do you know who measured blood pressure for the first time?" I ask.

"Don't know. Don't really care".

She isn't sold on "useless" information.

"Stephen Hales, a British bishop, sliced into his patient's artery, joined the vessel to an 11-foot-tall glass column, and saw the blood pushed up the 8-foot-mark. The patient was a horse. That was in 1711."

Hypertension has made Priti highly health-conscious.

At times when she's annoyed with me, she's apt to remark, "You're the one raising my blood pressure".

Her BP, I imagine, stems more from being a perfectionist, both at work and home, than from deficiency in the functioning of kidneys or liver or arteries. Anything big or small going remiss causes her irritation, anguish.

Meantime it's a pill—mostly Natrilix—at breakfast. Priti skimps on salt, almost to the point of making cooked dishes slightly insipid. She tries to make up by other condiments, particularly black pepper. And she's known to leave a dish untouched if the cook has erred in putting in too much salt.

"Excess salt damages only those who happen to be salt sensitive. And that's a small percentage of people", Ravi tells her. "In a lab they can easily check whether you're salt-sensitive or not, before you deny yourself the pleasure of salt".

"By now I've come to like food with little salt. No need of a test, even if a reliable one exists".

Jogi, another health freak in the family, gives the same treatment to the sugar bowl. Sugar is fattening, and refined sugar, he is convinced, is the cause of many ailments.

Butter stands banished from our table. I dip toast in milk to soften it. It's not an elegant sight but works out fairly fine, taste-wise. Since the last visit to Cranford, I've taken to marmalade on toast, having found that the delectable St. Dalfour marmalade from France—the orange rinds invitingly visible—is available in shops.

At Cranford, Priti forsook all dietary restrictions, declaring it a holiday from her health concerns. But she did double the dosage of her BP pills.

Priti is in a hurry in the morning. Gives quick instructions to the cook about lunch and is at her nursery school by 9.00.

The school is in a rented house close to the sector market. It has five teachers and some fifty kids. Priti doesn't teach but is there till 1. She's busy guiding teachers, meeting parents, ordering supplies, doing accounts, and looking after the general upkeep of the place. She's a perfectionist in whatever she does.

The venture had a discouragingly slow start. But by now it's doing gratifyingly well. It nets her a tidy income.

Her initial idea was to have the school on the ground floor of the house itself, with us moving to the first. I opposed it.

"The house is too good to be turned into a playpen for little devils. Urchins let loose in the garden, trampling flower beds, hurling stones at fruit".

Ravi, when he heard of her move, was horrified. Rang up, "No mama, no. Enjoy the house and the garden".

At that time Priti was upset about my refusal to have a part of the house turned into a kindergarten. Now she concedes it was one of the few sound decisions I ever took, not to mention my marrying her.

Gauri, the cleaning woman, is a buxom unmarried girl around 18 who comes on a creaky Atlas bicycle. She dresses in tight clothes. Uses lipstick. One or the other of her bra straps is usually showing. The tall girl, possibly drunk with the joy of youth, is either singing or giggling, often without ostensible cause. She sports a flower in her hair, mostly a rose or gainda, plucked at our place. At one time, Bhura chose one for her. Now she seems to be doing on her own.

I have a suspicion that the bad blood between Gauri and Bhura stems from Gauri rejecting Bhura's advances. A rejection so categorical it has turned Bhura's unfulfilled longings into hostility.

Gauri's job is to sweep the driveway, clean rooms, dust furniture, and wipe bathroom floors. She tends to skip corners and remote areas. And there's always a tussle with the mali whether a particular part of the compound or stairs was her duty to sweep or for the mali to clean up.

Gauri also does the daily wash. Garments needing professional ironing, such as my shirts and pants, are sent in the afternoon to a dhobi doing ironing under a tree at the road corner. Priti mostly does her own ironing, and does a neat job of it. She says she likes ironing, more so the fresh scent of cotton when the steam iron hits the shirt. To her, ironing is a sort of relaxation.

Rano, our live-in cook with her servant-like looks, is a widow over 40, a Pahari from Kangra. She sports a pair of huge shapeless breasts. Enormous hips. Old-fashioned thighs rub against each other when she walks. Once there was a waist. It lies hidden between two bulging flesh rolls. And she has by now several chins that shift when she talks.

Rano still retains her fine cut of face, helped by wide kohl-coloured eyes. And she's markedly fair-skinned for her strata of society. Rano had a definite sex appeal when she came to us two decades back. Pity she has let herself go. Maybe, she overeats to compensate for other tribulations in life. And she's clad solely in two garments, shirt and salwar. One can easily make out the total absence of underclothes.

Her chowkidar husband, an alcoholic and wife-beater, mercifully died of liver failure years ago. The no-good son, a brawny wild-eyed teenager with shoulder-length hair, currently does cycle repair, sitting in the verandah of a nearby market.

Unlike Gauri, Rano never laughs or smiles. She's ever morose. And if you care to ask how she's doing, looks heavenward to the gods and moans her lot. But she does cook half a dozen dishes well—items like meat curry, biryani, dal makhani, aloo gobi, fish pakoras, and rice pudding. Invariably she produces inviting duly-puffed thin phulkas. Priti's attempt at teaching her new dishes has been a signal failure.

Rano is an inveterate bidi smoker. Could be smoking two to three bundles a day. She's strictly forbidden to smoke inside the house. But you get a whiff of tobacco whenever she shuffles in with her noisy rubber flip-flops. Priti gave her money to buy canvas shoes to make her move soundlessly. But Rano refuses to part with her flip-flops; says, these are so easy to put on and off.

"You'll die of lung or throat cancer", warns Priti.

"Bibiji, who knows?! Bhagwan may grant me a better afterlife. At least not the same husband".

One thing is there. With two wrong persons marrying, at best two people are made unhappy, instead of four being made miserable.

While Priti buys vegetables and fruits, more or less on a daily basis on her way back from school, I do a fortnight's requirement of meat at one go. Priti dislikes standing before the butcher's smelly stall with its splattered blood and street dogs. She insists that the chicken I bring is freshly slaughtered and cleaned before my eyes. And I better ensure that the butcher doesn't neglect to pack in its liver and kidneys, even the bird's head. She has a fondness for chicken.

"Do you know Napoleon had a special weakness for chicken", I tell her.

"What's that to do with us?" she says dismissively.

Usually she has a good word for me over the purchase of meat. Lately I've discovered that one of the choicest parts of a lamb is the neck (*puth*)—ideal for biryani. Between lamb and goat, our clear preference is for the softer lamb meat.

I've started liking my butcher, the one I patronize out of half a dozen stalls. He's a heavy-set youngish Sikh with a thick beard right up to his eyes and cauliflower ears. You see a pair of huge hands, I suppose, with an iron-like grip. He ties a yellow headscarf in place of the turban. And wears a knee-length pleated *kachha*, his pajama pair hung on a nail nearby.

The man seems possessed of a cheerful disposition. He smiles seeing me come, the white teeth peeping out of the black beard thicket.

"Don't give cause of complaint to the good wife. Both you and I would be in trouble", is invariably my opening gambit after placing the order.

His standard reply: "Uncleji, what I give today would make Auntie happy; the choicest cuts of lamb and the softest chicken".

"I leave it all to you. Mind, no complaints".

And I begin attending to other market errands. It's no fun standing in front of hung carcasses and swatting sticky flies from one's face. The only thing worth watching is the dexterity with which my butcher friend wields the knife. One marvels at the ease with which the frighteningly sharp blade slices through flesh as if cutting into butter.

After lunch, an afternoon siesta is a must. And that means a regular nap.

In summer I'm at the golf course by 5.00 for a round of nine or fourteen holes and in winter by 3.00. Early morning game on dewy grass, mostly played by people with a busy day schedule, is not for me.

I started golf at the age of 55; started soon on promotion to the IAS. I got six half-hourly lessons from the club pro. Ravi sent me a 14-club Ping set, though he himself doesn't play golf. Says, he hasn't the time for it. And Priti never evinced any interest in the game. Indeed, she thinks that golfers, mostly talking of the sorry state of their game, can be great bores at parties to non-golfers.

Over the last two decades, my official handicap stands frozen at 18. In fact it would deteriorate but for my putting in only my best cards. As golfers grow older, they hate their handicap to rise, for that would be an admission of their prowess declining.

The days I go for golf, Priti plays bridge. And that way I have a regular golf foursome—all retired gents, one of them doubling as my doctor; another, the vet, the fourth, a retired air marshal; Priti has a bridge foursome. The four neighbourhood ladies meet by turn in their homes. The 3-hour play includes high evening tea.

I, too, play bridge. And I soon introduced Priti to it. By now she possibly plays better—at least bids more cautious than me.

We never play as partners. A few occasions of partner-play had given rise to such acrimony, she's dead set against a repeat.

The days I don't play golf and she bridge, we take walks in the Rose Garden or a longish one in Leisure Valley.

The game of golf not only affords exercise and open air, it has enlivened my life. So many hours spent nicely immersed in the game. There are few satisfactions sweeter for a golfer than hitting a good short; seeing the ball soar high and straight, landing on the green, more so at a frog's leap from the hole.

It is fun, gathering at the first tee, exchanging jokes and pleasantries—golfers are at their happiest and jolliest on the first tee.

The next three-four hours may not be free of spats—say, over a contested stroke-count. Yet an elaborate niceness tends to prevail. We repress coughs when others are swinging, join in hopeless hunt for lost balls, and on the green avoid stepping in one another's putting lines. The behaviour is often better here than elsewhere, possibly because we are happier here than elsewhere. It's a part of the good feeling that golf generates.

And then the pleasure of recalling the game when we sit for tea and snacks; the loser pair signing the bill.

On days Priti has nothing else to do, she accompanies me to the club. Takes a long walk on the waterfront—since her going round the Golden Temple *sarovar*, she fancies walking by the waterside. Thereafter, she either waits for me to join her at tea or gets driven home earlier.

CHAPTER 11

How's the equation shaping between me and Priti?

With the passing of years, Priti is doing well in her school venture while I'm floundering in my writing "misadventure". She's gaining in self-confidence, me sinking into self-pity. She is getting surer of herself. Maybe women as they advance in years often acquire greater awareness of their strengths and the correctness of their convictions. Women earning money clearly gain in confidence.

At times Priti perceives that she has three sons, not two, with a husband so dependent on her.

She is apt to make light of my misgivings. At times, she tends to be sharp, even sarcastic over my perceived plight. Once, exasperated over my dismal mood in writing, she cries out, "Heaven won't fall if you don't finish this book. Already too many books in the world. Who's going to read them all?"

Things have changed between us, I tell her, as she asks me to attend to some household items while leaving for school. "You go out to work every morning, making money. I stay at home, doing nothing except playing unsuccessfully with words. You think up things for me to do to earn my keep".

"That's a terrible thing to say".

"It happens to be true".

"It isn't".

"You're now the sole breadwinner. It's bound to have an effect on you, and so on to the equation between us. All relationships that way are about power, if not power now, power later. And the sources of power are so simple, so fixed. On top comes money".

"Must be some nonsense you read in a book", she retorts. "You're the one raising my blood pressure".

And she hurries off to the school. Her voice, I find, is gaining the authority of a school marm.

She has invited the Director of Education (Union Territory of Chandigarh) to evening tea. Priti's angling for a plot of land from the government at a concessional rate to build her own school building.

I am for avoiding the gentleman. She's keen that I—a high government official at one time—should be there to impress him.

The Director, a patronizing chap in his 50s with net-tied beard and precisely-tiered turban, turns out a bit bumptious for my liking.

"What are you doing?" he asks me.

This sort of question I often get asked by genuinely busy acquaintances. I have learnt to ignore it, after a few humiliating episodes.

He, however, repeats it. Waits for a reply.

"Retired", I say.

"Oh, retired! But what are you doing with yourself?"

A little irritated I say, "Killing time till time comes to kill me. Life insurance salesmen no longer bother me".

"Your wife tells me you're into writing novels".

"That's more of wishful thinking".

"What are you doing then?"

"Living off my wife".

Priti listens outraged.

"So you do nothing", he persists—with a man over 70.

"I just sit at home all day, doing nothing".

"Nothing?"

"Absolutely nothing".

Lucky the conversation gets sidetracked with the arrival

of tea things. And soon I slip out, leaving Priti to tackle the bounder.

And she does wangle an undertaking from him to recommend allotment of a 1000-sq.-yard piece of land.

"You were rather rude to Raunak Singh", she says as the gentleman left. "He was just being friendly. Didn't mean to offend you".

"He was too persistent. People always assume everyone must be doing something after retirement".

"I'd say that you are intelligent, funny. But you can't manage people. You have no people skills".

"People skills!"

"Yes, some have got these skills in ample measure. Others just don't".

And she may not be far wrong. I do nurse a feeling I could have had a more successful service career, even gratifying government jobs after retirement, if I had displayed what she calls "people skills".

Indeed, my worse weakness may not be the lack of people skills but a pronounced tendency to be impatient with the failings of others. This must have resulted in my having very few friends, as well as missed opportunities, in the absence of well-wishers.

As she's winding up the tea things, Priti can't help repeating what she has been telling me so often, "Don't live in isolation. Integrate with people. It energizes creativity; good for your writing".

While lunch is mostly vegetables, curd and rice, our dinner must have a meat dish, followed by dessert. And for me, it's a large whisky at bath, before. I own a silver peg measure but gave up measuring with it, as anything above the measure generated a guilt feeling. Now I pour myself half an inch of the golden liquid in a flat-bottomed glass.

Red wine, as advised by Ravi, is yet to be introduced.

I eat fast, more like a dog, till hunger pangs subside. Everything I heap on the main plate, ignoring katoris meant for curried things. Often, I start eating before others, on the plea the food would get cold. But I'm made to wait for the dessert till she catches up.

Priti eats like a cat, eats a bit and pauses. Eats slow. Goes more for curds, vegetables and salads, and less meat.

A trivial area of spousal conflict is the differing approach we bring to wastepaper baskets.

I rate wastepaper basket a prime invention; the brainchild of some genius. And insist on one in every room. These are no fancy stuff, mostly cane baskets that have been emptied of fruit.

As many as 20 times in a day I may be enjoying the teeny-weeny kick of discarding something, getting rid of it, putting it out of our life. And there's no end to discards: leaflets that flutter out of newspapers, ads in post, plastic bags, wrappers, used envelopes, out-of-ink ballpoints, torn socks, nail cuttings.

At times, the good wife retrieves an object discarded by me. "What's the urgency about it?" she often remonstrates. "This plastic bag, for one, can be of use. Indeed, you yourself may be asking for it". One whole shelf in the kitchen holds her collection of empty plastic bags.

My study-room basket—a large, wide-mouthed basket that once carried Amri apples from Kashmir—could be holding plenty of crumpled paper, often pressed into balls.

What upsets me about wastebaskets is the disappearance of anyone from its designated place. Doing her cleaning chores, Gauri takes a wastebasket out when she can't reduce its contents to a size she can carry in her fist. And, in line with her policy to minimize physical exertion, she often fails to bring up the empties unless she can combine it with a trip for some other work.

Imagine my irritation when I want to discard something and find the accustomed wastebasket missing. On occasions I have carried the offending object in my pocket till the same could be got rid of.

After dinner, lying in bed, we watch Priti's favourite TV serials between 9 and 10. At one time we used to sit side by side, with her leaning on my chest and my right arm around her—a sort of TV hug. The most important thing about the TV hug is to stay focussed on your partner's needs than to get too engrossed in the programme itself.

Now we sit apart on our sides of the wide double bed.

Egged on by Noni, we've exchanged our old Maruti 800 for a new air-conditioned Esteem, a silver-white car with matching seat covers and foot mats.

And we have taken on a full-time chauffeur.

Banta (Balwant Singh) was one of the official drivers in the Revenue Dept when I worked there. He has retired.

He's a full-bodied, tall Sikh, not known to pinch petrol. And, unlike his formidable appearance, Banta is patently non-aggressive in driving. With all those roundabouts of Chandigarh and their no-rule chaotic traffic, he'd let an aggressive driver go ahead, merely mumbling how bad people drove.

No more arguments with Priti when out for social calls or dinners. If there's any time in married life when we are apt to have a row, it is while I'm driving and she's sitting beside. The small, enclosed space of a car is a powerful symbol you're together.

While I'm reluctant to ask for directions every time there's doubt, she's ever urging me to seek assistance. Once looking for a house for dinner we became so bitterly argumentative, we gave up the search. Ended eating an omelette at home in stony silence, dressed in party clothes.

The driving scene stands transformed with the coming of Banta. We sit relaxed in the back. "Why didn't we get a chauffeur earlier", she's apt to exclaim.

In the beginning Banta had made out he was a teetotaller, didn't touch alcohol. This fiction got exposed when I saw him drinking at a marriage party, where drivers of guests were strangely being doled out liquor.

Banta returning to work after one of his binges is most contrite. And I don't have the heat to dispense with his services. Who knows we may get someone worse. Honest, competent chauffeurs are hard to come by.

I am in my study till breakfast, and thereafter till lunch, with a break for coffee. As a rule, serious work is over by lunch. Beyond that it's only light reading. Attention declines further in the evening with whisky.

The study is a sunny spacious room with bookshelves ranged from floor to ceiling on two sides. The large low windows afford a refreshing view of the back lawn and, beyond, of the public park. A climbing rose creeper covers a wall. You often see yellow roses peeping out, blowzy ones shedding their petals.

A potted rubber plant occupies a corner. It's Bhura's job to water it and periodically take it out for sun and air.

My most prized possession is the heavy teak desk, said to be over 100 years old. I bought it at an auction in Simla in 1960 for rupees 150. It was part of a European's household effects.

The dark-brown desk is one of the few good things around I personally acquired. The drawers still slide smoothly and the top is free of dents or scars. No cup of tea or coffee is allowed on it without a coaster.

Sitting immobile in study for hours makes the old body vulnerable to weather vagaries; the cold of winter, the heat of summer, the humidity of rainy season. The air conditioner Ravi gave me has made all the difference.

This piece of equipment alone—cold in a box—has transformed the room in terms of livability and comfort. Hope it helps my work output. But then I had slogged my hardest in sweltering heat with no cooling aids; at best a ceiling fan, with paperweights taking care of flying papers. Now even a water-cooler isn't deemed enough.

What do I do sitting the whole morning on a straight-backed leather chair with a computer screen in front? This calls for some explaining.

Seven years back, Ravi and Noni were here.

"Papa, what's the point of your running after consultancy work in land disputes. You have the means to live nicely. Why don't you write something creative? You're widely read, and fond of books", says Noni.

"I'm toying with the idea of opening a bookshop, a well-appointed bookshop stocking select volumes, with room enough for serious readers to sit and browse. I have my eyes on a shop in Sector 17, the one being vacated by an optical store".

"No Dad, no. Not a bookshop", Ravi intervenes, rubbing the bridge of his nose. "It won't survive. Nowadays you need to sell magazines, diaries, calendars, children's books, even toys alongside. And this you can't do".

Noni taking a sip of Kingfisher beer, a beer she has come to relish, "A bookshop will tie you up the whole day. And I don't think Papa has a head for business. He has been in service too long".

"I've worked in government. I should write about government. But it's so boring to write of official matters".

My only experience of writing anyway is office reports and noting on files. Creative writing, you begin in your early twenties, not in late sixties".

"Nobody is too old to write. Try your hand at autobiographical fiction. Nirad C. Chaudhuri, the well-known Indian writer, wrote the second part of his autobiography at the age of 90 and several famous novels have been written by authors over 60. You had an interesting innings. Leave something for Viki to read about your life and times", elaborates Noni.

"Any autobiographical fiction by me would largely dwell on the mistakes I made, the sorrows that came my way".

"Sorrows and mistakes are the stuff of fiction. No one writes a novel on happiness. And better start working with a computer. We'll get you one".

"To go straight from pen and paper to computer! I haven't handled a typewriter in my life".

"Doesn't take much time to pick up computer use".

And true to their word, a Compaq computer arrives next day along with a Hewlett Packard printer and a Brother fax machine.

As the equipment is being installed, Noni couldn't resist remarking, "Work, papa, work. I know writing is hard work. It can give you a stiff neck, an aching back, let alone an ugly mood when things don't go well.

Yet, you've to get on with it. Work is what made anything of this world. It's all we have. And it's what we have to do. I do concede creative writing is different from government work, the latter not particularly demanding of skill or imagination".

In time, I develop competency in the use of computer, mostly as word processor. I do enjoy the very process of reading. Writing is altogether different. A novel around one's own life proved a gut-wrenching undertaking. Yet I'm miserable the day I don't do any writing.

After umpteen false starts, revisions and suggestions from writer friends, I produce a 1,00,000-word manuscript.

And for ages it goes from publisher to publisher. Till one middle-level Indian publishing house signals acceptance, provided I'd buy 50 copies of it and pay in advance—they want to cover part of their printing costs. And the editors ask for so many changes, it has to be virtually rewritten. Thereafter, it undergoes endless language and format correction at the hands of my lady editor. She'd tear into my best passages, add things I thought were understood, and treat my writing as if from a college fresher. I mostly acquiesce, being a first-timer. All that I want is to get published.

The book is now slated to appear within a year. And it won't fetch much money. The contract stipulates that the first 200 of the 700-print-order won't attract the standard 10% royalty.

Meantime, I have begun a second one. This goes back to the times of my father rather than focusing on my life. And I hope to complete the first draft—a shorter volume of some 75,000 words—within a year.

What fate it would meet at the hands of publishers? Hopefully a notch better if my first novel is out by then.

Priti is not terribly excited about my writing venture. "I was quite happy with your playing golf and bridge, socializing and engrossed in hours of reading", she tells me. "You were mostly cheerful and often regale me with the interesting things you read. Now you sit cooped in your room. Any outside interruption annoys you".

"You know the whole story", I say, taking off my glasses. "I was taking life fairly easy till Noni pushed me into writing. Now the bug has caught me, and I can't withdraw. Some form of writing will be there till senility takes over".

"It's up to you", says she. "You've my support and good wishes".

"Creative writing is serious stuff", I respond. "You have to put up with the mood swings of the man at this work".

I'm not sure how Priti is taking this change. But then she nurses the hope that I may pick up as an established writer some day—at least gain recognition among our circle of friends and acquaintances. She appears reconciled to put up with my tantrums if it helps give me a feel of some importance.

Priti knows I pine for public recognition. And she'd love to have my pictures in papers she could show. Yet at times she must be feeling that I could be doing something other than writing, something that engendered fewer mood swings. Her main concern seems to be that I'm not perceived as a failure by our circle of successful friends.

Reading through the manuscript of my first novel, she remarks, "Why do you write such personal things?"

"My bundle of service memories is small, and most of those matters have lost their importance. So, I have to fall back on my personal life. All fiction that way involves some self-exposure. With good writers, their experiences become the experiences of readers".

"Are you sure you're succeeding there".

"No, I'm not satisfied. At times I despair I'll ever achieve it".

Meantime in a fit of bravado, I get my profession entered as 'writer' in place of 'retired IAS' in the passport while applying for renewal. Actually the most apt description of my present status would be 'househusband.'

I'm well aware that wifely support and good wishes may help but successful writing has to be sweated out by me. Whether I would be up to it has yet to be seen. But one thing I know that I'm not going to give it up now, whatever failings may dog me in creative writing.

On occasions, the midday siesta gives rise to sex. Curiously, I've scant inclination for marital sex after dinner. Maybe, I'm fagged out by then, feel too sleepy or too sated with food and drink. Things loom different after the light lunch. I'm still snappy.

Men are possibly at their smartest in the morning, going out for work. They deteriorate with work and tension as the day advances. Women, in contrast, start rather lethargic but pep up with the day, presumably reaching their peak towards early evening. The afternoon, that way, finds the two sexes—one on the downward curve, the other on the upward—at roughly the same level of zest and energy. No wonder, midday sex is known to find favour with some amorous nations and people.

In the beginning, Priti was more for sex after dinner than lunch. But she has gradually veered round to my frame of mind and body. The dame possesses a practical bent of mind. She knows how to make optimum use of limited resources—maximizing her hubby's declining libido to her steady sexual urges.

Now, with penetrative sex taking a backseat, oral sex appears all the more enticing. Pity, the home offerings in this activity are no more than meagre.

The urge to achieve ejaculation, once so compelling, has waned greatly, both to my dismay and relief.

With pressure of ejaculation gone, I indulge in extended love play. In certain respects it may be making me a more agreeable companion in the marital bed. Often the love play ends up with a finger-rub orgasm for her, while I'm quite content with nothing for myself. That way, with advancing years men become sexually far less selfish.

Indeed, the good wife may be having more enjoyable sex than when I was young.

One thing is manifest. By now my life is almost totally twined around this wife of 50 years: for food, for clothes, for sex, for conversation, for consultation, and for company, let alone her financial muscle from the nursery school.

My social life anyway would simply collapse without her. Of us two, Priti is the one talking to friends, writing to relatives, remembering birthdays and anniversaries, planning gifts, inviting people for food, returning calls, and otherwise keeping connections. She can be friendly to strangers, too. Easily picks up conversation with co-passengers in trains and buses, or the ones waiting at the doctor's.

She's particularly great in sending birthday and anniversary greetings. Besides putting her customary good wishes, she often asks me, "You're a writer. Write something interesting on the card".

I'm often at my wits end to pen an acceptable, friendly, yet jocular message.

When the telephone rings, I rarely pick it up, even if I happen to be nearer to the instrument than her. I know from experience that now 90% of the phone calls are meant for her. And when a common friend or relative calls, the caller is more inclined to talk to Priti than me. I anyway tend to terminate phone conversations abruptly while she can go on and on, on matters big and small.

Once I had friends. But by now, I seem to have lost the capacity to make new friends. The old ones are either dying off or drifting away. The trouble with me; I'm not cut out for making buddies. I disappoint people through neglect, lack of consideration, little communication, and an absence of warmth. Frankly I don't like men as much; I like women more. Maybe this absence of warmth stems from so few homely gestures and touches prevalent in my family. My main problem is that I'm highly self-centered, well-nigh selfish. For example, I don't take kindly to anything that disrupts my work schedule, even if it's visiting a sick friend. And this could at times show up as lack of consideration for others. To Priti, I lack 'people-skills'.

Lately, I joined a six-member book club, set up at the initiative of the librarian of Punjab University. We meet on the first Sunday of every month at breakfast in a restaurant to discuss one selected book for the occasion. I don't know how the librarian came to know of my literary leanings. The interaction with the other members, mostly university professors, is something I look forward to.

The doctor golfing buddy is clearly the closest at this time. Not only is he privy to my various ailments, I share some of my hopes and fears with him.

Harbans, a tall wiry Sardar, as a pediatrician is known for his concern for his young patients. Possibly he would have risen higher in government service but for his handling his patients in an uncommonly humane manner.

Harbans cuts an elegant figure with his greying eyebrows, the beard tidily pasted in position with a glue-like substance.

I simply can't visualize life without Priti. Good, she's younger by 8 years. And she takes extra care of her health. In all likelihood she'd outlive me. Women anyway are outliving men.

What if Priti died first? The thought is, no ... it cannot be, though.

"What would you do if I died first", Priti once remarks.

"I'd be completely lost".

"You'd manage all right. Of course, you'd have to look into hundred and one things that I take care of currently. But you'd manage".

And she says after a pause, "You could marry again".

"Who'd have me at this age? A dull old stick".

"Don't underrate yourself. You're a healthy, highly-educated man with money and property. No shortage of women for you among attractive spinsters and widows. It could well be Gyan, my widowed head teacher. Or, you can do worse by marrying my youngest sister living in London".

"Is that what you want?"

"But I don't want you to become a recluse, staying home all alone, simply reading books, and losing your hold on reality. I would want you to go out socially, to meet people, to live a normal active life".

"Don't waste your breath on such talk. I'm sure to go before you".

And on this note, our morbid conversation would have ended when Priti continues, "Of one thing I'm certain. You'd never get a wife who gives less trouble than me. And I am there to help whenever you run into a problem. If you are unsure about anything, I come up with the way out. I take care of the house and the garden. I run our social life. I rarely bother you with my health problems. Instead I nurse you when you're sick".

"Nobody's denying any of this. In fact I simply can't conceive of a life without you. Someone rightly said about man as an incomplete woman".

CHAPTER 12

Jogi, Girija, and the girls are here for a day. They are returning from Simla where Girija had gone to attend a Road Conference. This is their first visit to us after being posted in Delhi.

Girija is left-handed, the only visible left-hander I've come to watch closely. Her holding a pen in left hand or eating with the left never fails to tickle my curiosity.

"Must have had a tough time at school. Writing left to right, using the ruler, or sitting on chairs with the fixed arm as desk on the right".

"You're telling me! But the worst was using scissors in my primary girls' school, till Daddy got me a pair made for left-handers".

"Have you any problems in day-to-day work?"

"Not really. But I can say, even the telephone receiver held in the left—seemingly suited for left-handers—is actually designed for right-handers. While the left holds the receiver, the right is free to take down notes. Ballroom dancing is designed for a right-handed man dancing with a right-handed woman".

"The gene of left-handedness, which gives rise to manifest disadvantages in a right-handed world, hasn't been eliminated by evolution in its natural process of weeding out harmful genes. Around 10% of people everywhere have stayed left-handed.

I recently read that the left-hand gene is not rated a total liability. Left-handers process information faster between the two spheres of the brain and so can react quicker. Again in self-protection, a left-hander is in better position to inflict surprise blows on a right-hander who's more used to combat with right-handers".

"Give Jogi a left if he's nasty".

That sends Girija into giggles: "You better tell Jogi what awaits him if he behaves badly".

Jogi takes us all to a dainty dinner at the Mountview Hotel.

They are leaving next day before noon. Priti is packing a picnic lunch for them for the journey.

After breakfast, Jogi steps into my study wearing a natty safari suit and stylish Italian shoes. He's not only in top physical form, he cares to be smartly dressed.

Jogi closes the door behind him.

"Papa, I want a few words with you before we leave".

"Sure. Go ahead", I say, putting down pen and clearing away papers.

"I wish you'd reconsider your decision about the house" he says as he slides into a creaking chair in front, and takes off his glasses. He has this habit of taking them off when talking serious business. Apparently he's quite comfortable indoors without spectacles.

"We've discussed it often before. I had arrived at the decision after due deliberation. And I don't see any reason for revising it".

"Ravi by now is a multimillionaire. He nets over $2 million a year from his software business. That's rupees 10 crore. He doesn't need any part of the Chandigarh house. He's never going to live here. They're all American citizens".

"You may be right. And we're proud of Ravi's success. Yet, as a matter of principle, I'd give equal share of my property to the two sons. And as you're aware, this house is my main property.

"Ravi's in no need of it, while we haven't home. And there's no early prospect of our acquiring anything worthwhile. We don't save much from salaries".

"I'd be bequeathing the top floor to you, a full four-bedroom unit. You can comfortably live in it. Even build another floor on top, if wanting extra space. Anyway, you and Girija still have many years of service. You'll live in places other than Chandigarh".

"If I can't get the whole house, at least give us the ground portion. We can enjoy the lawns, the flowers, and fruits. An absent Ravi would have no use of it. He can't even sell it. Housing laws in Chandigarh forbid division".

Obviously Jogi has studied legal aspects that could further his plan.

"You know the whole background. My savings and loans didn't suffice to build this huge house. Ravi pitched in with $10,000. We named it 'Ravi Villa' because of it. He's certainly entitled to the more attractive half".

"But he doesn't need it. If you're favourably inclined, I can talk to him, persuade him. Offer him a deal".

"We don't want to move upstairs in our lifetime. Priti loves the garden, takes delight in it. And your mother is young enough to live another 15–20 years. If you ever decide to settle down in Chandigarh, you can only occupy the upper portion. She'd be living in the lower half".

"Oh, mother can surely live with us. In fact she must live with us. She'd be too frail to operate on her own".

"That's between you and your mother. I won't be on the scene".

"Do I understand you don't contemplate any change in your decision?"

"We can discuss the house issue again. No urgency about it. Ravi would be here for the anniversary celebrations".

And on that note the father–son sallies get interrupted, as the girls burst in. Their grandma has given them Rs 5,000 each. Nothing rivals a wad of crisp currency as gift.

Girija follows. She gets a gold necklace and two gold bracelets. The emerald-studded pieces once belonged to Priti's mother.

And then Priti saunters in, offering Jogi a silver Mont Blanc ballpoint and a light-brown full-sleeve cashmere cardigan. Delighted, Jogi gives his mother a hug. Puts on his glasses. And now he sits with legs crossed and his shining shoes in the air. The blue socks are a touch brighter than his trousers.

"The cardigan", I tell him, "is named after Lord Cardigan who led the Charge of the Light Brigade. He and his heroic cavalrymen used to sport special jerseys as a part of their outfit".

"That's interesting", says Girija. "Never gave a thought to its name. And I think, the cardigan would fit me nicely if Jogi can be persuaded to part with it".

The trouble with Jogi right from early boyhood; he displayed a pronounced streak of acquisitiveness.

"Where's my pencil", Ravi would rave. "It was on my desk yesterday". Or he'd moan, "I had 12 marbles. Now there are only seven".

Priti had a good guess where the missing items would be. "Calm down", she'd counsel. "I'll soon get them for you".

As Jogi dropped asleep, Priti would gently lift the pillow under his head. Usually she found the missing pencil, the marbles, even a pair of her hair clips. Jogi fancied knick-knacks and manifestly felt no compunction in pinching these.

Since then he hasn't been averse to acquiring an object if his heart set upon it. He's apt to pursue the same with uncommon single-mindedness and zeal.

For one, he's now an avid collector of art curios and miniature paintings. His collection is already worth several lakhs. How he got hold of so much stuff is a mystery. In a magnanimous moment, he gifted us a miniature of the Kangra School. It enjoys the pride of place in our living room.

No definite information is there with me whether Jogi has been extending his greed into official dealings. But he has been running into career complications. He got shifted from Collector Baroda under a cloud. And at Ahmedabad, the state headquarters, while his batch mates, including Girija, became secretaries to government, he was shunted aside as principal of a Subordinate Service Training School.

Indeed, it was a little embarrassing for Girija to be the Appointments Secretary, where she had access to his confidential CR (Character Roll). And she was privy to his inconsequential posting with the Training School.

Colleagues couldn't help conjecturing whether Jogindar would come to know of various transfer proposals in advance, even learn about his CR kept in Girija's custody. In real life, the chances of his being apprised of his CR's contents through his wife were minimal.

Office politics rests on the assumption that each person thinks and acts as an individual. What makes it trying for couples is that they are often clubbed as one unit.

Co-workers are usually hesitant to tell one partner anything they don't want the other partner to know. It is surmised that at home most pillow talk is work-related. Actually, much of the time couples talk of other things.

At Delhi again, after a lot of wire-pulling, he nets Rural Development, not a coveted ministry in bureaucratic parlance.

How much of a sobering influence Girija has on him would be hard to gauge. She has always struck me as a person of sterling integrity and high moral values.

Jogi has been pestering me for some years to will him the ground floor, if not all of the house.

I harbour a strong suspicion he has a grand design to grab the whole property, which could be worth a few crores.

Once he has the ground floor, he can make life impossible for the tenant above; force him to vacate. With the upper portion lying vacant for long, he could wangle to buy it off from Ravi for a nominal sum. Or humour him to give it away; Ravi's by nature giving.

And I suppose, Jogi is quite capable of taking forcible possession of the house if it came down to that.

He's a highly secretive chap. One is never sure with him as to what are his exact intentions? We always found it hard to fathom the full extent of his secretiveness.

A scenario where he takes over the whole house in our lifetime is most unwelcome. Ravi must have his share. He may be rich but Jogi isn't indigent either.

Jogi has this advantage. He's here in the country and is in a position to put on pressure. And he, I presume, turns into a near monomaniac in securing something he covets.

Ravi lives ten thousand miles away, and is deeply engrossed in making 'serious money' as he put it.

By raking up the house issue repeatedly, Jogi is creating certain unpleasantness and tension between me and him.

Why can't he lie low till I die? This is, what I understand, Ravi has been counselling him, too, "Don't bother the old man in his final years".

Jogi isn't deterred. He can be very persistent as well as impatient in gaining what he wants. I don't think talking to Girija would help. Jogi would fob her off; tell her it's his own family affair.

A situation where Jogi lives on the top floor while we live below can also turn out nightmarish. He would pester us no end with one thing or the other that furthers his encroachment on the property. He could ask for the better servant's quarter, a separate entry gate, extending an overhead balcony, or even a part of the garden for personal use. Off and on a new demand would crop up; he stays restive in such matters.

"There must be some mistake in our bringing up Jogi", I say, talking to Ravi about my will.

"We all make mistakes, Dad, all of us. Sometimes we do things that we're not proud of. No parent is all wrong, no child is all right. Be assured, both Jogi and I love you".

"I'd believe it. One's kids affect one most. And it's best to sort things straight with them. How I can do with Jogi, I haven't a clue".

"Solutions often do suggest themselves in time".

To me, the house issue is weighty.

In my last 3 years in the Provincial Civil Service, I had been on deputation with the Union Territory of Chandigarh. During this deputation, I may not have misused my position in any other manner. But I did secure one of the best residential plots going at concessional rate in Sector 16, a sector next to Sector 17, the main commercial-cum-shopping plaza.

Normal plots in the Sector are of 2 kanals, 1,000 yards. This one, an irregular corner one, measured nearly 3½ kanals. It's a prize plot that adjoins the miles-long Leisure Valley, bisecting the city with its greenery. The 30-acre Rose Garden with its unmatched collection of roses is just across.

Located in the heart of the city, the plot lies in the midst of greenery. Except for a house on the left, there are open green spaces on all sides. It's prime property, the land itself worth few crores.

I had pooled my resources and Ravi's contribution to make a pleasing large house, consisting of two independent units (despite Chandigarh housing plans that disfavour more than one living unit in a plot).

And I was fortunate to have a talented architect, a cousin of Priti, backed by a competent civil contractor. Her cousin disdained Corbusier's pattern of exposed brickwork and *jallis* as sun blockers in place of verandahs. He built a stone house, with deep conventional verandahs; saying, the occupants can sit therein and savour the surrounding greenery. Needing further space, a verandah could well be enclosed. You can't do it to a jalli gathering dust.

The layout, workmanship, and the fittings are considered first-rate. Rooms have marble floors. Windows and doors are solid wood, fashioned out of quality teak. A truckload of seasoned teak logs was obtained from Madhya Pradesh and sawn locally. Windows are recessed instead of having projecting sunshades—more of the Spanish villa style. Fittings are of brass. And imported fine-mesh wire gauze mounted on windows. This keeps out flies and mosquitoes, without making rooms unduly dark.

"Cut stone as outside finish is ideal", he said. "Periodic colouring of bricks or plaster paint eventually works out costlier, let alone the nuisance of scaffolding". I agreed despite the higher initial cost. And it turned out an apt decision. With rains, our outside walls gain a cleaner look; the ones with plaster coating get disfigured.

A broad corridor runs through from the front verandah to the back one, with three bedrooms, and my study on one side; a guest room, living room, dining room, kitchen, pantry and store (later converted into a small gurudwara) are on the other side. All rooms are spacious and airy with 12-ft. ceilings and tall windows. One bedroom stands earmarked for Ravi and another for Jogi. They are always put up in those very rooms. Jogi even keeps some of his clothes in it, a sort of unofficial occupation and claim to the room.

The same ground-floor pattern is duplicated on the first. While bedrooms on the ground floor have adjacent verandahs, those on the first floor have balconies.

In a corner of the compound is a block with garages for two cars and above it rooms for two servants.

With trees around, the house stands enticingly dappled in sun and shade all day.

This is the only immoveable property I own. And I'd like to do justice in the apportioning of it.

Jogi has been pressurizing Priti, too. He has a way of getting round his mother. To my mind Priti has always been much more than a good enough mother for him. They can sit together for hours, exchange jokes, and are at ease with each other. Jogi can be at his most endearing when he wants something of her. He's possibly proceeding on the assumption that, with women, if you persist long, you could have your way.

Rattled with his relentless importuning, Priti advocates some sort of a compromise over the house issue. I remain adamant. To me, any appeasement of Jogi in this regard would encourage him to make a grab for the whole property.

We are happy with our tenants. They live well. Keep the house in top condition. They have two cars, one chauffeur-driven Honda from the brewery, and an Esteem with Aarti. Ramesh sends us a case of his beer on occasions, such as Holi and Diwali. That's another matter; I hardly drink beer.

A uniformed guard from his firm is there at the high wrought-iron gate for the day, and another one for the night. It imparts to us all a feel of security. And it keeps off hawkers and mendicants.

A part-time mali tends their impressive roof garden.

They have no pets to mess up things, no children to make noise.

Over the years we have formed the friendliest of relations with them.

Ramesh is a short, neat fellow sporting an eyebrow-type moustache on a lively dark face. He likes to discuss politics with me, more so government functioning. He's a handyman who's good at repairing mechanical faults in gadgets, locks, or electric switches.

The man is known to be so tidy he can sleep in his work clothes and get up next morning without a crease on them. Priti can't help pointing out his example to me—by comparison, an untidy bloke, and helpless with his hands. If I try to mend or open something, I often end up breaking it as I tend to employ force when frustrated from lack of skill. Indeed, I have encountered more inert enemies, like a stuck bolt hurting me or a metal cap scratching my finger, than living enemies. Ramesh lives by the clock and the calendar. He has an electronic notebook to remind him of his engagements, insurance policies, and people's birthdays.

They are good paymasters. They pay rent every month on the first through an automatic bank transfer to a joint account of mine and Priti. Every 3 years the rent is jacked up through mutual agreement.

They like the house immensely: its location, the quiet, the views—better views from the first floor—and the quality of accommodation. Aarti tells me they'd never move till they build a house of their own. Currently, their attention and funds are focussed on expanding the buildings and facilities of her test lab.

Bad news from Amritsar; Priti's younger sister and her husband have been involved in a car accident with a bus. While Uma got away with a broken clavicle (the only long bone placed horizontally, I tell Priti, and one which often rejoins on its own) and a gash on the left shoulder, Hari suffered a knock on the head that rendered him unconscious.

Priti has two younger sisters, no brother, with her being the best looking of the three. Uma's husband is a wholesale dealer in dry fruits. Rati, the youngest, lives in London. She married an Indian doctor residing in England. But they got divorced within a year of marriage, he falling in love with his English secretary-cum-nursing assistant. Rati stayed on and lives on her own in London, working as a shop assistant.

Priti has to rush to Amritsar.

"I should be back within a week", says she. "Can't absent myself any longer. The nursery school will miss me. It's just the start of a new session".

"I'll miss you".

"You'd have all the time for typing".

She commonly refers to my writing as typing. Not exactly complimentary but then my writing hasn't fetched a single rupee till now.

"A week's too long. Everybody will miss you".

"I can always come earlier if needed. Amritsar isn't that far off".

I see her off at the railway station. To my waving her Godspeed, she responds with a smile from behind the air-conditioned glass. Those days are gone when you could put an arm out.

Even in the flurry of unforeseen departure and her distressed state of mind, Priti doesn't neglect wifely chores. The stock of eggs in the fridge door will last me a week. "You can always fall back on eggs".

Priti writes down in the kitchen notebook (she believes her husband reads better than he listens) in her clear bold hand that we need two bottles of milk instead of three, Johnny's medicine is in her bathroom cabinet, and there's need of a new gas cylinder. She lets Aarti know of her trip, which is as good as saying that the hapless husband left behind could do with an occasional meal.

She rings next morning. Hari's showing signs of improvement. He should be out of danger within days, say the doctors.

The fault lay entirely with the bus driver. He was dangerously overtaking a truck. And in doing so, came over to the side of the opposing traffic. Even veering their Maruti off the road, they couldn't avoid being scraped by the overtaking bus.

Priti wants me to ring her up every day. I suppose, this is to boost her image with the hosts—the image of a loved, wanted wife.

As to her queries about the household, I decide to give only good news, none bad. Over days, I make no mention of Rano chipping the spout of my favoured clay teapot, or of Gauri not coming for work. But I do tell her of Banta getting a grandson and bringing a box of laddoos.

Why upset Priti for nothing? Why spoil her stay? Why give evidence of my incompetence in handling household hassles?

The first two days are OK. Thereafter, the quality of meals begins to suffer a significant decline, with a consequent rise in alcohol intake.

The bed mostly remains unmade. Priti has a thing about a tidy bed and smooth sheets. For me, what matters is orderliness in the study, not bedroom.

Never seen so many people wanting to get paid: the newspaper boy, the dhobi, the bread man … . The household annoyances are beginning to mount.

When the cat is away, the mouse is supposed to play. This particular mouse hasn't anyone around to play with. I content myself with playing more golf, and doing a little more 'typing'.

Priti is being missed increasingly with every passing day. A sense of loneliness is seeping in. Nobody is there to talk to, nobody to argue about things, nobody to point out my failings. Through years of living together, I have learnt to take comfort from her presence without being unduly distracted by it.

CHAPTER 13

How goes it with Priti at Amritsar? Better, let her tell in her own words:

After the first three days when Hari's condition began to stabilize, I start enjoying my stay; no school work, no household worries, no pressures of any sort. Nice meals, and cuddly talks with the childless Uma; she has always been my favourite.

Every morning after breakfast I walk to the Golden Temple half a mile away. I, a Hindu girl, have always been fascinated with the Golden Temple, its atmosphere of piety and peace, its beauty and orderliness, and the presence of all that water in the sarovar. Living with my father-in-law—a devout Sikh—for 20 years made me take more and more to Sikh prayers and gurudwaras.

Daddha once expressed the fond hope of our boys keeping long hair. But this was mere wishful thinking. With Sawrup continuing with cut hair the boys would naturally follow suit.

I like to walk, and walk briskly. Cyclerickshaw pullers calling for customers find me shaking my head firmly.

The pious atmosphere of the Temple soothes my spirits. I take a round of the holy sarovar, walking barefoot on the marbled prakarma, said to be some 60 ft wide at most places. And then I go over the causeway to the inner sanctum.

It all brings on memories of my girlhood days when Temple-going doubled up as a measure of piety and clandestine rendezvous.

Doing the prakarma one morning I run into Rattan. He recognizes me instantly.

Rattan was my first love at fifteen, my only love before marriage. A year older than me, he was a strapping Sikh youth with sharp facial features, a light sprouting beard, and sunny disposition. Rattan worked as errand boy in my dad's cloth shop, and a helper at home.

Our secret meetings mostly took place while visiting the Golden Temple. These never went beyond loving glances, some handholding. Once he made bold to put his paw on my left breast, a hand I made haste to brush off.

"I want to marry you", he'd repeat in his endearing manner.

Let alone marriage, I didn't dare disclose anything about our affair to my quick-flaring father. Rattan was no marriage match: no schooling, no money, and no good family.

At seventeen, I was married to Sawrup, a promising young Naib Tahsildar. In dad's circles those days, a NT was deemed a great catch.

And this union has lasted half a century. No regrets.

Since then Rattan, as I learn now, has blossomed into a prosperous businessman with a chain of cloth stores. He has built a mansion for himself on the prestigious Mall. And he rides a chauffeured Mercedes.

"What do I see? Priti! Such a pleasant surprise!"

I nod in salutation.

"Seeing you after 50 years. You look just the same. No, you look better".

What can be my response except blushing?

"How are you here?"

"Came to my sister. Her husband suffered a serious car accident".

"I know Hari. I'll go, see him in the hospital. Meantime can we have a few minutes to exchange news?"

"I'm rather in a hurry".

I have no inclination to renew our former association.

"Just a cup of coffee at a nearby restaurant. I know of a nice one across Darshani Deori".

Willy-nilly I acquiesce. He's proving particularly persuasive, a practiced salesman.

The restaurant is quiet and cozy. And the management knows Rattan. We're escorted to a secluded table and waited upon deferentially.

We talk of old days and present times. Rattan relates his life story over coffee and cream rolls.

"I got so depressed, indeed so furious at your marriage—the only girl I ever loved—that I left Amritsar and my parents. Went to Delhi to work in Chacha's cloth shop in Chandni Chowk.

With luck and hard work I struck it good. Started dealing wholesale in sarees. Made money. Married. Had two sons and by now 5 grandchildren. I built a large three-storey house in Delhi's Kalindi Colony.

The anti-Sikh riots of 1984, in the aftermath of Mrs. Gandhi's assassination by her Sikh guards, spread to our locality. Right at midday a howling hundred-strong mob attacked our home, set fire to an outhouse. And the marauders began clambering over the high boundary wall. My eldest son, a bold youth, opened fire with a shotgun. One bloke was struck down dead. Others began to flee.

The police, spectators till now, promptly moved in. They took us, all the males, into custody. Confiscated the gun. We got released after a week through the intercession of an influential Congressman.

In utter disgust at the attitude of authorities, I shifted back to the safety of Amritsar. Started business anew. Flourished. The two sons still live and do business in Delhi.

My wife died of colon cancer 4 years back.

And I've absolutely no intention of marrying again. None at all ... unless it's with you".

"Stop saying such things".

Rattan happens to retain his youngish looks. He's jovial, even funny. He jokes about himself, about his poor education, about his rustic manners. Makes me laugh a lot.

I warm towards him.

I wonder what would have been my life if I had been married to this chap? He was a dear; sweet, loving. Who knows, he may have proved smarter in gauging my moods, arousing me, and otherwise looking after me.

Over coffee in comfy surroundings, Rattan extracts from me a promise to see him one more time tomorrow in the same place at the same hour.

The next day I find him waiting in the restaurant. He seats me, orders coffee and slices of fruit cake. And then Rattan presents me a gorgeous, heavily gold-braided Benares silk saree. It's crimson bright, my favourite colour.

"A small token to remind you of old times!"

"I can't accept such an expensive item. It would make me feel obligated".

"No obligation".

"Not correct to buy costly presents for a married woman".

"I didn't buy it. I deal in sarees".

"Can't take it". I say half-heartedly. The saree is simply stunning.

"OK, buy it at a discount", as he covers my hand with his. "I sell sarees all the time. I can take it as doing business this morning".

And he quotes a ridiculously low price of rupees one thousand, something approximating to one-fortieth of the actual.

And eventually Rattan succeeds in making me accept it. As I open the big brass-clasp of my handbag—the pragmatically large purse that could even hold a sweet to quiet a crying kid in my nursery school—to pay one thousand, he snaps it shut.

Well, I can pass the sari on as a present from Uma. Or, better tell Sawrup, I bought it as a bargain with my money. He knows how niggardly Uma is.

With the saree out of the way, Rattan prevails upon me to take a drive in his car. This is followed by a lavish lunch at the city's best hotel-restaurant.

"What about a short walk in the Company Gardens?" he asks. He's holding my elbow.

The atmosphere in Amritsar, memories of meeting him in the Golden Temple, the fabulous saree present, and his winning ways may make me do things I shouldn't do, things I don't want to do.

So, his suggestion of a post-lunch ramble in city's best park—evidently an opening for some sexual dalliance—has to be declined. And I can't help saying, "I love my husband. He's the man for me, has always stood by me during all these 50 years".

"But no one can take away my love for you", he says wistfully.

"I'll ever remember what it was with you, my first love. We can have our memories, but that's all we can have".

A wave of tenderness towards him sweeps my heart.

Rattan drops me at our place.

It all remains limited to laughter, friendly chatter, admiring glances, and a light touch to my waist as he seats me in his Merc.

The good wife is due back today. Looks like she has been away for a year, not a week.

Her return is a relief, no doubt, but brings on a bit of anxiety. I may have committed some domestic sins in her absence. Made mistakes I wouldn't even exactly know, till she points them out to me. My situation is akin to the teacher who has an Inspector of Schools visiting.

She's travelling back in a luxury bus. I and Banta are at the bus stand half an hour in advance. I don't want to take a chance, with her finding no one there to receive her. The express coach doing the 240 km stretch arrives a little after sunset. Her luggage includes a sack. This, she tells me, contains dried apricots, almonds, and cashew nuts, the things Uma's husband deals with.

"Happy to be back", says she.

A 10-minute drive brings us home.

She steps in. The house, she beams, looks lovely.

She makes no mention of any omissions. No defects are pointed out, not even a minor lapse.

I'm puzzled, though amused.

Till she reveals that on the 5-hour-long bus journey she made a resolve: she would not complain about one little thing, whatsoever the house is like.

Being united with Priti after an unaccustomed week's separation, I also feel like saying, "Don't worry about the house tonight. Check me over instead".

Tomorrow is another day.

PART-II

Strolling Down Memory Lane

What one remembers and how one remembers is to some extent a function of what one has become during the intervening years.

CHAPTER 14

I married for mother.

Soon after we had to abandon our home in Abbottabad and sought refuge in Amritsar, mother came down with tuberculosis. One lung had nearly collapsed. She needed constant care, which it was assumed, only a daughter-in-law could render—and such service with personal attention comes at no charge.

Sister Pasho, in whose house we were putting up, was busy with her own two kids—the elder dying of typhoid at the age of nine. And she was called upon to lend support to her husband in the restaurant kitchen below.

Towards the beginning of 1947, life had become frighteningly insecure for Sikhs and Hindus in Abbottabad, the hilly district town in Frontier Province, where we had lived for 24 years.

Father had gone there as a young junior teacher in the Government High School. He mostly taught history and geography to classes 7, 8, 9, and 10. And he made extra money from private tuitions in his spare time. Jointly, he and another teacher had authored a text book on Indian geography.

In due course he rose to be the seniormost teacher in the school. His promotion as the headmaster was in the offing.

By now Father had managed to build a three-room house on a picturesque hillside plot. And he had every intention of settling down there after retirement.

All the three of us were born in Abbottabad (named after its first British Deputy Commissioner).

At the time of migration, I, the eldest, was in Rawalpindi Christian College, doing my second year in M.A. history. Pasho was married to a restaurant owner in Amritsar. The youngest was labouring in tenth class in the Abottabad school.

Luckily, father secured a teaching job in a government high school at Amritsar within months of his arrival.

The family had moved in with their daughter. Her young husband owned the narrow-frontage high-ceiling building that housed an eatery on the ground floor and residence on the first.

More of a *dhaba* than a regular restaurant, it specialized in *kharoras* (feet of goat, lamb, pig). Some 300 kharoras were picked up from the slaughterhouse every morning and boiled for hours in an enormous steel cauldron. The softened ones had the hair scraped off meticulously and laboriously by two kitchen helpers grown adept at it over years of practice.

These were then cooked and sold with a bit of gravy. Takeaway kharoras and tandoor rotis constituted the dabha's bulk business. And I can say, I never ate tastier kharoras elsewhere.

Mangal Singh's hobby–sport–obsession was wrestling. A broad-chested, middle-height Sikh youth with pillar-like legs and bulging biceps, he could wrestle to the ground persons bigger, taller than he. A daredevil; I've seen him pushing a rampaging bull into a side gutter.

In time, Mangal helped father build another floor on top. This had three tiny bedrooms, kitchen and bath, with a compound in the middle; light and air filtering to it and the other rooms through a large grilled ventilator overhead; this was a necessity, as the house was bounded on three sides by walls of other houses. When it rained, you ran up to put a tarpaulin over the steel grill. Perched on the rooftop was a pan-toilet open to the sky—and flies.

This would be our home for years to come. Situated in a congested, bustling bazaar, it was no more than two furlongs on a narrow, winding road to the Sarai side of the Golden Temple.

By March 1947, Sikhs and Hindus were being attacked openly in Rawalpindi, particularly the more visible Sikhs. Even our Christian College didn't escape communal clashes.

Father insisted on my immediate return to Amritsar. And I obliged. But he was in for the rudest shock of his life when he saw me. I was minus my long hair and turban.

Together with two other Sikh classmates, we had shed off our long hair, threw away our turbans. It was a panic reaction to being trapped the evening before in a Muslim mohalla. We barely escaped being lynched by a group of ruffians shouting, "Kill the Sikhas, kill the Sikhas".

"I'd have preferred death to losing my hair", was the father's laconic comment.

Mother interceded. "He could grow it back some day".

"The damage has been done", he snapped back. "I don't care what he does hereafter".

And for months, he avoided talking to me, even when sitting near me.

On my side, I harboured no serious intention of reverting to the former state. What was done was done. Only I took care not to leave shaving implements in the common bathroom or shave in father's presence.

In the beginning I kept a biggish moustache and thick sideburns—a hangover of the long hair. But over years I became clean-shaven.

I joined the pre-eminent Khalsa College in M.A. history. And despite difficult home conditions, stood first in the university. I had developed a deep interest in history.

This earned me a gold medal and a scholarship for further studies.

I enrolled for a degree in law. I had every intention to practice law or compete for the IAS/PCS.

Father was keen on my taking up government service forthwith. He was enamored of government jobs, especially executive jobs. And a job would supplement the family's strained budget.

He wrote to mother's elder brother, a member of the Punjab Civil Service, posted as Additional Deputy Commissioner, Jullundar.

Pratap Singh called us both to Jullundar. And he took me to see the Divisional Commissioner, a genial-seeming ICS. Pratap put in a fervent plea on my behalf. The young man, my uncle made out, was academically brilliant: first in the university in M.A. history, first in his college in B.A., and high first division in Matric. He played hockey for his college. And he was a refugee.

The Commissioner asked me to sit with his Head Clerk and write down a three-page essay on Partition. I wrote it within an hour, dealing mainly with what our family had undergone.

"That's damn good", the Commissioner said, perusing it. He fired a few questions of general knowledge at me. And then ordered my nomination as Naib Tehsildar.

Father was ecstatic.

With his drawing a heady picture of Naib Tehsildar's power and prestige, I yielded to his wish. I joined service as NT, underwent a stretch of training, and stood posted at Phillaur in Jullunder district.

And I got engrossed in the minutiae of the job. By the time I seriously thought of taking competitive exams I was past the age of entry.

I had absolutely no plans of marriage at the start of my service career. This stage would involve being shifted from one field job to another in small, far-flung places during the early years.

Meantime Mother's condition was going from bad to worse. She needed assistance in bathing and dressing, and so also in feeding. She had to be helped to the toilet.

Quite a few times she would take me into her arms, the boney arms and the emaciated rib cage, and moan, "My dearest wish is to see you married before I die".

At this juncture Pasho took the initiative. She proposed my marriage to Priti, the eldest daughter of a substantial cloth store owner in Amritsar itself. Pasho's husband and Priti's father were distant cousins. The families knew each other—both Khatris, we Sikhs, they Hindus. A NT was then rated high as marriage potential.

Besides being mentally unprepared for marriage, I was hesitant about the proposed match itself—the girl still in the last year of high school. Later, I learnt, Priti had her own misgivings.

The only concession the eager match-makers made was to let us see each other for a few minutes in their company, the casual meeting arranged by Pasho's husband at a friend's house.

We didn't exchange a single word. But I couldn't resist noticing that she had a fetching body and a captivating face—large dark eyes, fine thin lips, a firm chin, and fair complexion. She gave the impression of someone active and competent who knew her mind. If I had to marry for Mother, Priti seemed at least as good as anybody else.

We were married in a gurudwara at noon. It meant going four times round the Guru Granth Sahib. Unlike Hindu marriages bound to an auspicious hour, Sikh marriage rituals can be undergone at any convenient time, and are manifestly simpler.

I wore a black *alpaca* achkan and churidar. She looked bashful, beautiful in a bright red *salwar-kammez-dupatta*.

The short ceremony was followed by a ghee-dripping meaty lunch for some 50 people, hosted at a hotel by the girl's side of the family. Mangal, my sister's husband, took a few snaps with his Kodak; there wasn't a professional photographer at hand. Half a dozen indistinct photos are all we have of the marriage.

Priti's two younger sisters, playing pranks on me, provided the only light relief to the day's proceedings. Their favoured trick was to hide my shoes and extort money for their restoration.

Priti brought a sizeable dowry in the shape of cash, jewellery, clothes and household goods.

There was no honeymoon for us but for a day's tonga trip to the nearby Sikh shrine of Taran Taran. And we had two nights together at home, the tiny room decorated with garlands of gainda flowers. I promised Priti, we'd have a regular honeymoon during the coming summer, at least a week at a hill resort.

The more I saw of Priti, the more I liked her. Well-nigh fell in love with her: her cheerful disposition, saucy talk, and marble-smooth, firm body. Marriage, which at one time loomed a forbidding prospect, was turning out vastly agreeable.

And then I'm off on my job, leaving Priti in attendance on an ailing mother-in-law and an exacting father-in-law. And she has another three months of schooling to sit for the Matric exams. At 17, Priti is called upon to run a middle-class home on a teacher's salary and what little I'd spare.

Luckily my younger brother, hopelessly poor in studies, did manage to scrape through matriculation in third division. And the fact of being a refugee helped him secure a clerk's post in the Excise Dept at Ambala. To that extent, the family stood relieved of a burden. And my brother was destined to retire from the same office as senior clerk after 30 years of indifferent service.

Mother passed away within 10 months of my marriage. She died suffering awfully in body and spirit. Perhaps her only consolation; Priti is pregnant.

Two days after mother's death, father collected all her clothes (these weren't many, as few were brought from Abbottabad and hardly any added during her illness), tied them in a bundle and dumped the same on a nearby roadside rubbish heap. Pasho did protest, "We could give these to someone needy".

"No", said father. "I wouldn't be a party to giving away contaminated clothes. If anyone picks them up from the rubbish heap, that's not my business".

In a way, what remained of mother were memories. Father would sit in his room and cry silently.

It took eight long years of sustained work as NT before I got promoted as Tehsildar. During this stretch, I was made to move from place to place—in all, six times.

I did develop a flair for checking *patwari* "papers" and other land records. The format and upkeep of land records hadn't changed in the last 150 years. Drawn on cotton cloth with black ink, the village patwari map could be folded like a large pocket kerchief. Every inch of a village stood mapped therein.

The importance of patwari papers was obvious. These were the mainstay of the whole system that provided not only the basis of Land Revenue but stability to rural society. It kept record of every tenancy, every crop, and every payment.

If entries in it were to be accurate, conforming to actual possession and cultivation, these needed constant checking from the higher-ups. And such checking called for skill and time. It meant frequent trips for on-the-spot inspections (*mauqa*) with people present, the village map in your hand.

I learnt riding though it was always a borrowed mount. And I did a lot of cycling, with the right trouser leg secured by a clip against being caught in the chain. In time I'd put clips on both legs of the trousers, a precaution against insects crawling up one's legs in the countryside. And I learnt to keep control, cycling on pedestrian pathways. Higher officers, even IAS, wouldn't disdain cycling in those days.

The job included all sorts of duties, whether of Land Consolidation campaigns, famine relief, refugee rehabilitation, or supply of essential commodities. And there was no such thing as office hours. You could be called any time day or night.

Besides the quality of one's work it was of utmost importance that the visiting bosses, PCS and IAS, or other prominent personalities, enjoyed a smooth tour, free of hassle and discomfort. I came across a few top-class Deputy Commissioners and Commissioners. In the 1950s and 60s, higher officers moved about much more often than they do today, and that also unguarded.

Looking after the bosses entailed a good deal of management and public relations. And, of course, it called for raising resources to meet their needs and expectations. It wasn't exactly extortion, yet at times pressure had to be applied on affluent farmers to contribute money or materials. The trouble mostly arose when a visiting biggie was not only expecting whisky and chicken at dinner but looking for a bedmate thereafter.

I wasn't particularly good at humouring bosses. Yet I did succeed to operate competently enough not to give cause for annoyance.

In turn, my subordinates, *patwaris* and *kanungos, lambardars* and other village officials must be doing their bit to look after me. I didn't mind cadging a free meal, a free ride, a free night-halt in comfort, or free farm produce I could send to my people back home. But I did draw a line at accepting cash or women, despite quite a few enticing opportunities. And no affairs of the heart; I was in love with Priti.

One thing that really bothered me on night halts with my well-to-do village hosts was the usual absence of a privy. You had to go out before dawn, seeking some privacy, especially when you were someone higher up. In time, I started carrying a bottle of water with me. This often evoked a laugh as bottle carrying was not in vogue in those days.

What I felt as real deprivation was the absence of ready marital sex, the need of the other body in bed. So I was ever on the lookout to make a quick trip to Amritsar. Yet I must admit I was vulnerable to female charm. You came across some very pretty girls; it's another matter that their youthfulness and looks would fade soon from early marriage, followed by lots of children and heavy farm-cum-house work.

Life otherwise wasn't too bad as Naib Tehsildar or Tehsildar. The Green Revolution was bringing affluence to the countryside. Landowners, big and small, humoured you, respected you, and did everything to provide you with physical amenities. One got the feel of being someone of consequence in the area.

Oh, yes, the delayed honeymoon did take place in the succeeding summer. By this time the bride is showing a bit of belly.

Father insisted we go. He said he always regretted missing his honeymoon. Gave us a gift of rupees three thousand out of the money he got in lieu of assets left in Pakistan. And he volunteered to look after his wife during Priti's absence. "The young bride badly needs a holiday", he said.

How do you get that blissed-out, just-married feeling six months after the wedding? By definition, a honeymoon is for the just married, a transient phase, perhaps a bit overrated.

Yet there we were at it.

We booked into the Clarke's, Simla on the Mall. Enjoyed enviable accommodation (the honeymoon suite with its balcony overlooking the green valley), good service (breakfast in bed), and wholesome meals. Spent mornings making love. Afternoons were given to strolling on the Mall hand in hand, with high tea at the famous Davico restaurant. Simla was plain glorious in September, with cloudless skies and forested hillsides.

What an attractive hill station the British had built! Sylvan surroundings, clean upkeep, and an inviting Mall with its orderly flow of pedestrian traffic. Amazing, how they could carve out some 2 miles of a near-level stretch at 6000 ft.

We got ourselves photographed in a studio. That's the framed picture we hang in our bedroom. I haven't come out badly but Priti looks so happy, so radiant, so charming. Later, a copy each of the same was passed on to Ravi and Jogi. And this photo does adorn their walls, too.

It was agreed that Priti and the kids would stay on in Amritsar with Father. That would be a help to the old man who had retired on a paltry pension. And the boys had to have proper schooling at one place. Frequent change of schools could be very disruptive of their studies.

This meant my missing a great deal the company of the two sons. And it would remain with me a matter of profound regret. I was hardly with them when they grew up, and this can be quite alienating.

Father helped Priti with studies.

After doing Matric, she began preparing privately for graduation. This called for a Giani in Gurmukhi and a pass in English. And, notwithstanding household work and the care of two kids, she did graduate within 4 years of marriage. That was an accomplishment.

Thereafter, Priti took a degree in Teachers' Training. For ten months, she had to be absent from home for more than half the day. Here, again, the doughty father-in-law came to her aid.

By the time Jogi reached school-going age, she bagged a teaching job in a nearby government middle school for girls.

I worked as a Tehsildar for 12 years, till promoted into the PCS (Provincial Civil Service).

While my various jobs entailed much rural touring and being called to work at all odd hours, I continued with my reading habit. Bought books and borrowed books, borrowed from friends and from libraries, both public and college libraries. Read biographies, autobiographies, histories, travel books and fiction, mostly in English. Always carried a book or two while touring, and read whenever I got spare time. With hardly any place to put them up, the books remained in wooden crates; the same in which I carted them from one place of posting to another.

Besides providing me pleasure and information, my reading may have helped me in my career. As tehsildar, I once had a young IAS officer boss as Assistant Commissioner. Sushil Kumar had been a brilliant student of Indian history. He'd call me frequently for discussions. And he gave me glowing Annual Reports, spoke to higher ups, "about the quality of his mind and the range of his scholarship". He took pains to introduce me to some of the top officials. All this must have helped accelerate my promotion to the PCS and later IAS.

Priti taught in a government high school in the locality. Both the boys got enrolled in St. Francis High School, considered to be the best in Amritsar. Being situated outside the walled city, it had to be reached by a cyclerickshaw hired on a monthly basis. Only on joining ninth class, were they allowed to cycle to school.

Priti was keen on boys completing their schooling in the noted institution before they moved elsewhere for higher studies. This could mean her being stuck in Amritsar right up to 1972 when Jogi would matriculate.

"It isn't fair", I said. "For the first 22 years of our marriage we'll be living virtually separate".

"That's the price we pay for the career of our boys. The enchantment of being a mother lies in fantasies about one's children's success".

"A little foolish to suppose that dreams could affect reality. Parents fret so much over the children! Hope, the children will appreciate, reciprocate in time".

"Once the boys are away in college, I'll seek transfer to a school in the place of your posting—say, Chandigarh".

"Wish, I had competed for the IAS/PCS. Let alone the much brighter service prospects, our family life would have been far different; we'd have lived together. Father pushed me too hastily into the job of a Naib Tehsildar".

"What's done can't be undone. We have to make the best of it".

"Maybe it's a character flaw with me, this tendency to nurse regrets?"

"Everybody nurses regrets; some more, some less".

"You have any?"

"Yes. For one, with better care our first child, the baby girl may have survived".

Priti and the boys would come and stay with me during school holidays. I arranged horse riding for Ravi and Jogi, even some bird shooting. There was no shortage of obliging zamindars having horses and guns.

Father visited at each one of my postings. It made the old man happy to see me at the height of his ambition for me.

On promotion to PCS, I was appointed SDO Abohar, Ferozepur District. That was a prize posting, Abohar being one of the few places in Punjab that still retained big zamindars. And an SDO there was feted well.

Within 2 years I was sent to Phagwara, Jullundar District. And, thereafter, to Bhatinda as Additional Deputy Commissioner.

Meantime Punjab was undergoing important administrative changes. The demand for Punjabi Suba that had fizzled out by 1961 was renewed in 1965. And the new Suba became a reality in November, 1966. It comprised 12 districts, including the former princely states of PEPSU (Patiala and East Punjab States Union).

The day arrived when I took over as Deputy Secretary Revenue at the Punjab State Secretariat, Chandigarh. By now Ravi had moved to IIT Bombay for Electronics and Jogi joined St. Stephen College, Delhi.

Using contacts with a colleague in the Education Department, I got Priti transferred to a government high school in Chandigarh. Within a year she became the school's headmistress.

I was destined to be in Chandigarh on various jobs till retirement.

We had an official bungalow in Sector 7. Found ourselves settled into comfortable living as husband and wife for the first time.

In 1978, there came promotion to the IAS, a momentous milestone for someone who starting service as a NT 28 years back.

"You've done well. Now you go as Deputy Commissioner, Ferozepur, an important position", said the Chief Secretary.

"Thanks, sir. But it will mean staying away from my wife, a school headmistress here. We have already lived apart for the first 22 years of marriage".

"Oh, I see. Any preference?"

"Sir, I understand, the post of Joint Secretary of Revenue is vacant. That's an area of my experience".

"Let me look into it".

Soon orders arrived appointing me "Jt Secy Revenue".

And in due course, I got promoted as Secretary of Revenue, my last job before retirement from Service.

CHAPTER 15

How did life treat Priti in the meantime? How did it feel looking back?

I couldn't marry the youth I fell in love with as a girl, my first love. And, first love, I suppose, never gets replicated.

Instead, I got married to a man I didn't know at all.

Happily, he turned out to be an acceptable chap—smart looking, healthy, loving, and serious in his work. But for years he was hardly there with me.

I spent long hours nursing a sick, tubercular mother-in-law—a mother-in-law I had come to like. Her suffering wrung my heart.

Then, there was dealing with a dictatorial father-in-law, someone who was otherwise good-hearted and helpful. 6-ft. tall, the sort of tall that made you feel safe, protected.

Getting through my matriculation exams was there—not a little complicated with the vomiting of pregnancy.

And running the household smoothly and economical—unaided but for an untidy, unpunctual maid.

I began to see that in marrying Sawrup, I had also married his mother, and to a great extent his father. Lucky, his younger brother went away. Admittedly, I had dreamt of a large new family on marriage but this was not turning as idyllic as I had imagined; I began seeing happy joint families to be more of a myth.

The mother-in-law died in my arms.

A little later a girl was born, born at my parents' place with an old-style midwife in attendance. Sawrup was away at his job.

Sadly, the underweight baby girl died within four days of birth. I'd always miss a daughter.

Ravi came 2 years later.

And then I had Jogi.

Sawrup underwent a vasectomy. To us, our family was complete.

I graduated. Obtained a Teacher's Training Degree. This secured me a teaching job in a nearby government girls' middle school.

I went through all the highs and lows of bringing up the boys almost single-handed. This entailed a heavy drain on my energy, already fatigued with teaching at school. I often felt utterly exhausted by nighttime. The only relief was to spend a Sunday with my parents. The boys would play on their small patch of lawn instead of being cooped up on the second floor. And we enjoyed hearty meals without my having to cook for it.

Ravi was shaping up nicely. He stayed top in studies, and you saw him mostly reading in his spare time. Studious, serious, well--behaved, he received glowing reports from the Fathers at St. Francis.

Jogi was turning out altogether different. He lagged behind in studies and neglected schoolwork. And was quick to pick up fights with other boys. Even in a sibling fight, when Jogi got into a rage, Ravi would slink away.

Worse, Jogi brazenly pinched things that belonged to others.

He could be irascibly rude to grandpa when reprimanded for his wayward ways.

And once when Daddha slapped him for stealing a rupee coin from his purse, Jogi went missing.

It was nearing nightfall, and yet no sign of the 11-year-old. A frantic search was on. Ravi made a fruitless round of Jogi's all neighbourhood friends. Daddha was filled with remorse for causing this crisis through slapping the errant boy.

I discovered that Jogi had also filched rupees three from me, from the money I was keeping in a tin box for household expenses.

Jogi, we later learnt, walked up to the Hall Bazar, the premier commercial area he passed everyday going to school. There he took a bus to Tanda Urmur, his father's place of posting. Finding on arrival that the father was out on tour, he ate some food and slept.

By midnight, Mangal Singh, Pasho's husband, reached Tanda Urmur in a taxi to inform Sawrup of the missing boy. And he was greatly relieved to find Jogi asleep there. Mangal journeyed back forthwith to put me out of my misery.

Jogi returned next day escorted by his father. He deserved a thorough drubbing. Yet he wasn't administered any. The headstrong boy had given his parents a horrendous fright. Whatever scolding he got was from Ravi.

Since that fateful day, interaction between grandpa and Jogi—otherwise poor—ground to a near total halt. Grandpa liked quietness; maybe from being exposed for years to unruly boys in classrooms. Jogi would never stay still for long. Here, Ravi obliged. A boy who is reading is very quiet.

The episode also highlighted the lack of communication between home and Sawrup's places of posting. A telephone, an ugly-looking big black instrument, was installed within days at the Amritsar house. It meant at least weekly contact with the family. The days of cell phones and daily calls were not in sight.

At 14, in ninth class, Ravi came down with typhoid. The fever persisted for weeks. It reduced him to a skeleton.

Sawrup rushed home. Got Ravi admitted into Glancy Medical College hospital, the city's main hospital.

Ravi was diagnosed as also suffering from tuberculosis. That was terrifying news. The horror of his grandma's illness lived in everyone's memory.

Ravi was given a full course of streptomycin, the expensive wonder drug. His fever came down. But he had grown too feeble to move about. Complained of abdominal pains. He had to stay hospitalized for another two weeks.

Ravi, lying in a general ward crowded with patients and their attendants, was bogged by a peculiar problem. He was unable to pass motion on the bedpan with everyone around awake, moving, talking; no screens were available for patients in that ward. And he couldn't get a morning bowel movement without eating something substantial.

So I'd boil two eggs, pack buttered toast and a flask of hot Ovaltine milk. And I'd walk 3 miles to the hospital to be there before daylight, before people start getting up in Ravi's ward.

I took care to go in clothes that hid my figure. And I'd walk fast, both to cut travel time and to discourage unwelcome male attention.

On one of those pre-dawn trips to the hospital, I had the scare of my life. A burly turbaned fellow began following me. The faster I walked, the faster he followed. I broke into a run. And could only shake him off when I joined a couple on their morning walk.

I refrained from narrating this episode to Ravi or Sawrup or anyone back home.

The memory of those pre-dawn walks through empty city streets still haunts me.

For two days Daddha volunteered to go in my place. But he came down with severe sciatica pain in his right leg.

Ravi recovered. He was brought home and nursed back to health and strength. He had to be given costly vitamins and scarce orange juice. Ravi rejoined school. And he soon regained his accustomed first position in the class.

Ravi did his Matriculation in high first division. He took the IIT entry test, securing maximum marks in written papers. And he succeeded in the interview. Sawrup accompanying him to Kanpur for the combined allocation for IITs. Ravi got his first option of electronics at the Bombay IIT.

With 5 years of outstanding academic record at the IIT,

he begged a scholarship at M.I.T Harvard for a Master's in electronics.

Thereafter, he took jobs in the U.S.

In time, he started his own software business.

Ravi married Nonita, an MBA from Wharton Business School working in New York with Merrill Lynch. Her father had been with the World Bank at Washington for nearly 2 decades. The family had a home in Bethesda, an upper-class suburb. Noni attended a neighbourhood high school, said to be one of the best in the area. Her only grouse; the school was swarming with snooty Jewish kids. And her Manhattan experience didn't endear her to the ways of Jewish businessmen.

Ravi came in contact with Noni when he approached her company for venture capital.

The pundit-conducted Hindu marriage was held at Hotel Marriott on Pennsylvania Avenue, overlooking the White House, followed by dinner and dance. The bridegroom did the last hundred yards on horseback, accompanied by bhangra-dancing friends—a sight unusual for that avenue. I and Sawrup journeyed to the US for it.

Ravi was now an American citizen. Noni had become one much earlier.

Jogi blundered along, backward in school studies and involved in all sorts of scrapes. He had us worried about his future, despite the best schooling we could afford. No pep talk from Sawrup shook him, and no persistent coaxing by me. And he avoided his grandpa like the plague.

At times Jogi even dared his dad, and this would make me awfully nervous about how Sawrup would react.

When Jogi had been escorted back from his nightly misadventure, Sawrup accosted the 11-year-old.

"I've to talk to you".

"I don't want to talk to you", was the insolent reply. "I'll only talk to Mummy".

"Why, not to me?"

"You don't care about me, only about Ravi".

"Who gave you that idea? I care about you as much as Ravi".

Seemingly unconvinced, Jogi slipped away to me before Sawrup could say more. I was at pains to explain to the boy crying in my arms that the anger of parents was never anger.

Maybe, Sawrup as an almost-absent father, knew so little about his sons. Despite all his readings on parenthood, he felt he was making a mess of fatherhood.

"To Jogi, I'm a jerk", he once told me, more in sorrow than anger.

Jogi did figure most in our talk whenever Sawrup was visiting.

"Why is his behaviour so different from Ravi's", I'd complain, as I listed some of his latest lapses.

"May have something to do with his birth order", Sawrup would venture. "The birth-order theory is built around the appealingly simple idea that your place in the family determines your personality, your very mental make-up. According to it, if you were the first born or the only born, you received the full charge of your parents' attention and expectations. That made you more demanding, over-controlling, ambitious. One reason why such children are likely to develop faster, and show greater eagerness to assume leadership or responsible roles".

"What about those who come later?"

"The personalities of middle children are harder to define or classify. But they do suffer from some benign neglect. They have fewer pictures in the family album. To cope with the lack of parental attention, they tend to become rebellious, secretive".

"Tagore wasn't the first-born, as I read in his Reminiscences"

"An exception, it could be. The main argument is that interaction between parents and the children plays a crucial part in the formation of personality. And here, the order of one's birth matters a lot. You know our dynamics with Ravi was

different from that with Jogi—the first-born always remained someone special. This could have played a part in making Jogi wary of authority: parents, teachers, grandpa".

"Don't know", as I knotted my untied length of hair. In deference to the unspoken wishes of my Sikh father-in-law, I never cut my hair, and retained the same even after his death. "Jogi actually cornered more of my time and attention than Ravi. He needed it. Let's hope, he outgrows his irresponsible behaviour. Anyway I'd suggest you don't treat him too roughly. It won't improve matters".

I'll leave it all to you. Like a typical father of our times, I seem to have nothing to do with my children until they misbehave and need attention".

"A little more patience", I'd plead. "He may come round. I read somewhere that siblings employ adaptive tactics to compete with one another in currying parental favour. Create differing roles for themselves within the family system. Ravi, with everybody praising him, must be evoking Jogi's jealousy. I imagine, children become painfully aware when they are loved less than a sibling. They are extremely sensitive to inequality, whether real or perceived. We should try our best to give no such impression to Jogi".

"I entirely agree, though it may not be as easy in practice. The two boys being different doesn't bother me. Possibly it's good for a family to have children with differing temperaments and behaviour patterns. It makes for a richer mix.

But don't forget, mothers aren't required to produce perfect individuals. They're required to feed, clothe, and educate their children. In fact I've a feeling that with adolescents, peers exert greater influence than parents".

I proved right. On reaching tenth class Jogi, on his own, turned a new leaf. His brother's success may have hit him.

Overnight he became serious in studies. Left off all distracting activities. Worked late into nights. And with only one year's hard work, managed to get a high first division in Matric.

He succeeded in securing admission into St Stephen Delhi on the score of his marks and strong recommendations of his school head.

In college, again Jogi had his ups and downs. He lived beyond what we could spare for him. There were reports of his indulging in beer binges and girl chasing. At one point he had to be rescued from his incurred debts.

Sawrup stood his ground. No money was to be given beyond the stipulated monthly sum. But Jogi managed to squeeze some rupees out of me.

Jogi graduated in low second division. But, to everyone's surprise, figured on top in his Masters in Economics

And, after a year as lecturer in Delhi's Hindu College, he successfully competed for the IAS.

My personal life in Amritsar during the 22 married years could be termed both as busy and dull. Long hours of teaching at school left me fagged out. And then I had to run a household with two active, perpetually hungry boys, and an idled father-in-law.

It was work, work, the whole day long. I had virtually no evening life, no outings, few movies, and no meals in quality restaurants. And I lived cooped up in a congested locality, with scant access to open spaces or greenery.

The house itself was far from comfortable. The roofless pan-latrine with its swarming flies and poor privacy meant that I had to finish my business before daylight. The bathroom was nothing but a chest-high tap that kept the cemented floor wet and slippery. The stair—nearly forty because of the high ground-floor ceiling—stood perilously steep, the uppermost rungs so perpendicular your nose almost touched them ascending. And there was no supportive railing, because there wasn't enough room to put one in place. I was ever assailed with the worry of someone tumbling down.

The old man wasn't much of a bother. Yet he was growing increasingly touchy, a bit cranky. He'd get upset over minor matters, such as slight delay in his meals or not finding his slippers in their accustomed place. And he was ever ready with advice whether wanted or not.

Only when Sawrup was there on one of his infrequent visits, could we enjoy a dinner at a restaurant, a movie, or an outing. I still remember the highlight of an evening was the movie 420 with Nadira playing the naughty girl, followed by a nice dinner at Moti Mahal. And it was a welcome relief from work and routine drudgery when I visited his places of posting. Pity, the occasions were so few.

I yearned for the day when the boys would go to college and I lived a normal married life with my mate.

PART-III

MUSINGS ON MARRIAGE AND AGEING

CHAPTER 16

1985.

The two boys have got into prized positions.

We're settled in our own Chandigarh home; the best house we ever lived. Spacious sunlit interiors. An airy, roomy kitchen admirably convenient for cooking; Priti's cousin architect had brought his wife with him when designing the kitchen. It's another matter that Rano would have been happier if she could cook sitting on the ground instead of standing.

You see a pleasing compound with its lawns and flower beds. Newly planted guava and mango trees. A jamun tree, tall, spread-out, and so also a tamarind tree. Bougainvilleas with red and white flowers creep all over the stone boundary walls.

I have retired. The loss of work and position hasn't hit as badly as feared. Teaming up with another retired colleague in revenue consultancy work did impart a feel of being usefully busy.

Punjab is passing through a horrible phase of Sikh militancy. Mercifully, being no longer in government, I'm not called upon to fight it.

Orwell's *1984* has been a horrendous year with us. Mindless murders by Bhindranwala's followers, the army's storming of the Golden Temple, the assassination of Indira Gandhi, and the consequent slaughter of Sikhs in Delhi and elsewhere. No let up in terrorism by Sikh militants and, in turn, police brutalities. And, on top, the Bhopal Gas tragedy with thousands dead and maimed.

Sant Bindranwale's men had been doing their damned best to create animosity between the Hindus and the Sikhs, hoping Hindus will move out, leaving Punjab for the Sikhs. The worst was stopping a bus and shooting all the Hindu males travelling therein.

Close affinity between the Hindus and Sikhs has been the basic characteristic of the two communities for more than 500 years—right since the origin of Sikh religion. Sikh gurus and their teachings are held in high regard by the Hindus of the region. Social relations between the two still remain cordial, despite tremendous strains during 1965 to 1985.

How can any religious or political move produce disharmony between me and Priti, one Sikh, one Hindu. And she's possibly nearer to the tenets of Sikhism than many a Sikh militant.

I, on my part, am fully convinced that the proper place for Sikhs is to be integrated within the Indian union and not in any separate state. Such an entity, in the unlikely event of ever coming into existence, would have disastrous consequences. Some Akali activists voicing this demand don't represent the wishes of the entire Sikh community. And Akalis themselves are bitterly divided into factions.

Father is 85. Being born in the year 1900, it's easy to figure out his age.

"Daddha worries me", makes out Priti.

"Anything particular?" I ask.

"He's too old to live on his own. I'll never forget how well he looked after me and the boys for 22 long years; virtually the only man in the house. You can say, we shared all the intimacies of marriage minus sex".

"What to do? He doesn't want to move. Is mulishly stubborn. Even spurned my offers of financial assistance. Says, he cherishes his independence".

"He isn't independent. Has to come down to Pasho for his three meals. And Pasho herself is doing poorly. The dhaba is in bad shape after her husband's death. It's currently leased to the head cook".

"Father pays Pasho a fixed monthly sum for his meals".

"Meagre meals at that. It's heartrending how he lives. Buys no new clothes. Goes nowhere barring his daily shuffle to the Golden Temple".

"Not as bad as that. He borrows books from the Temple library. And has his morning and evening readings of Granth Sahib".

"Those steep stairs! I stood in constant dread of someone tumbling down. A mishap surely awaits Daddha with his arthritic legs and weak sight. And the wet, slippery bathroom! I slipped several times".

"I've repeatedly volunteered to have the bathroom redone and effect other urgent renovations to the house. He's adamant. Says, what's the point of spending money? No one is going to live there after him".

"We must get Daddha here. Provide him better food, better medical care, better living conditions. He deserves it. Daddha used to tell me what he missed most in the Amritsar house was the greenery and the quiet he enjoyed in hilly Abbottabad. He'd love living here amidst verdant open spaces. I know it'll mean additional work and responsibility for me. But I'm prepared to shoulder it. He has done a lot for me and the boys".

"And for me, too".

"We should try again to get him here".

"OK. We go to Amritsar. Persuade him. Bring him along with us".

Meantime fate intervenes. Father slips in the bathroom over a wet soapy patch and fractures his right hip bone. We rush to Amritsar. Get him admitted to a hospital. Pinned in position, the bone does mend after a fortnight in hospital and physiotherapy follow-up at home.

Of his hospital stay, his first in 85 years, he'd say, "Nurses giving a sponge bath took me back to my infant days, being bathed by mother, a long time back".

Now he's in no position to go up and down the steep stairs. The operated leg is half an inch shorter than the other because of faulty joining. He has to use a crutch for walking.

Eventually Priti persuades him to come with us to Chandigarh.

"Daddha, wind up at Amritsar", says Priti. "Sell the house".

"How can I part with it! So many of our memories are bound with that house".

"We can give away the house and keep the memories".

"I guess, Priti's right", I add.

"Don't rush me, Beti. I'll be with you till I recover. No house selling".

"As you wish", I say.

He sees us packing his scanty belongings. To our surprise he had been giving away many items to others, even the curios presented by us to him from time to time.

"What about my Granth Sahib?"

"We'll install it in a separate room. You'll have a proper gurudwara for it", says Priti.

"Good. Please carry it with the reverence it commands".

Father is fixed in Ravi's room opening on the back verandah and lawn. His bathroom has been specially rendered slip-proof by wall-to-wall coir matting. And the 3 steps leading up to the house have been given a railing to hold on to.

We mostly see him sitting under the shady jamun in one of the white plastic chairs; the light, indestructible chair he can easily move about.

He loves outdoors. It must have been an intolerable privation for him to be cooped up in a small top-floor flat of a stuffy, noisy locality for nearly 40 years.

"No two towns more different than Amritsar and Chandigarh", he's apt to repeat. "Chandigarh is a product of geometry, rulers, and set squares. It has wide straight avenues, umpteen parks, and an impressive artificial lake. Public buildings, markets, and houses are all conforming to a design and pattern.

The bustling walled city of Amritsar has narrow lanes that never go straight. It's another matter, these remain cool in summer, hedged by houses that have been built as their builders fancied. A lively, lusty city but its central parts too messy and grossly overcrowded".

The old man's long separation from the trees, plants, flowers, and grasses he loves has ended, and he is experiencing a fervent reunion with Nature. He seems to derive obvious pleasure and satisfaction from it.

He's frequently in animated discussion with Priti on gardening matters. And we see him watching Bhura at work, advising him, demonstrating for him, even helping him at times.

Father gets a vegetable patch to grow tomatoes and green chillies. And on his initiative half a dozen apricot trees have been planted. "Apricots I'd grown in the compound of my Abbottabad house. Such beautiful flowers in spring and juicy fruit", he's apt to exclaim. "I'd say, the apricot is the king of fruits".

During his 7 years with us, till he died, father developed the garden greatly. He used to say, "There's no such thing as an instant garden. It has to develop and grow. That is its nature".

And he'd repeat another message for me: "The more we enjoy nature—and change of seasons—the happier we are. Old age can be dull if one takes no interest in nature. Gardening is a basic instinct".

"Well, I'm not brimming with it. Maybe plants grow too slow for one as impatient as me".

"One thing I know, plants aren't as good at surviving transplantation as *Homo sapiens*. Haven't we all settled nicely after being so brutally uprooted at Partition?"

Father put in a birdbath. It's fun watching sparrows merrily bathing in it and crafty crows brazenly drinking from it. Johnny loves to run through it; he likes water. Father also wanted a fish pond. That didn't materialize in his time.

Our place turns into a veritable riot of colour in spring with gulmohars, amaltas, bougainvillea and white apricot flowers, and on the ground, petunias, pansies, geraniums.

Father would sit for hours in the garden, watching parrots, pigeons, and squirrels—Johnny no longer chases squirrels. He particularly liked pigeons in their gent-suiting colour and beady eyes.

Priti would remark, "Pigeons have a propensity to defecate frequently, and at places hard to reach and clean".

"What I like most is listening to a koel's ku ku, the questioning cry of a bird perched invisibly among leaves".

To this Priti nods her agreement.

He's particularly fascinated with the fragrance of freshly mown grass.

Father has a wooden bench built around the tamarind tree. And he moves a leafy rubber plant into my study.

My only lasting contribution to the garden is a bottlebrush tree. Sobti, the vet, gave me a sapling. Unfortunately the tree has developed an alarming tilt. Care wasn't taken to confine it to upright growth.

Priti is apt to say, "Daddha has made our garden 'owners' pride, neighbours' envy'—on the lines of the Videocon TV ad".

Looking for Priti, I mostly find her in the garden. She wanders out whenever she gets a chance—she loves the outdoors. She could be seen pulling out a weed, cutting a flower for a vase, or just enjoying the view.

Plenty of books and magazines are in the house for Daddha to read. And that includes a whole lot of novels I have been collecting in my endeavour to write fiction. Surprisingly he takes more to self-improvement books such as the ones on how to stay healthy, how to pass time gainfully, even how to make friends. Feels a little odd, a man around 90 avidly reading things that advocate a change in lifestyle?

Reading that way rarely stops. Scores of other activities stop or become irrelevant. Even money may not matter that much. But what never stops is reading.

And the old man does display enough energy and goodwill to teach reading and writing Gurmukhi to Gauri. A lifelong teacher, one assumes.

He still stays chivalrous. Opens doors for ladies, gives them chairs—the old-world courtesies. Does his best to tone down his coughing or grimaces of pain when others are around. Takes care to shake off bread crumbs from his flowing white beard.

Father gains weight with us. Gets colour back in his cheeks. Develops a fondness for freshly-brewed strong coffee. He has even relaxed his moral code to accept a small, highly diluted whisky.

"So many bottles!" is his comment, at seeing my stock that's no more than a dozen assorted ones.

"You've to see Ravi's cellar. Several hundred bottles are ranged there".

"Well, I'll pass away an utter stranger to this world of drinks".

And over his protests, Priti fits him with an almost whole new wardrobe: fine cotton pyjama suits, walking shoes and chappals, shirts and trousers, pullovers and socks, a couple of turbans.

Father's enlarged prostate is increasingly troublesome. A few times the prostate nearly blocked the passage, necessitating an emergency insertion of a catheter.

A student of his, now an eminent urologist, was contacted. After prolonged examination that included insertion of a finger into his former teacher's rectum (something unimaginable in his schooldays), Kandhari concluded, "Medicines won't do. No alternative to TURP, the surgical procedure whereby a part of the blocking prostate is lanced with a cutter mounted at the tip of a catheter".

I was for it. How can the old man move about with a catheter in place and a urine bottle strapped to his thigh?

A cardiologist is consulted. He finds father physically fit enough to undergo such surgery.

Father has been a hit with my friend Harbans. The two are often closeted in animated conversation.

"What's your view about TURP for me? Give me your frank opinion", he asks.

A bit ironic, his asking advice of a child specialist, a stage father had passed more than 80 years back.

"Pitaji, there's no escape from TURP for you. My only worry is about other health complications, such as infection or fever".

"Haven't you medicines for that?"

"Yes, we have. The problem is about their correct dosage. Medical science hasn't as yet fully figured out the exact side effects of various medicines on a man of 90. The older you grow, the weaker is your system in expelling the injurious component of drugs, such as antibiotics".

"Help me minimize their intake?"

"Yes, I'll be around".

The biopsy reveals no presence of cancer, though prostate cancer at that age is quite common. It's somewhat reassuring that my own enlarged prostate may also escape cancerous condition.

Father is successfully operated by his student-doctor. And Kandhari refuses to accept any payment for his services. "How can I charge fee from my revered guru?"

As to the hospital charges, Father insists on paying these, "I can afford it".

I am with Father at the hospital for 3 days during the operation and recuperation.

There, I realize how humiliating TURP could be, a thing in store for me someday. Doctors, technicians, even female nurses, are handling father's penis as a mere piece of flesh. They seem to feel no qualms in leaving it uncovered. Father, otherwise particular about his privacy, gives up as hopeless the struggle to keep it under wrap.

I have more than an eyeful of his wrinkled privates, a shade darker than his octogenarian skin. The shrunken penis peers out pathetic; a tube of flesh, veined, hooded, sewn into the body.

And this is the object to which I owed my existence.

Some days we find Father moody, even irritable. He appears vexed over his bodily infirmities. Says old age is no picnic.

"Every new infirmity is an enemy to be outwitted", he tells me. He's compelled to read with a magnifying lens fitted in a table lamp that Ravi had sent him. He has to cup his hands over the ears to listen. And he's often held back from walking because of pain in his steel-fitted right hip.

The growing incapacity is hard to accept for a man who was once strong and athletic, and has been rendered physically feeble with advancing years. He sits silent for hours, as if more comfortable with silence than speech, and more in tune with nature than human beings.

Evidently, the body is the reality in which each of us is grounded. And it's not easy for me to share his thoughts. The stage of life more advanced than one's own is always hard to comprehend.

Yet I see no fear of death in his eyes, as if he's steadily in a position to contemplate his demise.

"I'm ready to go any time", he once tells me. "Worn out".

I don't comment. Is anyone really ready?

He seems to have made his peace with past mistakes, flaws, and failures. Presumably, he finds the past bearable, having weathered the torrid troubles of Partition.

The old man remains mentally alert enough to discuss complicated issues of Indian governance, foreign affairs, and situations prevailing in diverse countries. Once, when we were discussing senility, he came up with an amazingly acute observation: "How would one detect the onset of senility, when what is being attacked is the very faculty of detection itself?" Another time he asks me, "What's a billion? A hundred million or a thousand million?" And I had to look into an encyclopaedia, being unsure of it myself—so much for my vaunted knowledge.

Father gifts his Amritsar house to Pasho. She needed it for her son, the college lecturer and his family, presently putting up with her in dire discomfort.

We approve of his decision. My younger brother raises a ruckus.

"I'm a poor person, living at the mercy of my son. I need the house badly". He declaims vehemently, sputum dribbling out of the corners of his mouth.

"You'll still live at the mercy of your son", retorts the old man. "You haven't the vigour to live on your own".

"Does your age entitle you to insult me?" he barks back.

"I'm not insulting you, merely stating a fact".

"Why did you have me then, if you always think so poorly of me?" he rants in his unmannerly fashion. Bits of the cookie he was eating are shooting out, a few as far as Father's face.

"If I had known how you'd shape, I would not have done so", the old man mumbled, wiping his face clean.

"I was always given a raw deal", he whines, picking his nose.

"Everybody gets his due".

"You're painting me in the worst possible colours".

"I'm being accurate, my son. The time has come to be".

And he continues, "Pasho needs the house, you don't. And let's not forget, it was she and her hospitable husband who gave us shelter when we turned up at their doorstep as refugees. They allowed us, even helped us, to build a storey over their property.

I compensate you by giving my Fixed Deposits in post office and UTI shares. Don't worry, it's not a bad deal".

"You can't part with your savings in your lifetime", I butt in. "It's not done".

"My grouse against Daddha was that he denied himself of necessities, let alone luxuries, to save money for his children, and not very grateful children at that", Priti intervenes. "The house is kept in disrepair, sagging furniture, fraying curtains, broken windows, near empty fridge".

"Beti, I've learnt to live frugally, to cut down my wants. Once made to part with so much at Partition, I lost all love for things. Anyway I won't get a chance to spend my savings. I may die before that. Sucha can have the money just now. Let him be happy".

In the end it is agreed that the UTI shares be given forthwith to Sucha, while the transfer of Fixed Deposits could wait.

Pasho's son renovates father's portion. The bathroom is relaid and the uneven brick flooring in rooms covered over with thin marble tiles. But even he can't reshape the steep stairs.

Much mutual respect and love prevails between Ravi and his grandpa. He was Ravi's role model during the boy's formative years, and to grandpa, Ravi's a model grandson.

They spend hours together when Ravi is visiting. I suppose relations with sons and grandsons are more a product of communication, not physical proximity

"Why not come with us to the US?" he asks grandpa. "You haven't been out of India. Never had a glimpse of the wide world. Not even ridden a plane or seen the sea".

"I can make a rough guess what the world is like. Don't forget I've been a geography teacher".

"Stay with us, a month at least".

"I'm nearing 90. Not the time to foist myself on someone in a foreign land".

Ravi gets him fitted with the best available hearing aid, a Danish one costing around Rs 1,00,000.

"Why spend such a colossal sum on me? The money on the two tiny ear buttons could have bought a mansion in my youth. And this device wouldn't see service for more than a few years. It may have to be burnt along with me, being of no use to anybody else".

"It's worth it, Daddha. Will enable you to listen to people, mix with people, enjoy music. An educated, sensitive man like you shouldn't end up doing rosary beads or sit all day at breakfast table with the paper".

And on Ravi's insistence, grandpa agrees to have a boy servant exclusively for him; someone to give him the daily oil massage, help him in bathing, sort out his clothes, to accompany him for walks, and to do odd jobs for him.

"Ravi wanted me to journey to the US. If I could make a trip at all, I'd love to visit Abbottabad, the place where I worked and left my heart", the old man says one day at dinner.

"I'll take you there. And Priti, too. Show her where I grew up".

Within a month visas are arranged. Three of us fly to Lahore via Delhi. And we hire a driver-driven Toyota Crown for t he trip.

We motor to Panja Sahib, the historic Sikh shrine so dear to father. Once a popular pilgrim centre thronging with devout visitors and shoppers, it stands deserted. Yet arrangements are adequate for us to take the holy dip, touch the panja, and perform obeisance.

We find Abbottabad vastly different. In place of a quiet, leafy town, it's a big bustling city. You even forget you're in a former hill station unless you look at the hills around.

We go to see our house. The same stands divided in three units. Plaster is peeling and several glass panes missing. Children are romping all over.

"Makes me sad to see the house in such sorry state", the old man says. "I had built it with infinite care. And the garden on which I bestowed so much attention is a barren patch with only two apricot trees left".

Thereafter, we reach the high school, where he had taught and I had studied. A former student, now a balding headmaster, recognizes father. Embraces him and takes us on a tour of the building that has vastly expanded and over-built. He also arranges for tea with some teachers.

For two days we go round the teeming city and its roads choking with motorized vehicles. The main gurudwara where father had spent umpteen hours no longer functions. Mercifully it remains locked up, not vandalised. Then we motor to Gallis, the small summer hill resorts, termed Nathia Galli, Dunga Galli, Ghora Galli, and so on. We used to trek to these forest-covered mountains every summer. Father was an ardent walker, mountaineer, and hiker. He could do all sorts of knots, pitch up a tent, light a fire, and find his way in the woods. I never heard him talking of fatigue or complain about facilities. We boys looked to him for absolute leadership on those trekking trips.

"This visit has been exhilarating", he tells me on return. "Many, many thanks for making it possible".

"A memorable one for me, too".

Priti, who hadn't lived in those parts, is not similarly enthused. To her it's a trip like to any other new place.

"Careful. Keep a hand on the railing", I say, when he negotiates the three front steps. I dish out advice how he conducts himself in the bathroom without risking a fall. At the dining table we heap food on his plate, instead of letting him help himself.

Father is a light eater.

"You want to kill me", he jokes. "The less you eat, the longer you live. And food doesn't interest me greatly. After all, what you eat is not with you long enough to care about".

When offered bottled water, he can't help remarking, "In my time, nobody ever doubted tap water".

And he adds nostalgically, "Everything English was then deemed as the best quality: bicycles, tennis racquets, shotguns, shoes, biscuits, chocolates. Japanese items provoked jokes".

What a role reversal!

Here's the man who was the most commanding figure in my boyhood, an overpowering presence. I believed in his omniscience; as if he knew everything and had the right answers. I used to hang on to every word of his. Tall, dapper, solemn, he was always dignified.

He taught me how to handle a shotgun and knot a necktie. Muscular and strong enough to fight off a robber, beat the hell out of a street bully, or be unafraid of a mad dog, so I imagined. So good with his hands, I thought my dad could fix anything. And when he was angry, the whole household shook. All quarrels and loud voices stood suspended when he was sighted coming.

With me, he struck a fine balance between affection and distance.

And now I dole him advice on trivial matters and lend assistance in petty tasks. The once redoubtable man is grown so light, I lifted him off his feet in a tight embrace.

Parenting is said to be an invigorating experience. And it's a good deal of fun, too, despite the usual element of hassles and conflicts. But 'parenting' one's parent is rarely a smooth affair. The role reversal, a truly complex phenomenon, is never free from an element of frustration or embarrassment.

Is it so because it goes against nature's very scheme of things? In the animal world, the old are never parented by their offspring.

The elderly parent, more so a widower, is often anxious to retain a measure of independence, at least a semblance of it. Physical assistance is accepted but with a marked preference for the unobtrusive variety, not the showy sort. Old men tend to be touchy about it. They don't want their physical infirmities to be broadcast.

The elderly again wants to preserve a modicum of his lifestyle. No surprise, my dad was very reluctant to leave his modest home to be a guest at an affluent one. Clearly, he wished to be no burden to his progeny, as long as he could manage.

"When the father helps the son, both smile; when the son helps the father, both cry", is the proverb he quotes at times.

If ever I find myself in the same situation, with a son looking after me, I'd dearly wish to be treated as a friend than 'parented.'

Only 25 years separate me from my father. What had once seemed a great gulf, has shrunk to near insignificance. Our genetic structure must be close to identical—moles all over the body, sagging mouth, sleepy lids, a throat ever needing clearance. We could stand more like brothers than father and son.

After living with us for 8 years, Father died at 93 of a brief illness from a lung infection. He simply stopped breathing, with me at his bedside. His last words: "Look after Priti". Pity, she was then at her school.

His was the nearest to what can ever be termed as 'death with dignity'. In fact, one could say he died of 'age', not of any mentionable disease.

Much grief for the one dying at 93 was not in order. Yet we were truly sorry to see the old man go.

At the cremation, my younger brother Sucha, howls in grief. He behaves like the most bereaved family member party. Condolences from the ones gathered, however, are being proffered to me and Priti.

I suppose, the death of a parent you love impinges on you somewhat more simply than the death of a parent you clashed with. In your heart you know that your squabbles with the dead parent were mostly uncalled for.

A few days after cremation, we had a visit from Sucha. He wanted some things of father to keep as momentoes.

Right since we were children we envied two items of Father's; a pair of hair brushes joined together and kept in a leather case and in a hand-held ornate magnifier, he kept on his writing table. The two brushes with which father would brush his flowing beard were of some high quality; brushes mounted on steel plate with shining wood support, and looked as good as new even after more than 50 years of use. We gave both items to Sucha, although with his beard tied up he could not have much use for the brushes.

CHAPTER 17

Father is no more.

We are again reduced to two residents in the huge house, a house that could hold a party for a hundred. The dining table seats 12.

Living together in a long marriage has its inevitable ups and downs. Old couples living together do generate a measure of irritability, impatience, and obstinacy, more so when living in too close proximity. No small ordeal for the wife when her man never leaves her day and night, stares at her, interrupts her, and picks on things she says.

Our marriage has been host to that peculiar feature of living mostly separate for its first 22 years.

And now a husband all the time at home! He can easily get on his mate's nerves, more so a husband who's trying to write creative stuff. The exercise is apt to send him into varying moods, ranging from euphoria on one side to extreme despair on the other. And worse still, when the writing isn't collecting cash or attracting recognition.

It's good for her that Priti is out half the day at the nursery school. And on three afternoons a week I'm out golfing.

Again, she isn't bothered by any interference from me in the kitchen. I rarely step into that holy of holies except to fetch a tumbler of cold water or a piece of chocolate from the refrigerator. Ice cubes for whisky are put up punctually by Rano at sundown in a vacuum flask.

As to any talk from me about the garden, Priti's pet domain, the same is straightway shrugged off as if coming from a parrot. If I persist in intruding, I'm asked to distinguish between a bed of phlox and petunias. A wrong answer produces a snigger, and makes me beat a hasty retreat.

If compatibility is a necessary condition of happy marriage, then ours would rate as a serious mistake made five decades back. We're very different, but somehow we stay reconciled to our differences rather than raving about them.

Theoretically, marriage is all about "two people becoming one". But that sort of fusion has made precious little headway in ours.

I am an early riser. She wakes up late. Her best sleep, she claims, happens between 5 and 7. So I sneak out of bed without putting on a light, hoping not to hit my shins or toe against an intruding piece of furniture.

She's a night person, often reads a book or watches television into late hours. I burrow my face under the bedclothes or don the black eye shade of an airline. Mercifully, the moment my head hits the pillow, I'm often asleep.

I eat fast, heaping everything on one plate. She eats slow, and is picky with what she eats. Often I finish the main course while she's half through. And then I wait impatiently for the dessert, drumming the table with my fingers. Piqued, at times she lets me have the sweet straightway, while her own she carries to the bedroom.

Television we watch differently. I prefer to watch attentively in relative silence. She can easily combine it with ironing, telephoning, and conversation. And while I'd like to slide into a comfortable seat, she prefers to perch on a sofa stool; easier to get up frequently for various household chores.

My main watching is sports—golf, football, cricket; she favours romantic serials and tear-jerkers, such as *The Bold and The Beautiful* or some favourite Hindi serials. At times, I have to move to the livingroom TV set for a prolonged sports viewing, as she takes over the bigger bedroom one.

She loves parties, while I'm rarely comfortable with these, more so when I'm now 'nobody.' Once I overheard her telling Noni: "Whenever he sees me having a good time in a party, he wants to go home". I do get a bit jealous seeing her in sparkling conversation with passable males. The gift of small talk has eluded me.

At times we run into an argument when she has accepted a dinner or drink invitation without clearing with me.

"Why ruin a Saturday evening in the company of that boring couple?" I protest. "We could see a picture instead".

"Sorry, I went ahead and accepted it without consulting you".

"Well then, call them back and unaccept".

"Sudha would mind. She's so friendly to us".

"You could say, your husband isn't keeping fit. I'm actually not that fit. My back is bothering me".

Priti indulges in fun shopping. I have a hearty distaste of any shopping. Having known prices prevalent in the 1930–40s, to me everything appears atrociously priced. She likes birthdays and the connected festivity. Birthdays don't excite me.

The list of incompatibilities runs endlessly long. Yet I can't imagine being married to anyone else. On her part, one can surmise some affection for a husband of 50 years.

We're together, but it's not because of compatibility.

Priti, I sense, remains earnestly engaged in correcting my faults and failings, evidently for my own good. My recent habit of biting off hair on the back of my fingers invariably draws her flak. Creative creatures, women can't resist the temptation of improving their man.

"If a woman wants to mould her hubby to her image, the ideal would be a malleable boy-husband of 12. You can't do much to someone over 25 whose mother had already spoiled him beyond redemption", I say one time.

"You must have read that somewhere".

To Priti, anything funny or original I say, I must have gleaned from a book or magazine. Reading, she surmises, is my primary source of information, not sociability.

She is the perennial teacher; I, the class dunce:

"Use your hankie, not the napkin, to blow your nose".

"Again you left your book open upside down".

"Use a shoehorn. You could ruin its back, forcing feet in with a finger".

"At yesterday's dinner you started nibbling at your food before all the ladies had been served".

"Why work yourself into a rage at every erring driver in sight?"

"Why rave against corrupt public officials, unless you can do something to improve matters".

Priti possibly apprehends that my reaction to life's petty irritations would grow worse with age. "As a writer you should be observant of public disorder, not upset about it", she says.

Apparently it's her way to help me improve, to tamper my imperfections.

Her correctional approach—it doesn't amount to nagging—is usually a light-hearted affair. And is indulged in private, or at best within one's close family circle.

We remain happily married. Indeed, our marriage has improved since we started living together in Chandigarh. I suppose, marriages get better or worse with time—they never remain the same.

I have never stopped touching her, just for touching's sake, not only as a prelude to sex. Touching her softly at the cheek as I get up from the dining table, I always get up earlier, having finished earlier. And I'm free with compliments when she's dressed for an evening out; genuine compliments evoked by her elegant appearance.

Maybe we have an intimate way of relating to each other. And this connection we may be maintaining through a mild sort of spontaneous, playful banter. The light-hearted attitude towards each other's failings could be keeping us from acting combative or too argumentative.

People tend to underestimate the role of humour in marriage. Indeed, few strategies are more useful than it in defusing marital tension or in restoring a wounded ego.

At times I play another game. I feign ignorance over some simple matter, or make a childish remark, provoking her to a corrective or dismissive response. But by now, she often ignores it, having seen through my game plan.

PART-IV

A Widower's Waddle

"The desires of the heart are as crooked as corkscrews".

W.H. Auden

'Never say you know the last word about any human heart".

Henry James

CHAPTER 18

Priti is dead.

Three months have passed since she died.

Yesternight in a dream, the dead one sent me a letter, a long letter listing my failings as a husband but ending with words of affection for me.

At times I nurse the belief she isn't dead. And there are some images of her that keep flashing on my mental screen. These remain unchanged with the passage of time. At will, I run them through my mental projector.

One such picture is of Priti inspecting damage to the garden with the heavy downpour we had soon after return from the U.S. She's moving between flower beds with her salwar rolled up to her knees, her shapely calves and ankles showing.

Another one is of her lying on bed at George V hotel, Paris, with me on top, as reflected in the big wall mirror. Yet Priti's most poignant picture that haunts me occasionally is of her standing at the doorway, atop the steep Amritsar house steps, when I bring in Jogi after his frightening escapade. Intense emotions play on her face. Memories and thoughts can change with time, but some memories never change.

At times I prattle—carry a two-way conversation—as if she's around in the house.

Almost every day it hits me as to how much I had grown dependent on her. This, in turn, generates a feeling of heart-wrenching loneliness.

How unlucky to outlive one's longtime mate! The whole web of family living, its accummulated habits, its petty pinpricks, and its private jokes lies sundered. Life looms altogether different. I miss her benign presence, her pliable body, and her smooth running of the household. Even miss her comments over my various acts of commission and omission, negligence and carelessness. For one, she'd show annoyance over my forgetting some simple household things she had asked me to do; things like bringing her shawl from the laundry, picking up some school stuff from a shop while returning from golf. "You can remember so many names and incidents. But you can't remember an easy chore. I suppose, you weren't listening when I asked for it".

"I was listening. But I forgot".

Over the years, she tends to remember more and more of various tasks to be done, and I less and less. Of course, I can't justify my lapse because she remembers more; perhaps she is required to remember more.

Pasho has gone back. And she won't return till July–August. And I miss her, too, her cheerful presence. It's a sight, seeing her talking to Rano, the two fatty women, inflated as though with a cycle pump, sorting out not only mundane kitchen matters but exchanging weighty views on life and death. It's somewhat of a comic situation, with Rano gabbing in bad Hindi and Pasho not budging one whit from her Amritsari Punjabi.

I'm up at five as usual. Previously the alarm clock was kept close so as to be silenced quickly; I didn't want to disturb Priti unduly. Now I position it far off on the dressing table, making it obligatory for me to rise and slap it shut.

Don't think I can ever run an efficient household. And there are always nagging little worries, such as of the house being securely locked at night, or a tap left leaking, or a light staying on.

The breakfast remains the same unvaried: one soft-boiled egg, unbuttered toast, milk, and seasonal fruit, backed by a multivitamin pill and the brain-food of five almonds.

Rano, at times, from sheer past practice, lays the table for two, And I stare banefully at Priti's empty chair. She used to sit at the head of the table, with me sitting on her right side. I still sit in the same position, leaving her chair unoccupied.

I'm not sure how much food Rano pilfers—she's not known to steal money. The pilferage must have been contained when Pasho was here; Pasho may have operated even stricter control than Priti. But now Rano enjoys a free run of the kitchen. There's precious little I can do about it without souring the home atmosphere. Locking up the pantry and issuing daily rations, as once suggested by Pasho, sounds too repugnant a step to me. In fact I don't fancy carrying keys. The only key, the key of my desk drawer where I keep money and some important papers, I hide behind a book than carry it around. And the same situation still obtains, with Priti's bunch of keys lying in my locked desk drawer.

Lunch stands reduced to one vegetable, curd, boiled rice, and an item of fruit; dinner to one meat dish, dal, roti and dessert.

I continue to take the two morning papers, having been habituated to this for years.

Bhura has well-nigh declared his independence. He does what he deems fit. Meets me only for his salary, or money for manure and plants. The garden doesn't seem any the worse for it. When Priti was alive, she made it a point to cut flowers herself for vases in our living room and my study. This is now left to Bhura, and he usually botches it.

Meantime, the tenant Ramesh who is fairly knowledgeable on horticulture has agreed to my suggestion of supervising the garden. He's down every Sunday for it. Spends an hour or two with Bhura. He has even got some exotic rose cuttings from his brewery nursery.

Gauri didn't turn up for a fortnight, putting more pressure on Rano and Bhura. She took no prior permission. And has offered no explanation on return. Now she goes about glum, her merry cackle missing.

"Is Gauri unwell? I ask Rano. "She isn't as cheerful as before".

Rano makes a wry face. And then shoots back after an unaccustomed pause, "The hussy; underwent an abortion. Got rid of an illegitimate brat".

I feel sorry for Gauri. Some bastard has done her in. I'd like to give her some money but for fear of being misunderstood.

"You look weak, unwell. Take it easy till you recover", I tell her, when outside the range of Rano's hearing and sight. "Here's Rs 500, an advance on your salary to buy medicines and food".

With Priti gone, I carry more cash on my person.

There's no intention to recover the advance.

Gauri stares at me with big dark eyes, grabs the crisp 500-rupee bill, shoves it into her bra, and continues with her sweeping as if nothing has happened. I have to make a pretty determined effort to drag my eyes from her breasts.

I've shifted my clothes to the wardrobes in the master bedroom and toiletries to the adjacent bathroom.

The tub curtain rod, once heavily hung with all her nightclothes, stands brutally bare. My solitary sleeping suit is strung on a peg behind the door.

Priti's bedside table, ever short of space, lies blank but for a photograph of her—a smile lighting her eyes and parting her lips. In this studio photograph taken on her fortieth birthday, she's a mature beauty. Another framed photograph is there of Priti with Ravi and Jogi. She, 35, is sitting on a stool, with Ravi and Jogi standing on both sides. All the three are smiling. Our 'honeymoon' photo from Simla stays perched on the TV set.

The white double bed looms like a vast empty expanse. The very sight brings on memories of the body that used to inhabit its other side. I often lie facing that way, with legs scissor-forked across the unoccupied part.

The whole master bedroom and bathroom have taken on an eerie look; these aren't the same rooms. And one feels as if the living room has expanded. The furniture pieces with backs to the wall stare as if watching me.

Indeed, the house has assumed a somewhat sinister look with Priti absent from it. I feel more at ease out of it than in.

On days I hardly talk to anybody in the house but Johnny.

It's now afternoon golf on all six days (the course stays closed on Monday to give the grass much-needed rest). Daily golf can tend to be boring, too; the same thick socks and studded shoes, a cap, and a glove on the left hand.

Games like golf and bridge, it appears, attract persons of gloomy temperament who hope to escape their gloom during the long playing hours.

I'm there by 4, after the post-lunch snooze. Nine holes of golf, tea, an hour of bridge, and back home by 7.30. A stiff Scotch and tub bath are followed by a Rano-cooked meal.

Thereafter, I watch TV or read in bed, before falling asleep by 10. This is the time when I miss Priti most. An intense sense of desolation sweeps over.

These days I'm tearful so easily, so quickly. Reading an old letter of hers, seeing some photographs of us together, even looking at a curio bought by her gets droplets in my eyes. A glimpse of her favourite armchair lying empty triggers a touch of melancholy.

My correspondence is now mostly limited to replying to all those condolence messages. It came out as a surprise that so many people knew Priti, and were keen to commiserate about her demise.

I can place most of the correspondents but for one: Rattan Singh of Amritsar. The writer professes his profound grief at Priti's passing away. Of him, I don't have a clue. Questioned about it, Pasho could only tell that some 50 years back one Rattan was a shop boy with Priti's parents.

On Mondays it's a long evening walk in the Rose Garden. You see plump Sardarnis almost trotting in a seemingly vain bid to slim down the lumpy posteriors. Elderly men sitting on benches could be looking for someone to sit beside and talk to. Children are being held back from plucking roses or wandering into rose patches. The main fountain is usually devoid of water.

Walking has always had a calming effect on me. And Chandigarh is well designed for walking. There are no open drains to negotiate, no houses or shops overflowing on to pavements, and no through-traffic inside the sectors. Unlike other Indian cities, you can walk here in dignified safety.

Occasionally I go out for a movie, a social call, or dinner at Aarti's. My rare entertaining of others is at the golf club or at a restaurant. I've little faith in Rano turning out an appreciative meal.

Once or twice when I ventured to dine alone in a restaurant, the experience didn't prove pleasing. In busy restaurants, single diners are often accommodated in odd nooks or near the kitchen, and attract poor waiter attention. They're deemed poor tippers, persons who don't even have friends to accompany them. A lone diner better equip himself with some reading material to overcome the embarrassment of waiting.

My social life has virtually collapsed since Priti died. Like most men, I have just a pleasant, jocular relationship with other men. I don't get emotional with them or seek their advice, except for Harbans. With the bereavement visits over, hardly any friend calls, besides the golfing buddies and the tenant. And I'm losing contact with relatives, barring the two sons and their progeny.

I don't call on people. But I do like visitors. Pity, these are so few. What a contrast from my service days when visitors had to be discouraged, as one got too many of them.

As my observance of Sikh rituals is patchy, Harbans has volunteered to transfer the Guru Granth Sahib to his place. Now our small room remains locked.

Every Sunday evening I get a phone call from Ravi and Noni. That's their breakfast time. They encourage Viki to talk to his grandpa.

Jogi and Girija ring on Sunday mornings, with Lovely pitching in.

On some Sundays the eagerly awaited calls don't materialize. Evidently people could be too busy elsewhere. And I don't see much point in my ringing them up, more so when there's hardly anything new to tell.

In the beginning of February I find my account up by $2,000 instead of the monthly $1,000.

"Some mistake, Ravi", I tell him. "$2,000 has been credited to my name this month".

"That's no mistake, Dad. We made a mention of it when you were here. Money's all the more needed as income from Mama's kindergarten has dried up".

"Expenses have also come down. Feeding and clothing one in place of two".

"The basic household outgo doesn't decline. Actually your kitchen may get more wasteful. That's what Noni thinks".

The additional amount is OK. I have a proper respect for money but am not obsessed with it. What I'm more in want is the love and respect of my sons, not their money, unless money itself is taken as one indicator of their love. What I sorely need they can't spare: their time and attention. I find myself a self-pitying loner, despite their consolatory phone calls.

Well, money cannot ensure happiness. But it could mitigate unhappiness, at least help you live out your misery in comfort.

And surplus money can make a man horny. It can loosen his moral brakes.

I've no inclination to visit Jogi and Girija for the time being, despite repeated reminders from them. My stay would dislocate their living arrangements. As Priti found, happy joint family living is more of a myth.

Jogi ringing up, "Dad, how are you today? How you doing?"

"Fine", as I always say.

"We haven't heard from you for some time. Anything new?"

"What could be new?"

"How's your health?"

"Engine running all right. Body a bit rusty".

"Take it easy, Dad".

"Can't take it any more easy".

After a moment's wait: "Dad, why are you sticking on to Chandigarh? Move in with us. You need someone around to look after you".

"Thanks for the offer. But I'm staying put. My mind's made up".

"That doesn't make sense. The Chandigarh house is too big, too unwieldy for you to manage on your own. A single person in such a vast place. Putting up with power cuts and water shortages. And there's always the question of personal safety. Have a cozy apartment in Delhi if you want to live separately than with us. I can surely find one conveniently close".

"There isn't going to be any other house or apartment for me".

Jogi may have his ideas about getting me out of the Chandigarh house. But I need my own space, and this need overrides everything else.

"Dad, you're acting like an old man".

"What do you think I am? A young man?"

"I mean acting older than you have to be".

"I hope someday you won't accuse me of acting younger than I am."

"Dad, you've this problem: You don't share your troubles with your near ones".

"A trouble shared isn't necessarily a trouble halved".

Indeed there's no way you can make the young understand how it feels to be old and unwanted.

Conversation between me and Jogi tends to grow patchy, tense. We don't see eye to eye on anything. Not on one blessed thing. Take money. Jogi is mad about money. Perhaps his love of money drained his faculty for joy. I'm just comfortable with money, lacking nothing that money can buy.

Jogi and his wife earn a fair amount. Why does he always crave for more?

With the conversation growing desultory, I switch over to a pleasanter subject.

"What about all of you coming to Chandigarh in July? The girls have vacation".

"I'll discuss it with Honey. Let you know". (He calls Girija 'Honey').

Jogi will probably agree. It'd give him another chance to renew his plea about the house. Maybe he's banking on my going weak with the passing away of Priti.

I have the feeling that Jogi harbours some repressed resentment against me since his boyhood days. To him, I must have been the outsider who came home infrequently and behaved like a dictator—with mother seemingly subservient, someone who brooked no protest or defiance from his boys. Pity, I may have given this impression to him, when it was nowhere my intent.

It's possibly too late to make amends, to erase that image.

Now in my middle seventies, leading a retired life, I find that a new address book is overdue. Most of the old entries—of colleagues in service and of business acquaintances—have been rendered irrelevant. Of others, addresses change, telephone numbers even more frequently. And you now need to include a person's e-mail address, cell phone, and fax number. So I succumb to buying a new one—plainer, smaller. Presumably this would be my last.

And soon it dawns on me that rewriting an address book wasn't turning out to be the routine exercise I had envisaged. The process signifies some sort of a watershed in facing the last stage of one's life.

Often an old entry brings on a flood of memories, of the good times we had with someone. Another entry would evoke a feeling of regret for missing out on better relationships.

And then there are umpteen entries of people who had blossomed into celebrities in public affairs or as captains of industry. Yet all contact between them and me have ceased over the years. Apparently, they felt no need to sustain those contacts. And this brings on a sense of dejection.

But what makes rewriting particularly painful is to score out names of friends who have died since then. The noted urologist friend is dead; he who was so full of cheer, and the one who operated upon Father. "I'd take care of your enlarged prostate when a surgical intervention is due", he'd tell me. Perhaps I've to look for another urologist. He died at 60, of a disease he knew was incurable. Yet I have admiration for the courage and poise with which he lived his last years.

Another friend, a journalist, whose company was fun and intellectually stimulating, died of a sudden heart attack at the age of 54. That was shocking. Till that fatal morning he seemed so busy, so active, a life of promise. I marvel at the fortitude his professor-wife has displayed in living her life.

Going through various entries of the old address book, I discover to my dismay that nearly half of the friends of my youth are no more.

One clear indicator of one's decline: of the recent entries, a whole lot pertain to medical specialists—dentists, ophthalmologists, orthopedic surgeons, cardiologists, ENT specialists, physiotherapists. I've reached an age when I call my physicians by their first names, being a fatherly figure to them.

In a way I am glad I am still alive, and the possibilities of new adventures aren't fully foreclosed. Interests have shrunk; interests in cinema films, movie stars, singers, even restaurants. Aches and pains keep coming at unexpected places. Yet a lot of life, I feel, is still left in me.

The early morning hours, the very time I should be at my sharpest and full of renewed hope, pass away in depressive idleness.

Work on the second novel has been proceeding agonizingly slow. Often, I sit for hours 'typing' nothing; diverted instead to daydreaming, flooded with memories of days with Priti.

Unlike the computer, the human brain has no 'delete' key. You don't forget certain things even if you want it. We all carry the past inside us in some shape or the other. That way it's an advantage to have a poor memory. You have less to forget.

On days, numbness seizes me. The feel of utter desolation is overpowering. Tears well up.

At times it's so bad, there's an urge to end it all, to kill myself. And a suicidal urge in the elderly is deemed more serious; they act more determined. Unlike the young, the old have little optimism left. My favoured method would be popping fifty sleeping pills. You curl up in your bed and soon it's over. I've a horror of violent means that are messy and painful.

But then another part of me argues, "Anybody can swallow pills. Living is the challenge. Suicide is for the faint-hearted".

To overcome the suicidal mood, I get up, walk briskly up and down the verandah. During periods of mental anguish, walking is one activity I turn to—a golfer's mentality. It helps boost the depressed state of mind into some sort of rhythm, the soul-calming language of walking beginning to dissolve the darting of the mind.

Robert Lowell has rightly said, "If there was some little switch in the arm which one could press in order to die immediately and without pain, then everyone would sooner or later commit suicide".

Well, I'd be pressing such a switch sooner than later.

Yet, the thought of dying hurts. To part permanently with the children and grandchildren. To forego warm baths, premium Scotch, thick percolator coffee, black bittersweet chocolates, a good round of golf, some interesting hands at bridge, an absorbing novel, winter sunshine, monsoon breeze, greenery of the garden, the looks of beautiful women.

"Why this peculiar early morning depression?" I ask Harbans.

"Depression is mainly a state of mind. Once he offered me for trial two dozen Prozac, the expensive "Happiness Pill".

"The only antidepressant I want is Priti back".

"That's not on the market yet", he jibed.

The morning reverie is broken with the coming of tea and the two daily papers. I gobble the banana, sip three cups of golden, fragrant Darjeeling tea, and get immersed in the troubles of the world, relinquishing my own for the moment.

My second novel revolves round the life and times of father. I spend hours trying to remember my boyhood with him.

"It's an old story—ours,
My father's and mine".

—Shakespeare

During Father's last 7 years at Chandigarh I had umpteen sessions with him, asking him to spell out his times, the physical surroundings, his childhood and youth, his marriage and offsprings, and the teacher tussles at school. He, however, stayed totally clamped on sex or love outside marriage, though his weakness for attractive women was no secret among family members and close friends. He'd recall his wife, who had been dead for 40 years, with unaccustomed detachment.

Ferreting through scanty belongings after his demise, I come upon his diaries, four book-sized well-bound notebooks. This presented a dilemma. Should I read them? Or put them away, at least for some time? Or, destroy them unread?

It is said that the diarist, though seeking privacy for the diaries, yearns that these would be read by someone.

Eventually my curiosity got the better of discretion. I argued to myself, these would surely be a help in my next novel that's based on father's times.

The diaries, I find, consist of sporadic entries since 1946. And these dwell more on negative happenings in his life than the positive: the Partition riots and forced migration from open, cool spaces of Abbottabad to the congested, steamy alleys of Amritsar; the elder son cutting off his long hair; the younger one proving an idler, a waster, no good in studies or job; and the wife's prolonged sickness and death.

I find the pen with which he'd write diary entries in his firm upright hand. It's an old-fashioned black fountain pen, thick in the middle, tapering on the ends. The make stands somewhat rubbed off but it looks like Waterman. Possibly this is the pen he was given as the Best Teacher Award.

Outwardly calm and collected, Father does come out in these diaries as more of an unhappy man. His state of worklessness after retirement must be the primary cause. Have I inherited my melancholic streak from him?

What possibly saves him from slipping into depression is his strong faith in the Sikh gurus.

Clearly the Partition with its accompanying loss of a satisfying job, a comfortable home, and prominent position in society must have dealt a deadly blow to his ego and aspirations.

Mostly when he livens up in his diary, the entries pertain to Priti or Ravi, the considerate daughter-in-law and the promising grandson. And he highlights his enjoyment of the Chandigarh house garden.

I hardly figure in any recent entries. Possibly he assumed his diaries may fall into my hands, and so the reticence.

The diaries are liberally jotted with Urdu couplets, quotes in Gurmukhi from Gurbani, and at places a proverb. In my boyhood he'd often render advice through proverbs. The most commonly quoted were: "No gain without pain", "Practice makes a man perfect", "Where there's a will, there's a way". Evidently he isn't aware that proverbs—conventional wisdom compressed in a quotable phrase—have been losing their sheen.

The last entry made three days before his demise is almost prophetic. He talks of an approaching end, and whether he'd die with somebody by his bedside or no one around. Ruminates who would remember him except for a couple of close relatives once or twice a year. And thereafter no one will, as if he hadn't existed at all.

Yes, it's hard to shake off the sadness that comes over towards the end of one's life. Your failures lie stamped, your successes rubbed away.

I always imagined life to be simpler and purer with Father and his times. But then he could be as wayward and unaccountable in his longings as any of us. Every life that way is both ordinary and extraordinary. It's the mix of the respective portions that make a life interesting or humdrum.

Pity, literature has largely neglected the old and their emotions.

CHAPTER 19

"Every man hath a right to enjoy life".

John Gay, *The Beggar's Opera*

By March end, it's the onset of spring. The city's multitude of flowering trees display a riot of colour: pink, lilac, bright red, and myriad others. Avenues of amaltas are laden with yellow blossoms. Another avenue has pink-coloured cassias. You see a whole sector lined with yellow blossoms of kassod trees.

The Leisure Valley is full of flowering shrubs and trees. At places the flowers fall so thick they cover the ground like a carpet. The laburnum trees provide a visual feast.

Sunny and cool, the weather is heavenly.

In the garden, chrysanthemums, phlox, and geraniums are still in bloom. Tuberoses are budding. The stately jamun is shedding leaves by hundreds. The apricot trees laden with white flowers present a superb sight.

Bhura is busy watering, mowing, pruning, picking leaves. He's told not to burn leaves but he often does, saving himself the labour of carting them away.

It's beautiful all around.

How many more Chandigarh springs will I savor?

The lawns are going lush by the day.

The way the lawn is casting away its winter torpor, I may be shaking off some of my grief. Is it because of the spring in the air? Or, is it the passage of time? Grieving beyond 3–4 months is said to be overdoing. Sadness, it seems, is not capable of infinite growth. And then Priti and I had a compact; the survivor should get along, not grieve unduly.

With the poignancy of grief losing its sharp edge, I discern a revival in sexual stirrings. I usually wake up with a transient old man's tumescence.

I feel horny, particularly after lunch. Am paying more attention to Gauri than in the past. I seek opportunities to gaze at her breasts, talk to her, banter with her. Even Rano's bulky body doesn't seem devoid of interest.

I'm watching female bodies at home and outside with renewed attention. Face-watching isn't a new interest with me. For years I've been fascinated watching faces.

But why continue with voyeurism? A veteran of marriage and being elderly, to what end was I staring obsessively at young women? If I was really appraising for an opportunity, I should only be looking for women of a certain age and disposition, not the nubile young.

I know, I've neither talent nor real appetite for philandering. Was this staring intended to remind myself of what it had once been like?

And I'm not unaware of the pitfalls an elderly bloke runs into in chasing women—the well-derided caricature of an old lecher making a fool of himself. Sexual relations in old age are deemed not only shocking, they loom comic, even ill-fated. Men in their 70s may harbour wicked thoughts but they are supposed to suppress sexual urgings if any left. And in no case are they to have an affair with a person of another generation.

Love affairs, the damaging ones, I eschewed once married. What happened before marriage were a few tumbles in bed with a live-in cousin.

In the last 20 years, it has been Priti alone. And she has catered to those needs to my satisfaction. Are we getting nicer animals as we age? Now Priti is gone. I sorely miss her body, let alone the companionship.

My doctor-friend Harbans is here on a Monday evening. Both of us are into our second whisky.

My friend, I know, is an orderly man with orderly expectations and pleasures. Conceded, those pleasures are not as strong as they once had been.

"Harbans, how do you manage sex? You've been a widower for nearly a decade, right since you turned sixty.

"What's there to manage! Whenever the urge comes too strong, one seeks relief in a hand-job".

"Wanking is no answer for me as the urge to ejaculate is no longer compelling. I yearn for a woman's body—a desirable form one can hold, touch in various ways".

"An acquaintance of mine knows of a couple of call girls in the town. I can get you their telephones".

"Paid stuff won't do at my age. It has to be someone who's unhurried and appreciative of the sexual limitations of a man of 75. Old men need understanding women for the purpose".

"Better go in for re-marriage if you could find someone suitable".

"You didn't remarry".

"I live in a joint family with two adult sons, their wives, and children. A mate, even if I ever find one, will give rise to all sorts of complications. With you it's different".

"I'm not sure of that. Jogindar will kick hell at the prospect of an extra claimant to the house. The courtship and remarriage of an old widower is always made more difficult when middle-age children are involved. They set out to save him from an ill-considered marriage. Even grownup grandchildren join in this game".

"Jogindar can lump it", retorts Harbans. "At one time love affairs of old men were dubbed as inappropriate. Even the old didn't support the old in such dotage, lest in so doing they occasioned merriment against themselves. The elderly were supposed to withdraw totally from sexual competition, learn to be properly old. Do you know, Kinsey's Report devoted a mere 3 of its 1700 pages to the older age group? Only the great or the very rich can get away with it, persons like Picasso or Murdoch.

That's our trouble. We live in the twilight of the old morality, and that's just enough to torment us.

But take heart, times are changing. People are getting more relaxed about these things. And the older you get, the less you care what people think. You aren't bound hand and foot with the shackles of public opinion".

"Let alone public opinion, a live-in companion poses its own imponderables".

"Some risks are inherent in such situations. How a woman of unchartered disposition would fit into the life of a 75-year-old, with his habits and preferences formed? Seemingly pleasant persons are known to turn vicious in the fray for an old man's money, his property".

"I think an ideal mistress is the answer, if there does exist such a creature".

"Wish you luck. My medical comment; the more you do sex, the more you can do it. And sex is the most powerful of all anti-depressants".

On that note we part. Harbans is getting late for dinner, with his extended family waiting.

I'm back from 18 holes of Sunday golf. Harbans and I won the bet of tea and snacks against our regular twosome. I played particularly well.

And wonder of wonders; on number 3 hole, the first short 3-par of 150 yards, I hit a shot that trickled into the hole. Finally, I'd realized the dream of every golfer, a hole-in-one. It was indeed a rare good shot with a 4-iron, my favourite club. That's the beauty of golf. An ordinary club-level golfer can sometimes hit a perfect shot—couldn't be bettered by the world's champion golfer. No other game allows a 75-year-old amateur a chance at such perfection. It could make him elated for days, even months.

Our caddies around the green set up a shout. The other three players thump my back. In due course it'll get me the momento, the trophy of a golf ball mounted on a silver stand.

"This is the only thing I can boast to my children and grandchildren gathered at my deathbed", I tell Harbans.

And then a rubber of winning bridge where I bid and make a smart little slam.

All this generates a mild euphoria. Back home, it's the usual Famous Grouse, tub bath, and dinner.

I casually mention to Rano to hurry up with the meal as I had a tiring day at golf.

She serves two lamb chops with boiled potatoes. For dessert, it's gajjar-ka-halwa, a favourite of mine. Preparing the same entails much work: scrapping carrots, shredding them, cooking in milk, adding cream, raisons and almonds.

She gives hint of a smile instead of the usual scowl when I compliment her on the tasty halwa.

I'm lounging in bed, watching English League soccer match between Manchester United and Arsenal, my favourite being MU.

Rano appears at the door.

"Sahib, can I give your legs an oil rub? Good for tired limbs".

And she's already holding a katori of olive oil in one hand, the oil she says, she warmed.

The offer is so novel, so unexpected. And yet enticing enough not to be refused.

"Thanks. That would be nice".

Rano spreads a bath towel over the bed sheet. And she starts an oil rub from the feet.

As is my norm, I'm wearing shorts and a sweatshirt for the night. And I don't change into anything else for the massage. Only the T-shirt will be pulled off if she reaches the torso.

Squatting on a side of the bed, that creaks with her weight, she gives my feet the best rub I ever had, massaging each toe, better than what my pedicurist does.

Rano proceeds beyond to the knees and above. She avoids touching the genitals.

She asks me to turn over and take off the shirt. Massages vigorously but soothingly the neck, shoulders and the back. Where did she learn it, or is it coming natural to her? Pushes a hand deep into my shorts, rubbing oil on the buttocks. All this time I keep my eyes closed. And there's no talk.

She bids me turn over on the back. Gives the chest and tummy a prolonged rub. Lubricates the belly button.

Then, all of a sudden, she jerks my shorts down and drains off the rise with her oily fist.

Thereafter, Rano goes out without a word.

There's no mention or hint of it from her for days to come. Only she eyes me a bit more benignly than before.

I have absolutely no intention of repeating the escapade, though I had enjoyed it immensely. Our relationship is too awkward for any sex play. Her body, anyway, evokes no real desire in me. I find fat women off-putting. And there's the fear of scandal. Her no-good son could blackmail me, even assault me.

CHAPTER 20

By mid-May, it's the start of scorching heat. Day temperatures are shooting up to 43–44. Wish, they had sited Chandigarh a bit higher and cooler, more like Dehradun.

The month also sees me getting involved in an affair as I approach my 76th year.

Where will it lead to? Well, it could turn out to be the classic case of a dirty old man making a fool of himself, if nothing worse—no such thing as a dirty old woman.

Gyan Kaur was second to Priti at the kindergarten. I had glimpses of her a few times when she came to meet Priti. And I did notice her prominent presence among the mourners at the house and at the cremation.

A month after Priti's death, Gyan comes to see me, accompanied by all the other four female teachers.

"We want to retain the school name, Pritam Kindergarten, the name of the founder", she says.

"I see no objection".

"Any conditions, like royalty payment?"

"No. You have it free. That should be in accord with Priti's wishes".

"Many thanks. I'll now run it with Pritam as my role model".

The women hold a mumbled conversation among themselves, while Rano is serving them mugs of tea and biscuits.

"The school has furniture, equipment, playthings, and books", says Gyan. "All these are the property of your deceased wife. What should I pay for it? I'm not rich".

"Maybe, a monthly sum as lease money. Details can be discussed after you draw up an inventory of the goods".

"A monthly payment would be most helpful", she says, giving a winsome smile, the parting lips revealing a pair of pearly teeth.

The women are all giggling as they depart. A big load seems to have lifted off their minds.

"I've got the inventory ready", Gyan rings up one morning in mid-April. Why the list-making took so much time, I haven't a clue.

"Let me look at it".

"I'm sending it through the school maid".

And she continues after a moment's pause, "How about coming to my place, combining discussion about inventory with a meal? Priti used to tell me, a favourite dish of yours was biryani with puth meat. You'll get the same".

"That's thoughtful of you".

"So it's dinner next Sunday. An early one. Please do come by eight".

"I'll be there".

Gyan is the widow of a Saini Sikh High Court lawyer. He died tragically 10 years back in a mini-bus accident. The man left her a substantial house in Sector 15, a brisk 15-minute walk from our place.

She lives alone on the first floor, with the ground portion rented out as an architect's office.

I'm the sole dinner guest. The hostess has another teacher to assist her, a young teacher in her twenties.

As is my wont, I have a drink and bath, even a shave, after a day at the golf course. With Banta gone, I drive out the Esteem. Don't feel like walking on that hot sticky evening when all the folded places in the body tending to stick together.

I ring her bell, the button of a bell.

She welcomes me to a pleasingly furnished room that combines sitting and dining. A formidable water-cooler is running at full blast.

Having seated me on the sofa chair, she offers a small glass of fresh pineapple juice, duly chilled. I'd have preferred alcohol but this comes as good as soft drinks go. Tells me she's happy with the tenancy, more so with the office closed by the evening and on holidays.

"Have you gone through the list I sent", she asks, proffering me a plate of *kathi kabab.*

"Yes".

"What royalty do you expect?"

"What sort are you contemplating?"

She hesitates, looks at the other teacher who'd remain mute during the whole evening, and says, "We can't afford more than rupees two thousand a month".

And she appears quite relieved when I reply, "That's OK with me. In fact we'd go on reducing lease money every year, as the goods wear out".

With the school business out of the way, Gyan begins to speak about herself and the family. An unmarried son is in London, working in hotel management with the Marriott group. The married daughter lives with her banker husband in Bombay. They have two kids, a boy and a girl.

Her main source of income is the house rent and earnings from the kindergarten school. Fixed deposits in a bank left by her husband yield a few thousand per year. Somehow he neglected to take out life insurance.

A graduate, she was just a housewife when her husband met his sudden end. This meant loneliness and depression, with a total loss of identity.

Through a common friend, she had approached Priti and was given a teaching job. Priti even helped her secure Montessori training. "I'll ever be grateful to your wife", she says. "Pity, she died. She was a perfect employer; compassionate, kindly, incredibly decent, the nicest person I've known".

The meal is savoury, not too spicy, not too greasy. The *puth biryani* is superb. She has cooked it herself, giving ample evidence of her competence in the culinary department. The rest is prepared by the maid, an old one who has been with the family for decades and lives on the premises.

The youngish teacher begs leave after the meal. She has a baby boy to attend to.

The talk now veers around to our widowed lives.

"I feel terribly lonely at times", she says, sipping tea. "The workday passes all right. It's the evening that hangs so heavy. How much TV can one watch?"

"What takes care of my evenings is whisky and book reading".

"Maybe, I should take to a daily drink".

"Not a bad idea. Taking red wine, you possibly help your heart too. I'd send you a couple of bottles to try it out".

"What about you?"

"For me, it's always Scotch. Had one today before starting out for dinner".

"I'll offer it when you come next".

"A nice thought".

By this time I'm looking at her more closely. She may have been in possession of meagre body resources, but at 48 (her date of birth found in school records with Priti), she could be surpassing her better-endowed contemporaries. Short in stature, shorter in the legs than torso, she retains a compact figure that hasn't been made flabby by child-rearing or overeating, yet no lack of meat on her bones. I harbour a particular weakness for small women. They make me feel strong and over-powering. Gyan has full rounded breasts that seem to have stayed firm. Skin smooth, remarkably smooth and saved of wrinkles. A sharp nose tipped nicely. Thin lips, the upper one with a hint of hair. Dark, well-spaced eyes. A thick mass of glistening uncut hair—a woman's crowning glory— reaching below her hips. Priti, in contrast, had a light crop, which in later years she henna-dyed but couldn't hide a thinning patch on top.

Gyan surely retains sex appeal.

They say, women come into themselves around their forties. It seems true in her case. The earlier era when women got physically worn out by fifty is evidently on the wane.

Time to go. I feel like giving her a parting hug as she stands alongside. Her hair smell of shampoo. Haven't smelt a female head for some time. I hold back from clasping her. Only touch her lightly on the shoulder.

Yet something has passed between us. We become aware of a shared desire, instinctively, wordlessly. When will this desire turn into a reality? A matter of time, I suppose; it has to happen sometimes.

Six weeks pass by without further communication between us. In my youth I'd have striven impatiently for a move. It seems, the older you get, the longer you could wait for things. A paradox indeed; with less time left, it should be the other way round.

Maybe, in youth I was never sure of getting what I wanted. Now it's a little more definite. Like a spider with a spun web, waiting patiently but attentively for the prey, one looks to an eventual catch.

Meantime I'm full of sexual cravings for her; picturing her nude, fantasizing about her in bed. Maybe she's having loving thoughts, too. But what's the point of having dirty thoughts separately—you've to have them together?

My reciprocating with a dinner invitation, with the eagle-eyed Rano in attendance, is out of the question. And I'm not sure whether we are intimate enough to ask her out to a restaurant.

Gyan rings up. "The school is having problems with the landlord", she says. "The greedy fellow threatens to evict us unless we double the rent".

Probably she wants me to waive off or reduce the lease installment. I'd easily accede to such a request, in pursuit of my designs on her body—promising mistress material. With the stepped up remittances from Ravi, I can afford to be generous.

"Could you come to my place this coming Sunday to sort out the crisis?" she asks. "I'll serve an early lunch. You'll have time to go for golf".

She's familiar with my routine. Yet she doesn't know that during the heat of June, we play only nine holes, starting around 4.30 pm.

I agree to be there by 12. Drive to her place, leaving a message for Banta I'd be back after lunch.

And I take along three bottles of red Merlot, the delectable French wine.

Since some years I've had a regular supplier of imported drinks; a fat Sardarji with one leg, the other lost in a motorcycle accident. He can deliver any drinks within a week of the asking—and genuine stuff at that. He got me twelve Merlot at Rs. 450 each, a reasonable price.

My main demand is for the Famous Grouse Scotch that he supplies at Rs. 1000 each for one-litre bottles. I mostly order a dozen at one time, a full, unopened carton. And I've come to like Famous Grouse. Premium whiskies, such as Chivas Regal or Black Label, may be smoother but of the non-premium brands, possibly none matches Famous Grouse in taste and mildness. Ravi and Noni, when they were here liked it, too. And they surely know what drinks are.

Gyan is alone in the house, clad in a low-neck blouse—I get a glimpse of the lacy bra beneath—and a cream-coloured cotton sari. The cook, she tells me, has gone on a month's leave to her place in Solan.

Wonder of wonders, she produces a chilled bottle of Kingfisher beer. I pour two thirds in my mug, the rest in her glass. She doesn't demur. The inch of cool froth feels fine to the lips.

It's a light meal of cucumber–pineapple salad, fried pomfret, and Kwality *kulfi*.

Gyan, I can make out, is hanging back from broaching the awkward subject of lease money.

"I've decided, you don't make any lease payments for the next six months. This should enable you to tide over the rent crisis".

"Many, many thanks. I'm so relieved", she exclaims. And impulsively takes my right hand into both of hers.

The meal over, she wants to show her family albums. We move to the bedroom that holds a shelf of albums. Her husband was an avid photographer. The room is delightfully cool with a window air-conditioner on.

Standing by her as she sits turning over an album, I get a grand view of her breasts. I lightly touch her hair. Bring my mouth near her ear. Lower a hand to her supple, wrinkle-free neck and collarbone.

That glass of bitter beer—her first, she said—must be softening her. Or, is the chilled brew actually warming her?

She strokes my hand. I lower it into her inviting cleavage. Slip it over one fatty rise. Encounter no resistance. That's bonanza for a breast man. I grasp one, I grasp the other. These are firm and smooth like large apples. I rub a nipple, at once taut, between the thumb and forefinger.

If you've the nipple, she's yours, they say.

Fervent embraces, fervent kisses, though she's avoiding eye contact. Hardly any conversation.

And then we tumble onto the bed, followed by a fast, feverish bout of sex.

In one afternoon I've gone from the first breast touch to the first kiss, and then all the way. Felt cheery.

I suppose men get an inkling of women's vulnerabilities. It is surely instinctual to them as predators.

What about Gyan? It must have been more than a decade since she had touched naked human flesh besides her own. Now she renews her familiarity with the nude male body, though one 76 years old. At forty-eight she refound sex and sampled an orgasm. Even if it never happened again, the experience would be worth it.

I give her a quick kiss and depart. The whole thing has happened too sudden, too fast. One needed time to ruminate on it.

To cap it all, I play satisfying golf that afternoon. Hit some excellent shots, long and straight. The best was the quiet laugh at our opponent, the Air Marshall, who took a mighty back swing at a crucial hole, in the process losing his balance and sending the ball deep into the bushes.

Harbans and I won with a wide margin, mainly on the strength of my performance. At a couple of places I chipped so smoothly, I came within 'gimme' distance.

Maybe, one plays better after a satisfying copulating act. Some say, this makes your eyes focus better and your nerves calmer—things so crucial to good golf.

I'm being drawn into a full-fledged love affair.

Virtues like dignity or fidelity get a go by, given the right stimulus. Maybe sublime conduct only exists in scriptures or in some novels. Do I have the forte for a regular affair; the needed vitality, the demanding secrecy, the gnawing preoccupation with it, and the constant threat of scandal?

It's come to a rendezvous almost every Sunday noon for lunch, followed by lovemaking. Post-lunch lovemaking suits me. I'm horny in the afternoon, not in late evenings.

Kissing. Playing with her ample breasts, sucking them. She shows me everything, lets me do everything. Her sexuality, presumably lying dormant for a decade, is bursting forth.

Gyan has now gone in for a shaven-smooth crotch and hairless armpits. That's evidently her idea of appearing more alluring. To me, the presence or the absence of pubic hair or armpit hair is acceptable either way—both situations have their plus and minus points.

I've decided not to comment on it. Let this remain entirely Gyan's business.

Yet I do take time to peer at it.

This strikes me as looking no different from that of a woman of twenty or of Priti's in her late sixties. Apparently a woman's face is a better indicator of her age than the nether parts.

Breasts are beautiful but the vagina is a wonder, tucked brilliantly and compactly between the legs, all folded up so neatly. And what an economy of nature! A relatively tiny area performs multiple functions; urination, menstruation, conception, birth, let alone lovemaking.

Gyan gets a finger-induced orgasm every time, sometimes twice—the second coming easier and quicker. My pleasure mainly lies in giving her pleasure. By now I have a map of her body by heart.

Gyan is seemingly getting a glow from sexual activity that's developing into a joyous necessity.

Sexual intimacy rarely remains restricted to episodes of sex. It commonly generates feelings of mutual attraction, regard, respect, and love. And this is what has been happening between the two of us.

We're fast coming closer. We revel in each other's company, look forward to being together. In fact I feel younger when I'm with her.

Gyan is efficient, practical, and inherently cheerful. She never utters an unpleasant word—a woman can easily put off a man with a mention of his weakness. Laughs a lot on my witty remarks, accompanied by hand clapping. Laughter is assumed as the first sign of sexual attraction.

Gyan is an excellent cook—a positive predicator of a happy marriage. The taste buds titillate the stomach, and the stomach is so near the heart. She's well-organized to be a hostess and could do better with encouragement and material aids. All in all, she's coming out an agreeable companion.

As foreseen and feared, our affair is now an open secret, despite every conceivable precaution we take to keep it under wrap.

Do people figure out just looking at couples whether they are doing it? Surely outsiders can't be privy to that secret intimacy between two persons.

Rano knows it, and her face is wrier than before.

Banta knows it, and laughs it off.

Gauri knows it, and doesn't seem to give a damn either way.

Harbans knows it, and welcomes it.

The golfing Air Marshall openly frowns on my behaviour.

The vet Sobti observes a stony silence. And he has sent Johnny back without asking me about it. That's all right with me. Johnny is again his cheery self in the familiar surroundings.

The tenant Ramesh finds it hard to hide his annoyance.

Aarti stays the same, if not friendlier.

Don't know how the thing reached Jogi. Maybe, he has an informant or two planted around me.

"What a pleasant surprise", I say, as he arrives unannounced one evening. "How about Girija and the girls? You had promised a family visit".

"I've come on an urgent meeting with Punjab officers. It's scheduled for tomorrow. I'd drive back after the business lunch".

Dinner over, we sit in the living room with coffee; he maintaining a glum expression, mostly looking at the sharp crease of his trousers.

"What will you prefer, a cognac or single malt Scotch? I've got a couple of great ones from Ravi".

With any luck, Jogi should soften up after a whisky.

"Single malt, if it's no bother".

I bring out an unopened bottle and two whisky crystal glasses.

Jogi volunteers to open it.

“Macallan 25-year-old! That’s rated as the world’s best”, he exclaims.

Jogi pours two generous measures. He disdains water or ice.

We lift our glasses to each other. There’s something pleasing about a whisky offer from one’s son—even when the whisky is yours.

Jogi is eerily silent for some moments, as if debating what to say.

“Dad, what are we hearing? An affair with a teacher in mother’s nursery school”.

“For curiosity sake, how you came to know of it, sitting in Delhi?” I ask, idly rotating the whisky glass under the light of the table lamp.

“These things have a way of getting out. As they say, murder can’t be hid”.

“I’m not murdering anybody”.

“Isn’t an affair sinful?”

“Who isn’t sinning these days? Take government. Prime minister Narsimha Rao and minister Buta Singh are convicted by a court for bribing MPs in a no-confidence vote. I’d say, everyone suffers some vulnerability, unless you happen to be Mahatma Gandhi”.

A beep on his cell phone. Jogi looks at the number and shuts it off. Maybe it's a call from one of his informants.

“Dad, have you slept with her?”

“That’s rather an impertinent question for a son to ask”.

“Sorry. But is it now a full-fledged affair?”

"Yes. I'm getting friendly as well as sexually involved with the widowed teacher. I'm still an active man. And if you think it implies an interest in women, you aren't wrong".

"How long has this been going on?"

"None of your business".

"Of course it is. I'm your son", he shouts.

"Please don't yell. I have many bodily afflictions but have not gone deaf".

Jogi mutters, "I'm not pleased. Not pleased one bit".

A sudden shower of rain—unseasonal rain—peppers the large bay window.

He's scowling into his whisky. Scowling and great whisky do not go together.

And continues, "Do I assume, you don't care about the scandal it's causing? People must be laughing at the spectre of a 76-year-old consorting with someone 28 years younger".

(How the hell he has come to know of Gyan's exact age?)

"My life's my own. Am well aware of what I'm doing. Hold myself answerable to no one. And that includes my sons and their wives", as I go for a little water to dilute my drink. "Possibly the worst thing about growing old is having to listen to a lot of advice from one's children".

"Dad, she could be a money grabber. May have an eye on the house. Your sons, I suppose, have a right to save you from risking your property".

"She has a goodly house of her own. Rest assured, as long as my mental faculties are intact, our house won't be disposed off without consulting you and Ravi".

"Rather cheeky of me to ask. Do you propose to marry her?"

"Till now the matter of marriage hasn't figured between the two of us".

"Is it likely?"

"I can't say anything definite at this point of time".

"But you'd be continuing the affair", I presume.

Jogi refuses a refill. He's clearly rattled.

His cell phone wakens up again.

"Can't you switch off the infernal thing when we're talking?" I ask in exasperation. I hate cell phones.

He complies reluctantly.

"Your presumption is correct. I'll continue the relationship, if the other party stays amenable, and no insurmountable complications crop up".

"In that event, marriage is inevitable. No woman is happy to stay ever as a midday bedmate".

(Jogi seems to know quite a lot about the affair, even the fact of our clandestine meetings during daytime.)

"Dad, think the whole thing over. Give yourself a year or two".

"A few more years, and I'd be dead".

No one speaks for some moments. Evidently both of us are running short on conversational gambits.

"How can you object to a situation which can only affect you for the better?" I say, having bitten off the dead skin of my thumb nail. "A marriage, while making me happy, will also free you from having to look after me when I start falling to bits".

"I and Girija won't mind looking after you. Dad, your problem, as I see, you're too much alone. A man can get into all sorts of trouble, being home alone all day".

"I expected more awareness from you of marital loneliness. You and Girija had postings at different places for years".

"Now, you're talking of a different generation".

Changing tack, I ask, "You think, in some way I'm disloyal to your mother?"

"No", he concedes, after an agonizing pause.

"Do you very much dislike Gyan?"

"I hardly know her".

"Every vibration of yours indicates you have no wish to understand her".

"We're afraid of losing you".

"Thanks for the sentiment. Now come on, freshen up your drink. It's great whisky. Better, take the bottle with you. Let Girija try some".

He pours himself a small measure.

"I respected the choice of brides my sons made. Can't they, in turn, extend me the same courtesy?"

Jogi just gives his shoulder a shrug, as if mate choice by the young fell in an altogether different category than that by the old geezers.

I can read Jogi as a pilot reads a chart. And I imagine, he thinks he can do the same with me.

Telephone rings. It's a call from Cranford.

"How are you, Dad?" asks Ravi.

"I'm fine. How's Noni? How's Viki?"

"Fine, too".

"Jogi's here. Came down today on official business".

"He told us, you're having an affair. Appeared terribly upset. Must be talking of it".

"You're absolutely right. He's grilling me on my indiscretion. Dubs me a dirty old man, without saying it in so many words".

"That's between you and him. But let me tell you one thing, you've a rock-solid supporter in Noni. To her, you're perfectly entitled to seek your own happiness. She has already mailed you a letter on the subject".

"What about you?"

"I welcome any development that brings cheer to your life, otherwise rendered a lonely life".

Jogi, listening, gains a fairly accurate gist of how the phone conversation is going. He makes a face registering disgust, as if to condemn a footloose father to his two one-woman sons.

"Let me tell you one thing", I say. "The affair with Gyan won't make me forget Priti. That would never happen. But it could save me from remembering her obsessively, depressively".

This doesn't register at all with Jogi. He looks at his watch: "Eleven already!"

"I had a tiring day", he says. "And I've to get up early for my morning jog". He takes the Macallan along.

Inwardly, I fear, the way anger shows on his face, he could well swing the bottle at my head.

CHAPTER 21

Jogi possibly awaits more information about the woman through his contacts. Maybe, he can hatch a scheme to scuttle the clandestine relationship. He can be quite ruthless in such matters.

He, however, knows that tackling his dad head-on could be counterproductive. It can put the old man's tail up. He's aware how stubborn the gaffer can be.

Jogi's main apprehension seems to be that once this woman—barely 5 years older to him—gets installed on the ground floor portion, it will be ages before the same gets vacated.

Ravi has another sort of misgivings. Will Jogi's fury against Father's contemplated remarriage take an ugly turn?

"I'm fearful of Father's wellbeing", he confides in Noni. "Once Mother had mentioned that Jogi seem to have an elephant's memory for the wrongs done to him, whether actual or perceived".

"We shouldn't worry unduly. Girija is sure to exercise a restraining influence on her husband".

"Hope so. Where property is involved, any family matter is bound to become more complex, more unreasonable. Jogi may be doing well financially but the windfall of property is something most alluring. And this he feels threatened with Gyan coming into the picture".

I find oral communication with Jogi rather trying. We could communicate better through correspondence. And for him it will be easier to tell lies, which isn't as easy talking face to face. Lying is quite an art, and he has been good at it.

The only subject on which we can converse congenially these days is golf. Jogi has recently shown interest in the game, taken it up in his accustomed serious manner. He likes to talk of golf.

Looking for support on the affair issue, Jogi doesn't find any at home.

"Grandpa stayed a widower for 40 years", he tells Girija. "Papa can't weather it for half a year".

Rather cheeky of Jogi to cite grandpa as an example to emulate, when the two were not even on speaking terms.

"Forget grandpa. Comparisons are odious", says Girija. "My views are clear. No interference from children in papa's personal and sexual matters. The man has seen enough of life to judge what's good for him and what's bad. And I can tell you, he's a cautious man. He does not take undue risks".

Seeing a smirk on Jogi's face, Girija goes on to say, "Be sensible, darling. What could be better for him? Why should he live a lonely life? People do prize happiness and love ahead of everything else. I'd say, it's illogical of you to be so resentful of the affair or of an eventual marriage".

"The woman would suck his money. She's a scheming bitch, out to steal our inheritance. She could make him change the will in her favour, notwithstanding the assurance given by dad. And then poison him. Or, simply wear him out with too much sex—assuming he can still get it up. She could even remarry on dad's death as a wealthy widow by then. At the very least she'll draw him away from us".

"Your fears may be unfounded. Give papa a few months of happiness and you'll benefit. You know how generous love makes one".

"And the woman is a Saini, a caste that find inclusion in the list of Scheduled Castes.

"Come on, one can't harp on such distinctions these days. Not you anyway, a part of the ministry whose main mandate is the welfare and uplift of Scheduled Castes".

"I'm most concerned about losing our house to this vulgar, manipulating woman, a woman as young as the man's sons. She could make him move to her own place, sell the big house, and pocket a colossal amount of money. Dad once mentioned casually of a realtor offering him 10 crores. I feel like wangling a posting in Chandigarh and living in that house itself to thwart her machinations".

"The very idea is preposterous. A Gujarat IAS will find it extremely hard to secure a suitable berth in Chandigarh. Anyway, I won't be going".

"That bitch is going to get us disinherited. I could have her bumped off".

"Why not get Dad bumped off before he changes his will?" Girija shouts back in disgust.

Later I learn that without informing me, Jogi called on Gyan.

"I am Jogindar, Sawrup's second son".

"I've heard of you", as she motions him to take a chair. She sits across on a stool, giving him a don't-mess-with-me stare.

"Care for a soft drink?" she asks.

"No, thanks".

A surge of unease begins building up between the two.

"I warn you, I'm too old to be lectured to", she says in a sharp tone.

Gyan has a good notion of the opposition Jogi is whipping up against the love affair. And she's in no way cowed down by him. Taken aback, Jogi mutters, "I haven't come to lecture. I'm just trying to understand".

"What's there to understand? Your dad and I have come to like each other". "That's nice", he says. And he gets up to leave, adding "Will be seeing you soon".

I had assumed that men understood men's weaknesses and concerns better than women. Men, anyway, had simpler motivations: work, money, ego, sex. And so I expected that female relatives and friends would show greater annoyance over the affair than their male counterparts.

It's coming out the opposite.

Maybe women aren't as laking in understanding of the companionship and sexual needs of older men as their menfolk.

Noni's letter arrives through Fed Express, along with a box of Godiva bittersweet chocolates and snapshots of helmeted Viki on horseback.

"Dear Papa,

Hope this finds you in excellent health and spirits.

How's the writing going? Keep up with it.

Jogi tells us you're into an affair with a 48-year-old widow of a Sikh lawyer. He's most worried she could trap you into marriage, make a grab for your property. And he wants us to use our influence in dissuading you from what he terms a "scandalous as well as a suicidal course".

Ravi tried to calm him down.

The two of us have been discussing the development, though we aren't privy to much of it.

Wish, you could confide in us.

We're sure the person you're consorting with must be a proper person, sincere and dignified, besides being physically attractive.

How about sending her photograph!

Here you see people living together, if they're so inclined, without the trappings of marriage. Back home public opinion does not easily brook this sort of co-habitation.

Papa, I have a proposal.

Suiting your convenience, come and stay with us for a month or so. Arrange that the lady leaves India at the same time on some pretext and comes to the US

Both of you could stay in our guest wing. If you're keen on greater privacy, we can easily get you an apartment or a hotel room nearby.

This will give the two of you an opportunity to be together all the time and to live freely, away from prying eyes. It would also give us a chance to get better acquainted with the lady.

In the light of the experience, the two of you could then decide whether it's matrimony or something else.

Frankly, we'd welcome an outcome where you get a wife or live-in companion who can give you company and care in advancing years. With such a presence, we'd be more at ease about your welfare; a bit selfish on our part, you could say.

With love from both of us and Viki.

Yours affectionately,

Noni

I write back.

It's sweet of you to think that at 76, I am still interesting to anybody in a sexual way.

A snapshot of Gyan is enclosed.

Thanks for your offer of playing host to us. Our coming there isn't likely in the near future. My relationship with Gyan hasn't reached that level of closeness.

Your invitation, however, has given me the idea; why not try a week in Simla?

Priti and I had honeymoon at Simla. Who knows, the proposed trip could turn out a precursor, a pre-honeymoon spree.

And I've your dollars—changed into stuff with Gandhi on it—to burn on an expensive holiday. Hope, you and Ravi won't mind such use or abuse of your remittances.

I show Gyan Noni's letter.

"What do you say to it?" I ask as she finishes reading.

Taking off her reading glasses, "You've got in them an admirable daughter-in-law and a gracious son. I'm not similarly blessed. My boy in London has been bombarding me with angry phone calls since he came to know of it. Says, I've disgraced myself, sullied his dead father's good name. Mercifully, the daughter in Bombay is supportive of me, and so also her husband".

"I think the London boy is getting too emotional, too charged up. He should pipe down in due time".

"It's so upsetting being raved at by one's own offspring".

"You're telling me! Jogi's doing something similar".

Gyan, pushing aside a thick strand of stray hair, "I don't care what my son says. I'll do what my heart tells me".

"The Cranford offer may not be practical at this juncture. But it has given me another idea. How about spending a week together, say in Simla? The place is gloriously sunny and green at the close of the rainy season. We share the same hotel room, check in as a couple?"

"That would be a drastic step. Let me think over it for a day or two", she murmurs, chewing her pretty lower lip.

"Sunday to Sunday at Cecil-Oberoi. I had my honeymoon at Clarke's. But that establishment is no longer top class. Oberoi is the place".

Gyan phones after two days.

"I'm willing to go along with your proposal. Indeed, I'd love it. But why not some faraway place, such as Darjeeling, where we run less risk of coming across people known to us?"

"No point being hush-hush about it, hiding like thieves. People who matter will anyway get to know of it".

"All right. Do as you deem fit".

"What about the second week of September?"

"It's OK with me".

Arrangements for the trip are made on the quiet. Harbans, however, has to be informed, I'd be missing golf.

"Taking the big leap! Best of luck", says he.

"A leap in the dark, and an expensive one at that".

"Living in close proximity for a week should make you understand each other better. Give you some idea of how the marital scene would look like. You aren't young to stay all engrossed in sexual activity. It affords you a chance to study the other party's habits, mannerisms, moods".

Harbans goes on to say, "Old age for serenity, old age for austerity! I think this is one of the great conspiracies of the youth. And it's a wider conspiracy because the old collude in the belief. The old sitting in rocking chairs and nodding; our revels are ended, fires gone out.

It pleases me that you are declining to play this game".

And I better inform my tenants. I'll be out for a week. They'd wonder what has happened to me.

So I hop up barefoot before dinner.

Aarti alone is home. Ramesh has gone to Delhi for brewery purchases.

"Just came to tell you, I'll be travelling to Simla tomorrow morning on a week's holiday".

"You eat here. It's lamb cutlets".

"Rano's waiting with the meal".

"I'll send her a word".

And she fishes out a beer bottle from the fridge.

"Already had my evening quota of whisky. But I can do with a glass of beer".

Pouring the chilled drink, she says, "You need a holiday badly. You haven't had one since the tragic event last December".

"No point hiding it from you. Gyan is coming with me".

"Oh!"

"What do you think of it?" I ask, lapping the frothy brew.

"A right move. To know each other better before entertaining thoughts of matrimony".

And gulping her cola as she rises for dinner, she says, "Unlike Ramesh, I've always taken your side in this affair".

"Thanks. As with Priti, you're like my daughter. And I can't visualize anyone better".

A near-new Toyota Corolla arrives with a seasoned Sikh driver; the idea of taking our own car and driver deemed too intrusive.

After breakfast, I pack. I'm good at packing from years of moving from one job to another.

I pick up Gyan from her place. She's ready with a large suitcase.

It's an enjoyable, unrushed, 107 km ride to Simla. We do it in four hours, with a leisurely break for lunch at Barog Hotel on the sunny lawn, sitting under a sunshade.

"Where does the name Barog come from?" I ask the youngish manager as he came to see us off. "It doesn't sound Indian".

"Mr Barog was the English engineer laying the rail track on this stretch of Kalka-Simla link. Due to a calculating error, the two ends of the long tunnel being dug from both sides into the hill here didn't align as expected. Barog shot himself dead for the miscalculation. The British named the high hill point in his memory".

Our Sardar Ji turns out to be a silent, competent guy. That's good. I don't fancy garrulous drivers.

At the hotel register, I sign as Mr and Mrs S. Singh. We are conducted to a spacious third-floor room, its wide window overlooking a pine covered hillside.

The five-star hotel sports an enormous high lobby, topped by a skylight. Our inviting double bed is mounted with a padded headrest. And there's the usual complement of a fresh-fruit basket and a vase of white lilies. One sees heavy teak tables and chairs, solid table lamps. The bathroom has a deep tub, two bathrobes, and pairs of slippers, half a dozen soft towels, and all sorts of soaps and shampoos.

Gyan is delighted with the room. Embraces me, the moment the door shuts behind us. And we fall on the broad springy bed.

It's an hour of relaxed sex.

After a longish bath, we are out for a walk on the Mall in the cool, breezy evening, followed by a drink at the hotel bar and dinner at the well-appointed dining room. On return, we find the bedspread pulled back, a chocolate on each pillow, a bowel of fresh fruit on the table, and two bottles of mineral water. What luxury, she exclaims.

The room offers the facility of watching porn movies. I feel tempted to see one—the same could boost our libido. But I desist, unsure of Gyan's reaction. She doesn't appear liberated enough in these matters.

Our holiday routine: sipping cups of morning tea, lazing about, making love. We go down for a late breakfast.

Everyday by noon we drive out. One day it's Naldera, another Chini Bungalow. A full day trip is made to Chail, with lunch at the Palace Hotel. Chail, with its heavily wooded hills and controlled build-up, continues to be a charming resort.

On two days we motor to the Wildflower Hall, a super luxury Oberoi Hotel but frightfully costly. It's so exclusive they don't allow outsiders for lunch. Our hotel manager had to intercede for us.

The Wildflower Hall, built for Lord Kitchner, the Commander-in-Chief, exudes a grand atmosphere of opulence. After a disastrous fire, it has been rebuilt. The location, sited on top of a hill, is breathtakingly beautiful. A classic dining room has been fashioned out of Burmese teakwood. Food is no better than our hotel's but doubly priced.

There's scant chance of our running into anyone known at this exotic establishment.

The Mall is somewhat of a disappointment. It's no longer as clean and orderly as I had seen on my honeymoon 50 years back. Too many small shops are vending snacks in place of former elegant restaurants. On the honeymoon, Priti and I used to walk hand in hand. Because of her pregnancy, I often kept a supportive hand on the small of her back. Gyan walks so slowly, hand-in-hand walking degenerates into almost dragging her along.

Our lovemaking is mostly before bath and breakfast. Her being 28 years younger is an unfailing source of sexual stimulus.

At night, with Priti, we'd start sleeping face to face, arms and legs entwined. Now when we get inside the light hotel blankets nude, Gyan usually has her back to me. I begin by rubbing my toes against the soles of her feet. She commonly responds by pushing her bum against my lap, till she finds the right fit.

I love the warm roundness of her body.

A new bedmate is akin to living in a different country.

During the day we are out. And when we return in the evening, at least I'm fagged out. I drink two large whiskies, having brought my own bottle of Macallan. Gyan has been persuaded to try it, duly diluted with water. And she has begun to relish it. We've another bath before going down for dinner, followed by watching TV in bed.

Returning after lunch on Sunday, we're back in Chandigarh before dusk. Gyan is dropped at her place. Rano gets busy cooking dinner.

End of a 'sample' honeymoon. A trial run that's gone well. No untoward incident, no jarring note.

CHAPTER 22

What is Gyan's side of the story?

We're back from the Simla trip.

Are we going to marry? The notion now figures uppermost in my thoughts.

Sawrup didn't propose marriage. In fact there was no discussion at all on the subject during the whole week-long holiday. He seemed to avoid it, and I hadn't the heart to broach it.

Sawrup behaved throughout the trip as if we were husband and wife. He signed me in as such in the hotel register. And there was no question of separate rooms.

He took leadership in ordering meals, calling for hotel services, and planning outings. Conceded, he sports a higher lifestyle and is more experienced in the ways of the world, yet he operated as if he was with a newly wedded wife.

And we were husband and wife in bed. He proved a practiced pleasure-giver, despite a certain diffidence in the penetration department.

What about his son's invitation to stay a month or so with them—a sort of trial marriage? It'd be luxurious living with the rich hosts. And I'd get a chance to see new countries.

With marriage I move to a better house, and a more affluent lifestyle. At the least it'll be a car and a driver.

The nursery school won't have to pay lease money for its furniture and equipment. We can actually shift the school itself to the ground floor of the house—a far superior accommodation to the one we're having, and rent-free. No more hassles of the landlord. The large compound would be ideal for kids to play. With the superior premises, the school can be expanded, upgraded, modernized, made to yield more money.

We can comfortably live on the first floor. It'll be much easier for me to supervise the work of the school.

What should be my strategy? To stay pleasing—agreeing with his views rather than differing. More hospitable—stocking quality food and drinks for his visits. And sexually alluring—taking greater care of my body and clothes. It's like being young again, without the hormonal uproar.

Rushing Sawrup into marriage may misfire. He seems a pretty determined character. Better if I leave it to him to propose. At 76, he's more pressed for time than I.

Don't know why, after the Simla trip, I daydream a lot, something rarely indulged before. I daydream even during school hours when alone.

And I keep going a lot over my past life.

Father was a central secretariat clerk in Delhi. We lived all the time in a two-roomed official quarter in Sarojini Nagar, said to be the biggest residential colony for babus.

Father was dictatorial at home; often angry, impatient. He kept complaining of ailments that were no more than chronic constipation and periodic headache.

Mother was a housewife, weak, ineffective. She did what her husband directed, never stood up to him.

I had an elder sister, beautiful, taller, and fairer than I. And she was smart in studies. Everybody doted on her. Eventually she married an officer of UP Civil Service, doing her parents proud.

I was deemed plain in comparison, 5 ft. 3 in., and what they termed as 'wheatish' in complexion. Weak in studies, I managed graduation in third division.

At 18, I fell in love with a neighbourhood youth, working as an assistant in a Bata shoe store. We did indulge in surreptitious petting and kissing at Nehru Park, but nothing beyond that.

Father came to know of it. He went into a towering rage. Arranged my marriage to a distant cousin, a Public Prosecutor at Chandigarh. Father always fancied a government official as a son-in-law.

I was a virgin on my bridal night. Within half an hour of our getting together, the strongly-built, bearded bridegroom deflowered me. And then Amrik snored away, relieved, drunk.

Things improved over the years. Amrik resigned as Prosecuting Officer. He took to private criminal practice. And did well. He worked really hard at it.

In time Amrik secured one marla plot in the popular Sector 15 and put up the present house, a fine double-storey house. I would have been nowhere without it.

Simran was born in the first year of marriage. Actually she was born on the very day of our marriage anniversary. By the time we'd finish with her birthday party, we were too fagged out to celebrate anything else.

Basant followed 2 years later. I suffered greatly at childbirth, both babies being caesarian.

I entreated Amrik to go for vasectomy as our family, I said, was complete, a girl and a boy. He refused pointblank. "It'll make me impotent", he shot back.

Whereas Simran helped in the house and was good at studies, Basant proved bothersome right from his early years. He must have got my father's temper and impatience. Basant could be very rough and rude at times. Grown tall and brawny, even Amrik was afraid to chastise him.

Simran got married nicely to a young man in the State Bank of India Service, a prestigious service. And Gopal, the ambitious husband, later resigned it for a better paid job at Bombay with a Dubai Bank. They have two kids, and it's a happy, well-off family.

Basant was labouring through his college when the tragedy struck. A dozen lawyers, including Amrik, had hired a tourist mini-coach for the 70 km outing to Kasauli for a day. On a sharp turn on the Kasauli incline, where some road works were in progress, the coach hit an unloaded truck rashly coming down, and rolled into a khud. Amrik and another lawyer died on the spot, two others dying in the hospital.

My world collapsed. In one day I had gone from the security of a well-set housewife to a grieving, helpless widow. People commiserated: I was still lucky. How much worse it would have been if I had to spend months, even years, nursing a terminally sick husband.

Luckily, Gopal using his business contacts, got Basant admitted to a hotel management course with Tatas in Bombay. And within 3 years, Basant moved to Marriott, London. He hopes to stay on there as long as he can, possibly for good. Finds London life more exciting. Says that at 26 he's too young to think of marrying.

Basant is here; the same fiercely-moustached, barrel-chested, hefty turbaned figure. He had come to Bombay on hotel business. And would be spending the weekend in Chandigarh before flying to London.

Basant has brought me a beautiful Waterford crystal flower vase and a Citizen's bed clock. The cordiality generated by his visit and the gifts soon fritters away when he begins haranguing me on what he calls the 'infamous affair'.

"Mama, I never expected such a thing from you", he scolds as he quaffs his one-litre jug of beer. "I'd have understood if Father had an affair but not you".

I don't respond; simply keep looking at the back of my hands with their prominent greenish veins.

"A man of 76 going on with a widow of 48. The whole thing is comic, farcical. People must be bursting their sides laughing".

I sit motionless, quiet.

His irritation level is rising. It brings on to me the image of my wrathful, raving father.

"Mama, I'm serious. What are your plans? Are you going to marry the geezer? Or, you just live with the old lecher as his mistress?"

"The question of marriage hasn't cropped up between us, not yet. And I'm living in my own house".

And I can't help flinging back, "Please do me a favour. Don't use abusive language against him".

Basant goes glum for a few moments, playing with his beard. And then he bursts out, "This can't go on".

"You'll be informed if there are any developments".

"You mean I've no say in your life?"

"We are adults. We're entitled to live our own lives".

"That's what Gopal and Simran keep mouthing parrot-like. I thought they'd be with me in dissuading you from this mad course. Gopal keeps repeating that what his mother-in-law does in her private life is not his business. To Simran, remarriage isn't such an atrocious idea".

I keep mum.

He downs a deep draught of beer. "Mama, do you realize, the man is 76. You could be a widow again in 4–5 years, or slaving all day to nurse an invalid".

"No one knows when one's time is up. Your father died before he was 50. Left me shattered. Now I don't plan too far; think no more than 2–3 years ahead. The older I get, the more I believe in luck".

"Once he dies, his sons will turn you out of that mansion in no time. The fellow in the IAS is said to be pretty powerful. At best you may get a bit of the old man's cash".

"I'm not after his mansion or his money".

"Sorry to be rude. Then what are you after? A 76-year-old body!"

"It's a question of friendship, admiration, love. What's age to do in these matters? Some men are old at 40, others young at 80".

He mumbles sarcastically, "I don't know what women want?"

"You wouldn't know", I counter. "It's the oldest riddle with men".

And on that note, we adjourn for dinner.

Next day at breakfast Basant brings up the topic again.

"What about my seeing the gentleman! Someone who could become my father. Someone to whom I give away my mother as a bride. I'm curious how he looks".

"Not a felicitous idea. You've no control over your temper and your tongue. Human relations are best conducted courteously. In any case, bad words are like eggs dropped from a height. These create nothing but a mess".

"I promise, I'll not say or do anything hurtful".

"Don't know. Possibly no good would come out of it".

I ring up Sawrup. "Basant from London is here for the weekend. Has expressed a wish to see you".

"You mean the bitterest opponent to our relationship".

"Yes, the same one. But he has given a solemn undertaking, he won't say or do anything nasty".

Nearly a minute's silence at the other end.

"All right, as you wish. But he has to come with you, not alone".

"Sure. Thanks".

"Come this evening around 7.30 for a drink. I'll be back from golf".

Swarup escorted Basant and me into his study. Johnny, who gives his study room a go-by, sneaks in as if sensing that the big, burly newcomer was dangerous. I and Basant are with him for half an hour, sitting in his study. It's Famous Grouse for Basant and a glass of red Merlot for me. Rano's hovering in the background after providing us with a plate of cashew nuts.

We exchange pleasantries. He asks Basant about his job and future plans. And he talks about his own sons, the one in the US and the other in Delhi.

He sees us off to our rented car.

"Rather sprightly for someone 76", concedes Basant. "And dressed in natty clothes".

"That's his golfing gear. Golfers, young and old, put on colourful trousers and stylish sport shirts. Gives them a semblance of youth, he tells me". "He appears fairly well-informed".

"Yes, he's a man of wide experience, held high government jobs—and now a novelist".

"Has at least an impressive collection of books".

Good that we went to meet Sawrup. I'm feeling a little easier with Basant, though he can be very temperamental. Meeting people face to face wears down some prejudice.

In whom can I confide, seek advice if not support, about my situation? I've been more of a loner, with no real friend, no confidant. Sawrup says he's a loner too. Whether two lonely people coming together would add to that loneliness, or do they cancel each other's loneliness?

I used to share some confidences with Kanwar, my youngest sister-in-law in town. She now avoids meeting me or talking to me on one pretext or the other. Presumably, since the scandal broke out, her husband has forbidden her to have any connection with me.

The only other person in whom I can confide is Simran, and she lives in Bombay.

On an impulse, I ring her up.

"Simran, Gyan calling. How're Rati and Rohan?"

"Fine. Basant was here. Raving at you for what he terms 'scandalous affair'. Gopal asked him to take it easy. But he was in no mood to listen".

"I had a full blast of his fury. But he calmed a bit after meeting Sawrup. Simran, why don't you come for few days. We have to talk a lot. You can also meet Sawrup".

Simran answers after a pause, as if consulting Gopal, "I'm keen to see Sawrup. But, Mamma, I can't come. Kids have their school. You better be here. Gopal will be in Delhi on bank's business next Monday. He'll arrange for your air travel to Delhi and then onward with him on flight to Bombay".

I and Simran talk for hours. I tell her all I know about Sawrup, and my Simla experience.

"Mamma. Don't be bullied down by Basant. Do what your heart tells you. I, for one, would favour remarriage. And, by all accounts, Sawrup seems a good choice".

"But he's 76".

"A younger one would have been better. But it's still a welcome break for you. If I'm permitted to ask, how does it work—I mean, in bed?"

"Can't be the same as with a younger man. Yet working alright; he's experienced and considerate".

"Good".

"Sex side doesn't bother me. It's about getting along. Sawrup is into writing books, novels. Writers are said to be stubborn people with fixed habits and ways of life. I'd have to make all the adjustments to keep the marriage going".

As Rati the 9-year-old saunters in, Simran tells her to go play in the other room.

"Mamma, you shouldn't worry unduly on that score. With his age, he's bound to become more and more dependent on you, increasingly interested in keeping you in good humour".

"You advocate my marrying him?"

"I and Gopal have been debating it for days. The marriage will give you a new phase of life, a livelier life. We both favour the relationship, as long as it is primed for marriage, not sex alone".

"It's not all in my hands. But your support is heartening".

"We'll see Sawrup when we come to Chandigarh during the Christmas–New Year break".

"I'm sure, it'd help".

What a day it was that saw the start of dalliance between me and Sawrup! After lunch when he stood up close, his face was hardly 3–4 inches from mine. I could move away, yet it felt good, very good to be so near him—a comfortable cushion of flesh. Reminded me of Amrik.

Since Amrik died, I haven't touched a male body sensually. A total of four married men—not a single unmarried or widowed—did make overtures during these 10 years, including a close relative. Such advances were clearly from lust than love. None evoked any interest in me. Actually one of them, a cousin, generated revulsion in me with his crude importuning.

The most persistent pursuer has been the neighbour across, a middle-aged fat Sikh with a doctor-wife and three teenage daughters. A journalist, he mostly works from home while the female inmates are out at the hospital or school. He makes free with gestures, chits through servants, and the occasional gift of a perfume bottle—that I refuse to accept. If he doesn't desist in his unwanted overtures, I've no option but to talk to his wife, a doughty female from the looks of her.

Of late, he's making fewer advances. He must have learnt of my liaison with Sawrup. I, however, harbour an apprehension that he, angry with his rejection, may create trouble; incite locals against us.

"The fat journalist living across seems to be mounting a near obtrusive watch on your visits, the time you come and the time you depart", I tell Sawrup one day.

"Bastard".

"I fear he might collect neighbours and gherao the house when you're here".

"Most unlikely. He won't dare it".

But since then Sawrup often leaves his car near a corner shop. And we have started varying our get-together, sometimes on Saturdays, or even on a working day.

Many a time I ask myself: What do I want? What do I desire in life?

Surely I want to feel young again. It's no fun getting old. And I want love. I want sex. I'm menopausal and nearing 50, yet I'd want a sexual partner. I fee, I'm still in possession of passable libido.

Indeed I had my first orgasm in my 50th year. It was a finger-induced fun manipulated by Sawrup that sent ecstatic shudders into my body. And since then there have been quite a few repetitions of the same. I do really enjoy his making love with me; so unhurried, so full of fondness, and so gently.

Do I want to marry Sawrup? Is he the sort of guy who will turn out exactly as I take him to be? A guy who comes home when he says he'll come. A guy I'd be happy to live with from day to day.

Should I agree if he asks for my hand? Or, even propel him towards a proposal? Will I be happier as a wife than living independently on my own? Will I be happier in my house—and in my own bed—than putting up in his mansion?

One thing is certain. The relationship with him has already yielded me much happiness. It brought fun and joy into a boring existence. At one time I imagined my sex life had wound up before 40 with the death of Amrik.

And it has made me take extra care of my looks. I dress better. I visit a beauty parlour every month for a facial, pedicure, and manicure. I'm also getting my leg hair waxed.

I pay more attention to food preparations and the upkeep of the house. An occasional alcoholic drink lightens my mood. And I had a glorious holiday in Simla, let alone the gift of emerald earrings and a Tissot wristwatch.

In a way my life stands transformed. There is the weekly get-together to look forward to. How I wait for his gentlemanly bell-ring! His visits mean lively conversation and consummate sexual activity.

And I couldn't have done without his generous financial support in running the nursery school.

What I like most about him is his jovial temperament and propensity to banter. He makes me laugh a lot.

The other day he said, "I hope you'd keep on asking me to lunch. It's the only decent meal I eat".

To which I had to retort, "Nobody gets a paunch like yours on a starvation diet".

And we laughed and laughed.

Yet this affair has extracted its own price. Amrik's three younger brothers and their wives have virtually boycotted me, cut off all contacts. Guddi, the wife of the eldest, is openly hurling accusations that my brazenly immoral behaviour could be the ruin of a good match for her teenage daughter.

Neighbours and many others are avoiding me, a manifest show of their disapproval. Even a few parents have withdrawn their wards from our school. One mother has been telling people that the head teacher's conduct can be a bad influence on her daughter—a girl of four. Another one dared to accost me with, "You should be ashamed of yourself".

Chandigarh, that way, is a place with small-town mentality. Wish one could enjoy the anonymity of a big city like Delhi or Bombay.

As yet Sawrup hasn't proposed marriage. That way, men seem to control their destinies. Women only help, organize, support, often doing so to escape their solitary existence.

At times, I feel the present state of relationship is possibly more suited to both of us than marriage—a lunch every week with its pleasing atmosphere and animated talk, followed by sexual activity.

Living together in Simla, I did find him somewhat bossy. He expected his views to prevail—I wouldn't say, to be enforced—on most day-to-day matters: what to eat, where to eat, what to drink, where to go, even advising me what to wear. He instructed me in the technique of tub bathing. Behaved a bit impatient when I took time getting ready.

Of course, he was playing the host. But it came down to more of an overpowering presence.

He made me walk more than I was inclined. He's a golfer. My feet begin to hurt over any long walk. Straightway he ascribed it to faulty footwear. Bought me an expensive Adidas canvas pair and Footjoy golf socks to go with. It did help but frankly, I'm not enamoured of walking in hill stations or elsewhere.

Sawrup, with his greater experience of the world, is bound to dominate me. Priti was different. She knew much about the world without having experienced it. In fact, she appeared to be the dominant partner.

At times I think I'd like to live my life the way I've been living. To do what I want, and the way I want, even if it means a smaller, less pretentious house and frugal existence.

Yet I don't rule out marriage to him.

A live-in without marriage is anyway unthinkable in our conditions.

Meantime, he can take me on holidays. Shower gifts on me, spend money on me. Enable me to enjoy his company. The idea of being together in the US for a month doesn't fail to excite me.

CHAPTER 23

It has been four months since Gyan and I became lovers. The tally till now is a dozen assignations at her place, topped by a week of living together in a Simla hotel.

Where does one go from here? That's the question I often ask myself. Has it to culminate in marriage? Or, can we go on like this?

One thing is evident; the affair has enlivened my life, diminished my loneliness, helped me fight depression, and kept my sexual side ticking.

On the debit side there's some unpleasantness in the family, more so with Jogi. And quite a few others tend to treat me a social pariah, or even a laughing stock. I can do without those people's company, but their ridicule does hurt.

As far as the morality issue, I've no regrets whatsoever. Maybe, I've grown amoral in such matters.

I suppose Gyan will eventually agree to a marriage if I propose. But will we be happier married? For myself, I can't reply in the affirmative with any confidence. One thing, however, is certain: that Gyan can't be a full replacement for Priti. To that extent I must keep my expectations low.

Marriage at my age is too complex an issue for an easy answer. Normally, widowers here don't marry in their 70s, not even in their 60s. I could have well masqueraded as a man of 60 instead of 76. But my exact age is too well known. The publicity of the 50th marriage anniversary has been there and so also the known age of a government official.

Today is Diwali. We are into woollen clothing and chilly nights.

Priti used to celebrate the festival of lights with zeal. She'd buy hundreds of earthen diyas (preferred diyas to candles or strings of tiny coloured bulbs). Presents were sent and presents received. The house would be chockfull of sweets and dry fruit. Scores of greeting cards were sent out. The ones received crowded tables and shelves for days beyond Diwali. To me, this prolonged card display looked like overdoing, with cards often losing their precarious perch.

This Diwali I send no cards, no gifts. And it's only 50 diyas put up half-heartedly by Rano. Luckily the roof of the house is aglow with lights, courtesy tenants.

Aarti has invited me to dinner. Yet, without Priti, it will remain a hollow Diwali dinner.

I miss Priti everyday: her supportive companionship, her humour, and her commonsense approach to living. I didn't mind her critical remarks; she meant to make me perfect.

At times I feel I didn't take enough interest in Priti's happiness. Maybe I remained too wrapped up in myself.

We may have made love a few thousand times in 50 years, and mostly with mutual pleasure. We came to understand each other's desires and inclinations. Yet, I may not have put my best in the non-bed side of the relationship. Didn't give requisite attention to her pursuits, such as the school and the garden; a bit unfair to her.

By and large, she accommodated, not me.

Over the married years, especially after my retirement from service, Priti gained in maturity and influence vis-à-vis me. And she learnt to overlook my funny gestures, questionable opinions, even rude actions.

I had come to accept her superiority—without hostility or anger. She had more balanced answers to everyday issues and problems. I'd say, we constituted a good combination; she, hard-headed, and me, daydreaming.

She had slid into middle age smoothly, gracefully, keeping herself physically desirable. Indeed, her body never failed to arouse me.

Yet I seem to have escaped the feared degeneration into an intolerable existence consequent on her demise.

I'm into an acceptable daily routine: some writing and reading, golf, bridge, drink, and television. Noni is right, the challenge of writing a novel does occupy my mind. I get up every morning with some purpose in view.

Work is going apace on the second novel. The first one is scheduled for publication in December. It has reached the stage of proof correction.

The other evening, I met a known Punjabi novelist at a dinner with Harbans. A dignified grey-bearded sardar of 70 discussed what I was writing.

"Why don't you write in Punjabi?. Why you people always write in English?" he queried.

"English is the only language in which I am proficient".

"You can write in simple Punjabi. That is your mother tongue".

"I can try, but the subject of my writing is not rural India like the one in your novels".

"Alright. Better get your novel translated into Punjabi. I can introduce you to my publisher".

"Thanks. That's a good idea", I say. "I'll send you a copy of my novel when it is published".

The new-found success in fiction-writing is making me a little more comfortable with my life, a little more tolerant of others.

Planning the Sunday noon rendezvous with Gyan—the way an athlete prepares for the race—adds zest to life. Only in the later part of the evening, the absence of an agreeable companion brings on a shade of depression. I long for someone to talk to at nightfall, go to bed with someone beside.

How different things would have been if Priti was alive?

Can Gyan fill up that void? I'm not so sure. Priti was a very superior person, superior to Gyan, even superior to me. I may have better sense of world history but she had much sounder sense about the business of living, backed by determination and willpower.

During the week stay in Simla I came to know Gyan better, her strengths and her weaknesses. She's energetic, ambitious, and good-hearted. Possesses a practical bent of mind; a perceptive woman with a fair share of feminine intuition. She's a competent cook and fond of good food. She has started taking more interest in books. I already discern an improvement in her English vocabulary.

But then Gyan can be needlessly irritating. She can take almost half an hour of washing and cleaning to get ready for the night. Waiting impatiently in bed, it did annoy me a bit. She has actually not much sense of time. Can easily be late for an outing or appointment, while I'm a stickler for punctuality or stipulated time—a lifelong habit from waiting on high-ups in service.

I had read somewhere that chronic lateness is a planned affair—something passive–aggressive. I doubt whether Gyan's lateness falls in that category, as something planned. It just happens. And my obsessive punctuality could also denote insecurity. I better learn to be tolerant of occasional unpunctuality in others.

Both I and Priti were avid walkers. She walked briskly. She kept pace with me. Many quality companionship hours were built around walks, starting with long hikes during the honeymoon—and mind, she was five months' pregnant. Gyan, by contrast, has to be virtually dragged along, and this was no fun at Simla.

Pasho's son Sajjan and his wife have come to see me, to offer condolences for the death of Priti and father. They are on their way from the UK to Amritsar, their return to India delayed by several months.

Sajjan promises to relieve Pasho to be with me. It seems they haven't heard anything about the Gyan affair.

And lo, Pasho arrives within a week, unannounced, lugging a bulky battered bag on a cyclerickshaw.

"Pasho, why didn't you ring up or write? Banta would have received you at the bus stand".

"I'm accustomed to riding rickshaws".

Pasho settles herself in the spare room as if on a long haul.

Here's a person who makes few demands. She's good and solid, like the daily chappati.

"Pasho, you run the kitchen. Handle all connected chores. I'd give you rupees ten thousand at the outset every month, to be replenished if you go short".

"Five thousand should be enough".

"Let's see how it goes. Don't worry unduly about money; there's enough going".

I'm certain Pasho will operate economically. Already, you see her switching off any light that's not strictly necessary. Hope she doesn't behave too tight-fisted so as to bring down the standard of food set up by Priti, or come too hard on Rano for food pilferage.

Pasho, it appears, hasn't heard of my affair. A bit hard to believe but it seems true. I'm sure, this state of innocence won't last a day or two. If nobody else, Rano would put her wise. And that's what happens.

"What do I hear about this woman Gyan?" she asks next evening as we finish dinner, a satisfying dinner with roast lamb, *dal makhani*, and fruit cream.

No point asking her about the source of her information; it is obvious.

"Yes, it's true. I'm involved with the Saini widow".

"You don't have Priti now to keep you in line. Never a whisper of scandal when she was alive".

"You have a point, Pasho".

"So soon after Priti's death! One shouldn't make a move for at least 2 years after losing a loved one. You need that much of time to make up your mind".

"I'm not getting younger. Crossed 76. Haven't got a lot of time left".

Next day she brings up the topic again. "Sucha is fuming. It's outrageous, he says, his elderly brother cavorting with a woman some 30 years younger. He's now with his son in Chandigarh but proclaims loudly his disinclination to see you".

"You know how quickly our younger brother flares up, insults everybody. He's hysteric, exaggerates everything. Let's go tomorrow evening to their place. I'd like to remain at least on speaking terms with him. And I like Satwant, his politician son".

"Will you be marrying this woman? You can be frank with me".

"Pasho, we haven't discussed marriage so far".

"You mean, she'll keep on sleeping with you as a mistress?"

"She has been doing so till now".

"I better return to Amritsar", she says and stands up as if going away that very moment. "My being here may make her think, you don't want marriage; you've got someone to run the household".

"Sit down, Pasho", I say, catching her thick forearm to make her sit back on her chair. "Relax. Our marriage decision would have nothing to do with your presence. We have to think of many other things".

And I continue, "Pasho, don't do anything in a rush. You're a great help and company to me. You've brought cheer to the house. I'm ever grateful to you. We've always been loving brother and sister. With Priti gone, we're also fast friends".

"I want to see her. Talk to her. Tell her my stay here is very, very, temporary".

I suppose, a woman can sense the level of sexual activity in another woman. And possibly feels it more if she herself is bereft of male companionship.

"You can tell her whatever you like. I'll invite Gyan to dinner for the coming Saturday".

The call on my younger brother doesn't go too badly. Pity, his son, as usual, is out touring villages. I enjoy discussing politics with him.

Sucha starts sarcastic, "I was a widower at 49. Didn't remarry or seek a mistress. You're past 76. And you had a matchless mate in Priti, an incomparable lady".

He talks as if Priti is still alive.

"Shows that in character, I'm weaker than you. I claim no moral moorings. And I do concede, sex could disorder our normally-led elderly lives. Is it not strange that desire should so many years outlive performance? Shakespeare says that somewhere".

"Why quote Shakespeare? I know, you'll do exactly what suits you. And such show of insouciance while indulging in crass behaviour".

"Don't we all do what suits us or what life decrees for us? Someone has said that if fate changes horses, riders ride along".

"That woman is after your money, your house", he whines, bouncing on the poorly-padded bones of his bottom.

"Maybe some money. It's mostly Ravi's money. And he tells me he isn't bothered how and where it goes. As to the house, I've promised my sons I'll do nothing without consulting them".

"Are you sure the woman is not after your property?" he shrieks.

"How can one be sure unless you're Muhammad Ali".

"Bhai Sahib, you don't admit. But your behaviour is most disreputable, even embarrassing to your relatives. People mock me for it".

Sucha took a doubtful-looking bit of cloth from his pullover pocket and began mopping sweat on his brow. He's essentially an unhappy man. Possibly finds unhappiness where none exists. The man's so frail, so sensitive to weather change, Pasho was once led to remark, "He never should have left his mother's womb—a wonderfully safe place, a perfect environment". He had been nicknamed 'Rondu' (cry baby) when small; he cried so much.

"I can only say, I'm genuinely sorry if my conduct has caused you embarrassment. But do visit us, now that you're in Chandigarh. If not me, at least come to meet Pasho".

Sucha made a studied attempt to conceal his disapproval.

"I'll come", he mumbles.

Sucha appears somewhat mollified with my abject apology. He had been anticipating a harsh exchange of words.

We rise to depart. Pasho heaves herself up from the white plastic chair—a chair made from a few ounces of plastic but bearing bravely a mound of flesh.

The only little problem with Sucha's visits: Johnny seems to have taken a distinct dislike to him. Growls at seeing him come. It's a bit disquieting for Sucha to have earned the disapproval of a well-behaved dog.

The dinner evening with Gyan goes off better than I anticipated. The two women, both widowed at forty; Pasho from a rail accident, Gyan from a road accident, have a lot to talk to each other. Pasho takes pains to reiterate she's here for a very short spell. She has to be back soon in Amritsar.

As Banta drives Gyan back to her place, Pasho rubbing a hand over her portly belly in the aftermath of a hearty meal, can't help remarking, "No patch on Priti. But she seems a sensible person. May make a good wife".

"Marriage is too important a decision. I won't be making it in a hurry".

Yet many an important decision in life gets taken viscerally, not rationally.

CHAPTER 24

December 25, 2000.

It's exactly a year since Priti died.

They say that time seems to go faster, years rush by, as one grows older. Is it because the young ones' days are packed with activity and excitement? Or, is it because as one grows older, a year becomes a smaller and smaller fraction of one's life?

For me the hours and minutes don't appear to pass more quickly—they are the same as they always were. At least they seem so to me in my seventies. Actually, hours and minutes still seem excruciatingly long when I'm bored or depressed—an exaggerated consciousness of time.

Noni confirms, they'd be in Chandigarh during the Xmas break—a year since they came last. Ravi is also entering into collaboration with an Indian software company in Bangalore and would be visiting them.

The same day I write to Jogi. "Why don't you all come to Chandigarh when Ravi is here? A family reunion!"

"Capital idea", he rings back. "We'll reach on the 23rd evening along with Ravi and return along with them on the 31st morning".

Aarti, learning of it, volunteers to put up one couple.

"Thanks. The two sons have their allotted rooms. Children can sleep in the living room. They'd possibly enjoy being together".

While Ravi's room-allotment is symbolic, Jogi always keeps some of his stuff here as if staking his claim to the house.

"At least, keep one dinner date for us", say Aarti.

"Sure".

On the next noon rendezvous, I tell Gyan of the impending arrivals. She's keen to meet them, especially the US contingent.

"They must have a lunch or dinner with me".

"Don't undertake that bother. You join us at meals, not once, but as many times as you can".

Harbans, whom I meet almost on a daily basis, can't do without asking, "What's the idea? Will you make up your mind about marriage with Gyan before your sons and daughters-in-law arrive, and face them with your decision? Or, do you throw it open for discussion to them?"

"Marriage will be entirely my decision, springing from my inner self. I won't link it with this visit. Surely the subject is bound to surface up. I'll hear what they have to say."

"I suppose that's a sound basis to proceed. The world is learning to recognize the rights of adolescents and the rights of women. But it hardly lets an old widower live out his life of choice, more so if he's rich or owns coveted property".

"To Jogi, my opting for a second wife would be a rank selfish act with no deference to my descendants. He sees it simply as the case of an old man going for his gratification, in total disregard of the family honour and preservation of its property. Jogi obviously apprehends that a new claimant, one more player in the shape of a wife in her fifties, is bound to mess up his inheritance prospects despite my repeated assurances to the contrary".

"Jogi's a greedy character. But you don't have to bother too much about him".

"Jogi's worst fear is that I may sell the big house, pocket the money, and move to Gyan's place. Generous people like Ravi, I suppose, believe others would be similarly generous. Selfish ones like Jogi see selfishness in everyone else".

"That would serve Jogi right".

Everybody's here. Priti would have loved such a family gathering. She revelled in family reunions.

Today is her death anniversary—and our marriage anniversary. The day has turned out rainy, windy, and bitterly cold. Last year it was sunny and warm, a day that would have proved perfect for the scheduled anniversary party.

Jogi moots the idea of holding the traditional barsi function, marking a year of Priti's death.

"We did away with the more imperative chautha. The same approach goes for the ritual of barsi", I say.

In her memory, however, we all go to Sector 15 gurudwara, the one Priti patronized. She'd walk to it every Sunday morning, a brisk 20-minute walk. Ravi donated rupees 30,000 in her name.

This is Viki's first visit to a gurudwara. He's intrigued to see the big book kept wrapped in silks and handled so reverently. Even a whisk used over it as if to deter flies.

Mala and Lovely are immaculately behaved; discrete enough not to make much mention of Priti to me. Maybe, they have been tutored accordingly by Girija. But Viki can't be stopped from talking of his grandma, the one who gifted him the yellow Porsche. He's at a stage where he weaves all sorts of imaginary stories; his being received at the airport, his driving away in a Rolls, with driver, in the backseat, his watching a road accident, and so on.

Pasho, seeing Viki hanging by Johnny's neck, is alarmed. "Don't. Johnny isn't trained for it".

"No dog bites me. Not scared of dogs. Am a big boy".

Noni doesn't intervene either way. Shrugs it off as a harmless, childish caper.

After dinner the adults collect in my study. Only Pasho stays busy winding up the kitchen. Ravi opens a bottle of vintage port. And people peer at Gyan's photo on my desk, dwarfed by a larger one of Priti.

Noni, handing everyone a glass of port, "Here's to Dad, a good mate to mother".

"Not as good as I should have been".

Everybody raising glasses: "To Dad",

"Father's last words to me, 'Look after Priti'. I'm not sure how well I complied with his dying wish. Maybe, I'll say the same to Ravi or Jogi whoever happens to be at my deathbed, 'Look after Noni' or 'Look after Girija', though I'm aware the two feisty ladies would manage quite competently without the benefit of those last words".

"Talk of pleasant things, Papa", cuts in Girija. "When do we see the lady?"

"She's keen to meet you all. Wanted you for a meal. I can ask her to join at dinner tomorrow".

"But where does the relationship stand?" calls out Jogi, sipping his port. "Shouldn't we know something of it beforehand?"

"If you mean marriage, the topic hasn't yet cropped up between the two of us".

"But what are your plans?" he persists. "That should be fairly simple by now".

"I don't think anything important is ever simple. I'm giving myself a minimum of 4 to 6 months more before deciding".

"By then you'd be 77. Time is not on your side, Papa", butts in Noni laughing, the wine goblet held in her painted nails. "Life is for living, not for ruminating".

"I don't see the need of a rush", says Ravi, as he gives everyone a refill. "Things here seem to be ticking pretty smoothly".

"Folks, hold on your comments till you meet the lady. Noni and Girija should spend more time with her. Women are supposed to be shrewder, more perceptive in judging other women".

"A union of two older persons may not have the same excitement as between the young. Yet I'm excited. It'd be fun participating, even if Papa insists on keeping the ceremonies low key", says Noni.

"You must admit Dad's brilliance", says Ravi. "I read somewhere that for older men, to find their perfect partner, you had to halve your age, and then add 10 years. By that reckoning, Dad's ideal mate would 48; 38 plus 10. Gyan's exactly 48, the optimum age".

"Counting chicken before they're hatched", quips Girija. "You can't easily figure out Dad's response to marriage, assuming the lady's willing. He's not the one to be hustled into a hasty decision".

"Dad's problem as I understand; he had in Priti an extraordinary wife. He just can't help making comparisons", says Ravi, gulping his drink and getting up.

The family dinner with Gyan present goes off agreeably. Noni plays the trick of plying everyone with plenty of Rhenish red wine, backed by Pasho producing a quality meal. After all, Pasho has run a restaurant. With two-three glasses of wine each, tongues get loose, jokes fly across, not a few contributed by me.

And I'm playing an active, almost an exaggerated role as a host, overseeing everybody's getting enough, calling Rano for more. "We can manage, Dad" says Ravi. "You weren't known for table assistance. Always others did for you".

"But then someone was there for it".

Gyan, clad in a pinkish silk salwar and kameez, is fetching. Presumably, she feels wonderful in her new dress—feels as floating and feminine as the dress. She looks far younger than her years. And wine has flushed her face.

In the beginning, she showed some awkwardness but soon relaxed in jolly company.

I notice that Pasho, sitting next, has a bit of fruit cream sticking to her kurta front. But you can't touch a lady's breast in the presence of others, even when she happens to be your 70-year-old sister. I even desist from drawing her attention to it.

After dinner men go into the study for cognac. Women remain seated at the dining table itself, quaffing tea, nibbling chocolates, and carrying on conversation.

Only around 11 when Gyan expresses a desire to leave, Banta, accompanied by Noni and Girija, drops her at her place.

"Come in", she invites them.

"Some other day", they say. "It's already late".

Seven enjoyable days fly by. Ravi and Noni go to Bangalore for a day, while Viki stays behind.

All of us make a trip by road to Amritsar. Noni, and so also the children, haven't seen the Golden Temple. Viki keeps exclaiming as he walked the prakarma: "So much marble, so white, so clean".

We partake of roti, dal, and sabzi at the gurudwara's langar.

And then we visit our old house where Ravi and Jogi had grown up.

Ravi and Jogi go into a reminiscent mood. They talk of their formative years in the house.

Ravi says, "To mother I owe my very sense of self and the capacity to deal with other human beings. She also impressed upon me not to rebel against our mostly-absent father, the supreme authority, whatever grouse one may nurse against him. You may now question the justification of such an advice, but I accepted it, and deem myself no worse for it.

"Nice of you", I say.

"I also carry fond memories of Grandpa", says he.

On return, Aarti gives a grand dinner, with Gyan also an invitee. Ramesh, otherwise hostile to my affair, is all affability, a perfect host.

Noni and Girija spend half a day with Gyan in an outing to the historic Panjore Gardens, the seven-tiered, high-walled, Mughal Gardens 20 km away.

Ravi and Noni insist I visit them this coming summer, preferably in June. They can celebrate my 77th birthday, and I can participate in Viki's, too. Separately, Noni invites Gyan to come along. Gyan's response: "I'll talk to Sawrup. Let you know".

It's the last evening of the family gathering.

"From whatever I've gauged, Gyan isn't for grabbing Papa's property", says Girija. "She seems perfectly content with her own house. Of course, on marriage, she'd enjoy a higher standard of living, a happy development for her".

"That should set Jogi's mind at a little ease", I say. "As to any higher standard of living, it's largely an offshoot of Ravi's money".

"We've been having some discussion among ourselves", says Noni. "If I'm permitted to sum up: we leave it all to Papa. We'd respect his decision. To us, Gyan would be a welcome addition to the family. But if Papa chooses to keep living on his own, we go along with it. In the latter case it'd be of immense help if Pasho auntie can stay on".

Pasho interposes, "I'm getting old, too. I need looking after, not the other way round".

May 2001.

My novel has been published, causing no ripples in the literary world. The publisher tells me the sales from the first edition of 700 haven't been bad. He may print another edition. But till now I haven't received a rupee from him. Anyone not wanting money for his writing is said to be phoney.

The draft of the second novel is nearly ready. It isn't coming out too badly. Ravi and Noni want to read it, before I undertake revisions.

Gyan consents to the US trip. I inform Noni of it. A June trip will also afford welcome relief from Chandigarh's gruelling summer heat with its merciless, pounding sun. Pasho would be going back to Amritsar in my absence. She seems to miss the hustle bustle of her Amritsar home.

In time two business-class return air tickets by SAS arrive. Noni wants us to stay in their guest wing, at least in the beginning.

"How are we putting them up?" asks Ravi. "In separate bedrooms or a shared one!"

"Both the bedrooms of the guest wing will be kept ready. It's for them to decide".

"I understand they stayed in one hotel room in Simla for a week".

"If I were Gyan, I may join at bedtime but later move to a separate room. Get up alone in the morning—women don't look their best at waking. Give myself the needed space and time to collect my thoughts about a matter as weighty as marriage".

"Did you give as much thought when you were marrying?"

"I was 25, not a widow of 50 with adult children and grandchildren, marrying a widower 27 year older with his children and grandchildren".

"I'm not sure whether I'd remarry in Dad's position. But I wouldn't fault him for doing it", wonders Ravi.

"His life will be incomplete, lonely, and depressed without regular female company and support. Of course, the ocean holds a lot of fish. There could be older women who are free, with better education, professionally advanced, and socially superior. But Gyan is at hand. And in my reckoning, she should be good for him".

"People who marry very late have got into habits they find hard to change or adjust".

"Between them two, dad will possibly get away without being forced to change overtly his routine and lifestyle. It's Gyan who will have to make more adjustments".

"Yes, it may begin by his being the dominant partner. But the equation could change dramatically within a few years. To give oneself over sexually and otherwise to a much older man allows a younger woman the sort of authority she won't get over a younger man".

"Well, we've to be reconciled to such a situation", says Noni.

By this time Viki is calling loudly for dad; he's bogged down in his Lego build-up of a road bridge.

"Does Gyan see any advantage in the change? That's the question. It's her choice between an independent, do-as-you-like existence and falling in line with someone offering a more interesting, a more affluent lifestyle. As to loneliness itself, women, I believe, can bear it much better than men", continues Noni, making for the kitchen.

We are here in Cranford since June 5. The whole day we are left on our own in the guest wing, unless visited by Viki or Othello, the family bulldog.

Viki's loveable as ever, with his engaging chatter and winsome ways. He often comes driving in his yellow Porsche. And he keeps proclaiming it's a gift from grandma.

Gyan, a swimmer since her girlhood, finds the facility of a private pool plainly fascinating. She revels in the pool. Noni has given her a couple of her bikinis—both women are of nearly the same build. How lissome, how supple, how youthful a body felt when supported by thousands of gallons of water. I sit by poolside, enviably watching Gyan and Viki at their water games.

I bring in the morning tea tray, followed by a leisurely breakfast. By noon we walk out for lunch to one of the town's restaurants: Japanese, Italian, Chinese, French, or Mexican. Somehow, I haven't taken to Mexican cuisine though their place is ever full of diners. Most Mexican dishes contain minced meat, something that I don't fancy. We mainly patronize the Italian eatery. I'm finding to my pleasant surprise that Italian dishes are as good as the French while markedly cheaper.

Gyan has learnt to cope with the ample American helpings, even their large plate. If you order tiger prawns, you get a dozen instead of a couple back home.

Ravi is usually back by the 'cocktail hour'. We sit out during the long twilight.

All of us have dinner together, either at the house or at an eating place outside. Gyan and Noni often talk late into the night. The two have hit off well.

Our lovemaking is mostly during the afternoon; the time I'm at my best. By now we are more relaxed about it. Feel no compulsion doing something if we aren't inclined to it.

After dinner and saying goodnight to our hosts, we sit in the guestroom watching TV. By eleven, feeling drowsy, it's usually Gyan who gets up. Kisses me goodnight and proceeds to her bedroom. The subject of sleeping in the same room and bed or separate hasn't cropped up formally between us. But I'm going along with Gyan's inclination to sleep separate, giving us space and time to think of our future relationship.

Ravi and Noni have come to know of our sleeping arrangements, possibly through Gyan to Noni. They, however, refrain to comment on it.

My choice is getting clearer by the day, and that's marriage to Gyan. I'd gain welcome relief from loneliness, help in house running, and attractive female companionship. I'm almost in love with her.

And I imagine I lose practically nothing in the bargain. I can carry on with the lifestyle of reading and writing, playing golf, and meeting my friends. Gyan, I expect, would fit into my life without rocking it unduly.

Of course, in 2, 3 years sex will take a back seat, losing its current clandestine edge and the novelty of a new body. Anyway I'd be entering my eighties. What will remain is the need of female companionship.

As I understand, old age can be enlivened by two things; a love for gardening and interaction with young people, particularly teenagers. I love gardens but have been able to evince no serious interest in gardening itself. Again, I am denied the company of my grandchildren, the two girls away in Delhi and the boy in the far-off US. My only contact with the young is at the golf club where I meet youngsters taking to golf.

In the absence of the love for gardening and hardly any young company, I have to fall back on a helpful female companion to make my old years livable.

Jogi wouldn't be happy with this marriage but he may get reconciled in due course, especially when I'll assure him of his first-floor portion. Whatever new property claims may crop up with remarriage, Jogi's share will be kept intact.

CHAPTER 25

How is it going with Gyan?

I find Sawrup pleasant and interesting. And in bed he is keen to give me pleasure. He really attracts me. He really does. Right from the day I saw the grief-stricken widower of a greatly beloved wife, my heart warmed to him.

But then I see in him a streak of bossiness; he wants things to go his way. And he does display a certain impatience. Makes a fuss about punctuality.

I think I can put up with his pet peeves and mannerisms. Like all older men he could be fussy about his personal comforts, viewing me largely as an adjunct to his well-regulated life. His writing, for one, would enjoy priority. But I can easily put up with all this.

As far as I can make out, he's essentially a decent man. And it should be more fun living with him than being alone on my own. Even if I've to surrender a part of my independent existence, one feels superior living with a partner than being without one.

I can't ignore the fact that Sawrup is 77. If at all I marry him, it is not likely to last over10 years, possibly less. That's a pity. Yet it makes the marriage to him a less momentous decision than marrying a younger man.

Within 10 days of living together, I decide to marry Gyan. It would give me a second chance to find the love I lost, to have another go at a happy ending.

In a way what could be more hopeful than a second marriage. I do look forward to a good deal of pleasing existence beyond 77.

As usual, I bring morning tea to her bed room. Today, I have experimented with the Chinese green tea. Taking a few sips, Gyan exclaims, "This is so smooth, so invigorating".

It occurred to me that I better take a bag of genuine Chinese tea. Who knows? Back home, we may soon be drinking morning tea together.

After tea, I come out for a short walk. It's a brilliant morning, with sunshine and cool breeze. I walk to the rivulets edge and sit on the wooden deck. The picture upper most in my mind is of Gyan merrily sipping tea in her floral house court.

It's evident that life would be more fun if every morning would begin with such pleasant companionship. There and then, I make up my mind that we have to be married.

So after breakfast, I grasp her hand and ask, "Will you marry me? I love you".

Gyan is taken aback by the proposal. All she can do is to blush, and then she stammers, "It's so sudden".

Any uneasy silence prevails. Yet I can observe a glow on her face.

In minutes, she makes an awaited nod. We embrace, kiss.

Gyan knows she's marrying an old man. But then you can't have all things your own way. The younger men who had pursued her in the widowed state were simply odious.

In comparison, Sawrup is considerate, loving, and affluent. His mind is sharp and is still busy at his intellectual work. Life with him should be pleasant and interesting, more so in comparison to my lonely existence.

Gyan is taken somewhat by surprise with the abruptness of my proposal. She stares at me for some time.

"It'd be the beginning of a new life for me, acquiring a new family", she says.

"You know you're agreeing to marry a man old enough to be your father".

"I know it. And I like that way. I feel safe with you".

"You deserve a younger man".

"It is the companionship that matters most with me".

"We've decided to marry", I tell Ravi and Noni at dinner that evening.

Congratulations, they say, vastly enthused.

And forthwith they get up to embrace both of us.

"Calls for a champagne toast", Ravi gets up to bring a bottle and four narrow flutes. We drink a toast to the new relationship.

"Did Papa propose on bended knee?" Noni asks.

Gyan merely smiles back.

"Priti would bless remarriage", says Noni. "During my long talks with her I learnt that she always wanted Papa to be happy, doing her best to ward away unhappiness from him".

"If Manu, the ancient lawgiver, is to be followed I should be renouncing the world, moving into a forest. Instead I'm marrying a second time, and that someone much younger".

"Manu is not for modern times", makes out Ravi, heaping Caesar salad on his plate; he has a weakness for salads. "Manu had divided life into four equal portions of 25 years. Now the third stage of active old age is getting longer and longer, while the fourth stage of decrepitude is getting shorter. One day you are active, healthy, even playing golf. And then you pop off with a brief illness, sometimes as brief as a few days".

And he continues, "As they say things change. Nothing ever remains the same—that's the only feature that stays unchanged. Anyway everybody ages differently, not only in physical and mental condition but in attitude to ageing.'

"A bit ironical, isn't it? Venturing into a wedding within 18 months of a cremation".

"All plays of Shakespeare—your favourite playwright—end either in a funeral or a wedding. You happen to have both", quips Ravi.

Noni piping in, "Gyan, you're nothing short of a miracle for Papa. It's written all over him. His face glows. He looks sharper".

"We'd like to have the simplest possible marriage ceremony", I say. "More like the way Adam and Eve married: no elaborate ceremony, no music, no caterer, no photographer, no one but God as witness".

"Papa, if you want real simple, have it here itself. Return to India married", says Noni. "A marriage back home, howsoever hard you may try, will not be free from fussy ceremonies, controversial guest lists, and other complications, not to mention the inevitable sniggers and snide remarks".

"An excellent idea", calls out Ravi, now got up to operate the coffee machine. "Our marriage also took place here. Didn't turn out too badly. Isn't it so, dear Noni?"

"Let's talk of the coming one. The marriage can best be in a gurudwara. There's one twenty miles away. Won't take more than an hour with four of us present and the granthi. Gurudwaras here issue you a regular marriage certificate on their letterhead, duly witnessed and stamped, even registered.

Better marry on June 20, Papa's birthday. Fly next day to Bermuda for a week's honeymoon—one of the best places in the world for it".

"At the ceremony, I'll be on the groom's side. Noni, you take the bride's side. Viki will watch. If an additional witness is wanted, I'll ask my secretary to join in".

"This is so sudden", exclaims Gyan.

"Give us a day to think over it", I say.

"Fair enough. Tell us tomorrow at dinner. That would leave another two days to get Gyan a bridal dress, sort it out with the gurudwara, and collect presents", says Noni. "Papa, you get busy buying a beautiful ring".

"A champagne dinner that night", says Ravi. "At Bermuda, you stay in the same hotel we stayed. The Princess, a first-rate place".

"I'll get them the hotel's honeymoon suite. I've seen it. Right on the top floor, it affords a panoramic view of the sea".

"An old couple honeymooning! Enjoying each other's

company! It can induce amused glances, more so from young honeymooners, musing what on earth are they up to?"

"You can easily ignore them", says Ravi.

"Who says old? Papa doesn't look more than fifty-five, Gyan, hardly thirty-five", chimes in Noni with a merry chuckle.

"The sort of age you give me would render Ravi illegitimate".

That produces a guffaw all round.

For women, fifty may be the new thirty. But Gyan is not unaware that the sort of expectations a 30-year-old harbours hardly extend to a woman of 50.

The marriage ceremony at the gurudwara turns out delightfully short, simple, and elegant. We make the customary offering. After the four pheras, followed by ardaas and karha prasad, we receive the marriage certificate, duly signed and stamped. This document, both in English and Gurmukhi, bears our signatures and those of two witnesses which include Ravi's secretary and the granthi's assistant.

Gyan is the very picture of a bashful bride. Viki, a scarf tied over his head, seems to take serious interest in the proceedings. Thereafter, we adjourn for lunch to the kid's favourite Japanese restaurant.

Next day we fly to Bermuda. The narrow 21-mile-long group of islands is as pretty as its postcard pictures. Evergreen islands lush with the famed Bermuda grass, no high-rise buildings, no billboards, no litter, no graffiti. Beautiful coral beaches with pink-coloured soft sand. And we have a lovely hotel room with fantastic views, and some superb meals.

On our return, Ravi rings up Jogi who grunts his congratulations for the news. Pity, Ravi's call catches the couple at a raging marital tiff. Jogi is hollering at Lovely coming home late on several evenings, particularly that evening by nine.

"I don't like this one bit, drama rehearsals or no rehearsals. Today, a boy dropped her home".